BY DEAD RECKONING

*Recollections
of a
Master Navigator*

BY DEAD RECKONING

Recollections of a Master Navigator

Ralph Lewis

Paladwr Press

To Mina
my wife of fifty-six years
for her patience, understanding and love

Published 1994 by Paladwr Press,
1906 Wilson Lane, Apt. 101, McLean, Virginia
22102-1957

Manufactured in Hong Kong

Maps by R.E.G. Davies

Edited by R.E.G. Davies and John Wegg

Typesetting/Layout by Spot Color

Pre-press Production by The Drawing Board

ISBN 0-9626483-6-1

First Edition

Contents

Maps
by R.E.G. Davies

Cartoons
by Jerry Daly

Foreword

by Donald S. Lopez
Former Deputy Director,
National Air and Space Museum

I have been interested in aviation for most of my life and directly involved in it since 1941, from flying in China in World War II, six years as an air force fighter test pilot, teaching aeronautics at the USAF Academy, working as an engineer for NASA on the Apollo program, and, for more than 20 years, at the Smithsonian Institution, helping to direct the shape and form of the National Air and Space Museum.

In all those years I have read hundreds of books by pilots but I cannot recall ever reading, or even seeing, one by a navigator. I had come to the conclusion that, perhaps, they either could not write or did not wish to, but could only communicate in terms of true courses, magnetic headings, and other highly technical navigators' language. But after reading *By Dead Reckoning*, I found that at least one navigator, Ralph Lewis, not only can write, but can write very well.

Although he was born and raised in small towns in central Kansas, and did not begin his flying career until he was 29, he amassed more than 21,000 hours in the air, covered more than 3,500,000 miles (including 700 trips between California and Hawaii) and saw much of the world during his 21-year flying career as a radio operator and navigator.

His youthful interest in ham radio led to his beginning a career in broadcasting which, at the outset of WW II, led to his employment with United Air Lines as a radio operator in its air cargo logistics support operations for the U.S. Armed Forces in the western Pacific. On the long overwater flights, the only long-range communication link was the CW (dots and dashes) radio and the radio operator was a vital member of the crew, equipped with navigational knowhow as well as his own professional skills.

After the war Ralph Lewis joined the newly-formed Transocean Air Lines, a cargo and passenger non-scheduled airline that took over some of the runs that United had flown during the war. He was able to capitalize on another hobby when he became the official photographer for Transocean in addition to his flying duties. His skill as a photographer is evident from the many splendid illustrations in this book, all from his own camera.

In the early 1950s, radio technology had advanced to the stage when long-range voice communication was possible, reducing, and then eliminating, the requirement for radio operators. Ralph Lewis became a navigator and flew in that crew position for the remainder of his flying career.

This book is far more than the story of an individual. It covers the birth, life, and death of Transocean Air Lines, a pioneer air carrier with the well-earned reputation of flying anything, anywhere, anytime. Some of those anythings are the basis for many of the unusual and often amusing incidents in which he was involved. It also provides a glimpse at some of the lost arts of flying. The advances of technology and the advent of computers and satellites have virtually eliminated the need for navigators. Inertial navigation systems, Loran, and the Global Positioning System, have replaced celestial navigation and dead reckoning. Flying the long overwater flights to the small, isolated Pacific islands, using only celestial and dead reckoning techniques was difficult and dangerous. Writing this as a former Army Air Force and U.S. Air Force fighter pilot who hated to fly out of sight of land, the idea of crossing thousand-mile stretches of water seems to have been particularly difficult and dangerous.

The anecdotal, often amusing, matter-of-fact style is very readable and his descriptions of the many exotic locales and people will help to qualify the reader for at least three credits in geography.

From time to time, the author also intersperses his accounts of a lifetime in the air with progress reports on his personal life and the often-forgotten problems of pursuing a career that demands long periods away from home and family. While we can follow Ralph's flying life in this autobiography, we can also share some of the problems of raising a family (and his was not straightforward), house-hunting, and home-building, when the telephone was a constant threat to domestic serenity.

All in all this is a most interesting and enjoyable story about a period and type of flying that too little is written about. Since Ralph Lewis's recollections of a master navigator have clearly established that navigators can, indeed, write, let us hope that more of his fraternity will be encouraged to pick up their pens and share their experiences with us.

Author's Preface

During a trip to Kansas in 1986, my wife Mina and I spent an afternoon visiting with an aunt of hers who counts among the family treasures a hand-written journal, meticulously recorded in pen and ink by her great, great, great grandfather. Yellow, faded, and brittle with age now, it chronicles in detail certain events during his life.

Born in 1815 on a farm in Indiana Territory, he received only 18 months of schooling, and that was before he was 12 years of age, yet he writes with poignant eloquence in expressing his personal repudiation of slavery during the American Civil War. Vividly, he relates stories about homesteading in Iowa, carpetbaggers, Missouri river-boat gamblers, and Presidents Lincoln and Arthur. This pioneer's account, written 150 years ago, fascinated me and provided the inspiration for my own biography.

But today is a special day: it is Thanksgiving 1993, and both Mina and I have a great deal to be thankful for. Our lives have been blessed with good health, and we have maintained a close and loving relationship with our two children.

Our son David received his education at the University of California in Berkeley, became a biochemist, and for the past fourteen years has been engaged in enzyme research at the University of Maryland in Baltimore, and at Stanford University in Palo Alto, California.

Mary, our daughter, is accounting supervisor for a major law firm in Oakland, California. She and her husband, Andrew, have given us three bright and wonderful grandchildren—two boys, Joseph and Thomas, and a girl, Christina. To these grandchildren I offer this book with the wish that they, like Mina's aunt, will preserve its pages for their children and their children's children.

But now, about this book ... occasionally, the sudden unmistakable rumble of jet engines somewhere high overhead commands our attention, prompting us to shade our eyes from the sun and peer into the blue sky above. As the sound intensifies, we know that unless the jet's vapor trail is visible, we will never see the tiny speck that generates that distant roar.

Thirty-five thousand feet up, at the edge of the troposphere, that almost invisible object streaking through the sky is a modern jet transport with perhaps 400 human beings comfortably and safely encapsulated within.

You stand, watching the miniscule point of light and its streaming ribbon of silver until it finally disappears from view. Sometimes, if the aircraft is high enough, the setting sun may paint that meteoric pinpoint and its contrail a brilliant crimson, creating the illusion of a comet as it passes near the surface of the earth.

Invariably, when this scenario plays itself out above me, I pause in reflection at the spectacle, wondering what it would be like to be back up there on the flight deck ... but alas, the days of the flight radio operator and flight navigator are no more.

Today's pilots, of course, still experience the exuberance of flight, but for me there is solace in knowing that those who flew in my day had something else ... adventure, excitement, and the lure of the unknown—events that characterized much of the early days of the air transport business.

This book contains episodes from that period during the 1940s and 1950s when four-engined commercial air transports were driven by piston and propeller; a time when crews of fledgling supplemental air carriers "barnstormed" their way around the world; a time when passengers and cargo were picked up wherever they could be found; and a time when captains of these aircraft often carried cash to pay for gasoline at foreign air fields. This then is my story.

Ralph Lewis

Acknowledgements

For those Good Samaritans who helped make this book possible, I wish to remember the following:

Gene Crowe, for darkroom time in reproducing many of the photographs that had long been out of print; Bob Ringer for sharing his knowledge of airplanes and engines; Barbara Draper for her constant support and encouragement; Ron Davies for his expertise in doing the maps, Jerry Daly for his cartoons, and finally my wife Mina for putting up with me during my obsession in getting the job done. To these loyal folks I offer my heartfelt thanks.

The author ... in the cabin of a DC-3 during flight somewhere in the Aleutians. Accorded officer's privileges, United Air Lines crew members, flying for the Army Air Transport Command, wore regulation military uniforms with special ATC insignia. (Photo date: August 16, 1943)

In the Beginning

I would like to undertake this writing with a few facts about my immediate family. My father, born Ralph Earl Lewis in Wilson, Kansas, in 1885, was the son of a German watchmaker and railroad worker. My mother, Emma Amelia Olson, was the fourth of eight children born to Swedish immigrants in Assaria, Kansas, in 1887.

Upon graduation from high school, Father found work in his home town of Wilson with the American Express Company. A chronological transcript, written in his own hand, indicates that he was employed by that company for eight years as a substitute agent and clerk, spending short periods of time in each of several small mid-Kansas towns.

In January of 1911, after a period of understudy, he took a position in Sylvan Grove, Kansas, as a telegrapher with the Union Pacific Railroad. This became my father's life's work. My birth, in September 1912, was the first for Earl and Emma, who christened me Ralph Chester. A sister, born two years later, was followed by two younger brothers in 1918 and 1928.

Our father was a good man and gentle of nature, but as children we saw very little of him because of the hours he worked at his job. When we youngsters came home from school in the afternoon, Dad would have left for work. Returning home at midnight, he often slept the next morning until after we had again left for school. It was not until many years later that I really came to know and appreciate my father.

As most women did in those days, Mother stayed home to cook, sew, and take care of her children. Possessing a special talent and love for music, both parents played musical instruments and sang.

Sylvan Grove Then and Now

Sylvan Grove, where I spent the first six years of my life, was a small rural farming community with just enough inhabitants to call it a town. Dr. Shalksohn, the only doctor in those parts, came to our house to deliver me. Just how much most of us remember from the first five or six years of this earthly existence, I can only speculate. The passage of time is almost certain to rearrange our accurate recollection of events, yet I have managed to cling to certain images from my childhood.

1

My parents' closest friends owned and operated Behrhorst's Hardware Store, the center of social life in Sylvan Grove. With three children about my age, they lived on a spacious corner lot in the grandest house in Lincoln County. Facing the center of an intersection at the top of Sylvan's only hill, their property afforded a commanding overview of the town. As a small child, I remember being invited there to an afternoon tea party given for the Behrhorst's four-year-old daughter, Wanda. This gala event, held on the wide, well-groomed lawn in front of their home, was quite formal, and I was immensely impressed.

In 1976, while sojourning briefly in Kansas, I decided to visit my birthplace once more. Though sixty years had passed since the family moved away, the little town seemed much the same as I remembered it. Parking in front of Planters State Bank on Sylvan's main street, I left the car and headed up the rise toward the old Behrhorst home, treading the same sidewalk that I had coasted down in my little red wagon nearly seven decades before. Badly fragmented from the harsh Kansas winters, the cement sections were all askew now, pushed up and out of place by tree roots.

At the top of the hill the Behrhorst house was still there all right, but, as I approached, I could only stare in disbelief at its shabby, run-down appearance. What I had remembered as a near mansion was, in reality, a rather smallish house, set far too close to the street. What had become of the carefully tended, park-like expanse of green lawn that had made such an impression on me? Where, too, were the bright colorful flowers that had once ringed the front porch? Time has a devilish way of changing our perception of things. I turned away, preferring to live with the memory.

Dejectedly, I trudged back to the bottom of the hill and made a right turn up the main street toward the hardware store. Most of the structures that lined the two-block-long main street, as well as every fence post in the county, had been hewn from native stone mined from a nearby quarry. The two-storey hardware building was no exception, but I seem to remember that a large wooden awning had extended out over the sidewalk in front. It was gone now.

Deciding to go inside, I climbed the stone steps and entered. An elderly gentleman standing behind a counter near the middle of the store was cranking up a sale. His snow-white hair seemed in harmony with the ancient cash register as it clattered away in painful protest.

Glancing around, I took stock of the place. Clutter seemed everywhere. On the floor nearby stood a ten-gallon milk can displaying a variety of buggy whips. The sun's rays, streaming through the storefront windows, highlighted a row of horse collars placed high on the opposite wall. Laden with dust, they had obviously hung undisturbed for years. A "traveling" ladder that could be rolled to any point from front to rear still appeared to be in good working order. Relics of a bygone era, these items served to remind one of decades past, visions of which were fortified by the musty aroma of leather goods, paints, oils, seeds, and fertilizers ... a mixture of smells ingrained in the old building itself.

The clerk—of the same vintage as the store—appeared to be in excellent health, confiding happily to me a few moments later that he was ninety-five years old and the store's present owner. When I inquired about the manually operated freight elevator at the rear of the building that we kids had taken such delight in running up and down, he laughed. "Oh yes ... it creaks and groans a bit now, but we still use it to move merchandise to and from the basement." He remembered my father, too. Both men, he told me, had been charter members of the local order of the Masonic Lodge. My return to Sylvan Grove had been an experience in remembering, which left me with a bittersweet feeling and a reminder that our time on this earth is short indeed.

Salina Days

In 1918, the railroad transferred my father to Salina, where he bought his parents' home, whence he walked a mile and a half to work every afternoon, seven days a week, and it was not unusual to see him sitting on the front porch steps before he left the house, stuffing cardboard in his shoes to cover the holes. Through the Twenties, though, and even through the Great Depression of the Thirties, my father had excellent job security. As a result, our family of five was relatively well off.

Salina was a typical mid-western town of 16,000 souls when our family moved there. It served as a hub for dozens of small rural communities scattered throughout the wheat fields of central Kansas. Its economy depended largely on the production of wheat, corn, oats, and other grains, but livestock also played an important part in the welfare of Kansas farmers. The soil of the plains was rich and deep. The summer rain showers and the winter snows, in league with the industry and resolve of its inhabitants, caused it to produce in abundance.

Our town was located on the main line of the Union Pacific Railroad, about half way between Kansas City and Denver, and daily runs of the Plainville and McPherson Branch lines made up here. The Smoky Hill River meandered through the center of town; its water, as its name suggests, was "too thin to plow and too thick to drink".

Automobiles were still something of a novelty in the late Twenties; not every family could afford one. East-west Highway 40 was paved with two narrow lanes of concrete, but Highway 81 north and south was dirt, as were all the other interconnecting roads of that time. When it rained, they turned to mud, making travel by auto unthinkable. Those brave enough to try often wound up in a ditch and had to be pulled out by a team of horses. Salina boasted a university, a girls' college, a military school for boys, and three large flour mills, whose wheat storage elevators dominated the skyline.

Through the summer, my household chores included emptying the pan under the family icebox each morning. If not done on schedule, it ran over, triggering all sorts of ugly reprisals from Mother.

Ingenuity is what held our young world together, but it was ingenuity, too, that often got us in trouble. One day, in an effort to embellish my home-made scooter with a headlamp, I sawed a tin can in half with Dad's new crosscut wood saw. My sister and brother witnessed the misdeed and had to be threatened with instant extinction if they squealed.

During the summertime, several days in a row of unusually high temperatures occasionally brought on an afternoon thunder shower, which cooled things down a bit. More often than not, however, heat and humidity continued throughout the night.

Beyond the surrounding screen of our sleeping porch, myriads of glow-worms, which we called lightning bugs, glowed in the dark as the tiny winged insects gave off their intermittent yellow fluorescence. Continuous night sounds of singing locusts droned away in the giant elm trees outside, and the sweet fragrance of summer foliage, drifting in on an occasional wisp of cool air, gently lulled us to sleep.

A pretty little neighbor girl named Pollyanna Snyder lived in the house back of us. She became my friend one day when she crawled under the chicken wire fence behind Mother's garden. She showed me how to scoop out the rear end of the hapless "lightning bugs" to make lighted rings for my fingers. That was the end of a beautiful friendship - well, almost the end.

Pollyanna

Eighth grade graduation was not exactly a flag-waving event in my young life, nor was the student dance that was scheduled to follow the afternoon ceremo-nies. Some of the other boys had been bragging about their "dates", and, fearing that my macho image might be tarnished, I felt compelled to ask a girl to accompany me to the dance, too, but who might that possibly be anyway? Until now, I had held a vague notion that girls were something that boys just had to contend with, like it or not. I did not even know any girls, yet, suddenly, here I was, actually considering a short personal relationship with one.

Then ... I had a glimmer of an idea. What about the one who had climbed under the fence in our back yard some five or six years before ... Pollyanna Snyder. She too had been growing up, and had become even prettier during those formative years. I had seen her in school from time to time, but we had never had occasion to speak to each other.

Stealing a glance at her the next day in class—from a discreet distance, of course—I was surprised to notice that she had developed curves in all the right places. I guess I hadn't been paying much attention. She seemed quite popular at school. What if she turned me down? Would I be able to live with the embarrassment? After all, we had known each other only briefly once before.

Taking a chance, I picked up the telephone and called her. She answered so sweetly on the phone ... could this be the same girl who had shown me how to dissect lightning bugs? She must surely have noticed my awkwardness as I blurted out my question, but if she did, she gave no indication. Pausing only briefly, she agreed to be my date for the dance. Flattery consumed me; this was my lucky day—or was it?

In checking my limited wardrobe the morning of the big event, I discovered to my dismay that my one and only necktie was badly soiled, so I turned to Mother who usually had all the answers.

"We don't have the time to get it to the cleaners now," she said, "but don't worry, I'll clean it for you." Whereupon she went off to the garage for a pan of gasoline, and in no time at all the grease spots were gone. Then with obvious satisfaction, she said, "I'll hang it out on the clothesline to dry, and by the time you leave for the school program, it will be ready to wear."

While dressing I could not help being thankful for a mother who always knew how to cope with such emergencies. Pollyanna would be waiting for me when I came by for her at two o'clock. The only thing left to do now was to retrieve the tie from the clothesline and don my jacket, but, when I went out through the rear door, the odor of gasoline radiating from my tie had polluted the entire backyard!

Poor Pollyanna ... this brave girl spent the next two hours in my company, asking only once, "What is that horrid smell?" ... "Gee," I lied, "I don't smell anything," all the while praying that others in the crowd would not be able to identify the source. Of course, there were no words to express the shame I felt. The blow to my ego was devastating. Pollyanna? She never spoke to me again. Growing up can be very painful.

Swan Song for the Eaglerock

In western Kansas, so they say, you can lie flat on the ground and see to the horizon in any direction, but on the outskirts of Salina, there was a prominence known as Country Club Hill. On the crest of this hill, some two or three hundred feet above town level, was a large cornfield that doubled as Salina's airport. Occasionally, after finishing my paper route in the afternoon, I pushed my bicycle up the long slope to see if there might be an airplane in the little hangar building. It was usually empty, but, at times, itinerant aviators flew in on Sunday afternoons and sold rides to those who had the courage to fly and the money to pay. The year was 1928.

An Offer I Couldn't Refuse

On one such occasion I had my first chance to inspect a real airplane at close range. Standing just outside the hangar in the bright summer sunlight was this flying machine that I recognized from a picture I had seen in *Aero Digest* at the library. The craft, manufactured by the Alexander Company, was an Eaglerock open cockpit biplane with dual controls powered by an OX-5 engine.

Spellbound, I tried to move in for a closer look, but the rope barrier that surrounded the 'plane kept me at a respectful distance. As I stood there in rapt silence admiring this beautiful craft, a tall, rather lanky man, probably in his early forties, emerged from the hangar. Undeniably the pilot, he wore a white silk scarf draped nonchalantly around his neck and a pair of goggles contoured across his forehead. Glancing in my direction, his eyes landed on me.

"Hey Kid how would you like to have a ride in my airplane?" I turned around to see whom he might be addressing, but no one else was in sight. Turning back toward him in disbelief, I pointed a questioning finger at myself.

"Yes, you, son." he continued, "I'll take you up if you'll wash down my airplane and shine her up a bit." I could not believe my good fortune; I was being offered a free ride.

"We do have a problem, though, young fellow ..." He paused as though he suddenly felt the whole idea might not be a good one. "There's no water up here on this hill."

For a brief moment my heart sank ... then, suddenly, I had the answer.

"Sir, I can bring a bucketful up each day on my handlebars after I've finished delivering papers," I said with enthusiasm, "and in four or five afternoons I'll have enough!"

He contemplated my proposal briefly, then extended his hand and broke out in a wide grin. "My name is Jack Hidecker," he said. "You've got yourself a deal, young man."

I was on cloud nine that afternoon, for I knew I could never have raised the money to pay for such a treat. I literally floated the four miles down the hill toward home, but I was afraid to tell my parents of my bargain; I was sure they would not approve. Every evening for the next five days I struggled to push my bicycle up the hill with a pail of water dangling from its handlebars. A quarter of each pail sloshed out before I could reach the hangar, but I reasoned that an extra bucketful and an extra day would make up for the loss. Indeed, it was a labor of love. The following Saturday was to be my big day; I thought it would never come.

First Flight

Saturday morning, however, did finally arrive. I rose and fixed my breakfast before anyone else in the house was up, and left Mom a note saying only that I was going to the airport. With soap, brush, and rags in my paper bag, I headed full speed across town and up the hill to Mr. Hidecker's airplane. As I arrived at the hangar, he was on his back beside a wheel strut, apparently changing a tire.

"Hey, kid," he yelled when he saw me, "what did you say your name was?" He didn't wait for a reply, but added impatiently, "Hand me that crescent wrench over there." He jerked his head in the direction of the hangar door. I jumped to comply.

One wing of the airplane had been jacked up to lift the wheel off the ground, and he was in the process of removing the bad tire, when suddenly the jack slipped from under the wing support, driving the tip of the jack completely through the lower wing! Mr. Hidecker had an extensive vocabulary of colorful language, and at that point I think he recited most of it.

I missed my lunch that day and my ride as well, for it had to be postponed, at least temporarily. After the 'plane was again blocked up and the tire finally changed, I set to work with soap and water to complete my end of our bargain, finally finishing the job just in time to return to the newspaper office, pick up my papers, and head for my route. Mr. Hidecker spent all that week replacing the torn fabric in the wing, and not until the following Saturday did I finally have my ride.

It was the fall of the year and the dried corn stalks had been gathered into shocks. They stood in long rows throughout the field except for a corridor which had been cleared to allow landings and takeoffs for Mr. Hidecker's airplane. He had told me to be there ready to go by seven o'clock in the morning because, as he explained it, the air would be more stable at that time of day. The delay had only heightened my excitement, and I reached the hangar ahead of time.

Having regained his jovial manner, Mr. Hidecker greeted me with a cheerful "hello," a set of goggles, and a leather helmet, commenting that the airplane was again ready to fly. The headgear was a bit large but the chin strap, he assured me, would hold it on. After adjusting my goggles and showing me where to step, he helped me into the front cockpit, making certain that I was securely strapped in.

"Now, I'm going to pull the propeller through two or three turns", he said, "then, when I say contact, I want you to turn the ignition switch to `on.' " He reached in over my shoulder, pointing it out to me. "But after that you're not to touch any of the controls ... do you understand?" I nodded assent.

Suddenly, I remembered Mother and Dad. I knew then that I should have told them what I was going to do, but it was too late for that now. Mr. Hidecker donned his helmet, lowered his goggles, and walked around to the big engine up front. As he rotated the propeller, its tips were visible through the slanted windscreen in front of me. Then came the command, "contact!"

"Contact!", I echoed in return, and threw the switch. In a sudden flight of fancy I imagined that I was the pilot and in undisputed control of the aircraft ... the master of my own destiny. Now it was just me and the Eaglerock ... soaring upward to do battle with the elements.

Fantasy, however, soon gave way to reality when, with another hefty pull of the propeller, the OX-5 coughed a couple of times, then sputtered to life. The field was extremely rough from the corn stubble, so the aircraft—engine idling—remained stationary as Mr. Hidecker, with a wave of his hand in my direction, climbed into the rear cockpit.

With an increase in throttle the engine began to roar, and we were soon vibrating violently down between the rows of corn shocks, gaining momentum for take off. For what seemed an interminable length of time, we rocketed through the rough stubble, shaking so badly that I was sure the 'plane would fall apart before we could get into the air, but then, suddenly, the wheels left the ground and the vibrations ceased. Now I experienced a smoothness that I had not imagined possible as the runway and the cornfield dropped away behind and below us. I was airborne at last.

I remember the pressure on my back from the rapid acceleration during take off, and the sound of rushing air and engine as we soared upward. A pervasive feeling of exhilaration and freedom came over me. Whatever illusions I may have enjoyed in the past about riding in an airplane were eclipsed now by the reality of it all. We leveled off at about two thousand feet and a few minutes later went into a steep bank.

Looking down, I saw a toy landscape of tiny houses, miniature farm yards, and colorfully patterned fields. Segmented into patchwork by roads, the spellbinding scene extended to the horizon in every direction. It almost seemed that I could reach out and pick up one of those diminutive buildings and put it down wherever I chose. Near the edge of town, the rows of tall wheat storage elevators, gleaming white against the land, cast long shadows in the early morning light. The extraordinary view from the air left an indelible impression.

The most thrilling adventure in my sixteen years of life ended about twenty minutes later as we touched down back at the cornfield. I knew then that I wanted some day to be an aviator just like Mr. Hidecker. I could not thank him enough. He patted me on the shoulder and laughingly replied, "Thanks to you, too, kid!" As I got on my bicycle and headed down the hill toward home that Saturday morning, the idol of my life was the man with the white silk scarf around his neck.

I was never to see him again ... for this story, I must now tell you, ended in disaster. A few days after I had climbed out of Jack Hidecker's airplane, he nose-dived the Eaglerock into the ground not far from the airport and was killed. What happened, people could only speculate. I had gone to the newspaper office to fold my papers for delivery and was struck by the headline, "AIRPLANE CRASHES, PILOT KILLED!" I was stunned; I could not believe that I had lost my new-found friend. Of course, Dad read the headlines the next morning; I could keep my secret no longer. Had my parents known of my plans, I would have missed the most incredible adventure of my young life.

Ham Radio

My musical training began in the eighth grade. Enrolling at the Salina Conservatory of Music, I studied violin under the tutelage of an old German master, Hjalmer Bernhardt. He taught me well and by my senior year I was proficient enough to play first chair in the high school orchestra, an experience that would stand me in good stead later in life.

A small circle of close friends in high school had become interested in amateur radio, and were actually operating their own "ham stations". The thought of being able to communicate directly with other "hams" halfway round the world intrigued me too. I borrowed text books on electronics, sent away for still others, and with help and encouragement from my buddies, qualified as the newest member of an elite group with the call letters, W9IEE.

In a couple of months I was "on the air" with my new dot and dash communication station. Most of the components I built from scratch or scavenged from various sources. The power company had given me an old transformer core, so I purchased wire and rewound it to produce 3,000 volts AC. When rectified through two 866 mercury vapor tubes and filtered, the resultant potential was nearly 1,200 volts DC—a lot of power for a young fellow to be playing around with. Under the right conditions this was easily enough voltage, with sufficient current, to electrocute me. Only too soon I was to gain a healthy respect for my new hobby.

On an unusually cold morning, I had gone down to the basement to my "communications room" intending to fire up the transmitter when, to my dismay, the two 866s refused to vaporize because of the low room temperature. I hit on a sure fire solution. Wadding up a newspaper which lay nearby, I lighted it with a match and dropped it on top of the tubes. In doing so, I apparently touched an electrode on top of one of them, because suddenly everything went black. Waking up minutes later on the floor in the opposite corner of the room, I remembered feeling as though I had been struck on the head with a twenty pound rubber mallet. There is nothing like practical "hands-on" experience when it comes to learning a lesson. I was probably lucky to be alive, but the die had been cast. I was to spend many happy hours talking to people on seven continents.

One night I stayed up late, knowing that Australian signals skipped in well on the twenty meter band later in the evening. The dots and dashes were flying thick and fast when I heard my father enter the house upstairs. I glanced at my watch, knowing that he left the depot at midnight. It was 12:20 a.m. ... I should have been in bed! The next thing I knew he came thundering down the cellar stairway and, bursting into my room, yelled "What the Sam Hill are you up to now?" He was angrier than I had ever seen him. "Every light bulb in the house upstairs is glowing on and off", he shouted.

I laid a book on my telegraph key and, with Dad close behind, headed upstairs to take a look. He was right.

My Zepp antenna had been strung from the chimney on the front of the house to a pole fastened to the rear of the house. I then realized that the house's electrical wiring in the attic was parallel to, and obviously in resonance with, my antenna. They could not have been separated by more than six feet. Anyway, the radiation was intense enough to make light bulbs glow at half brilliance, which caused my father to light up to full brilliance.

"Who do you think is paying the light bill around here?" he roared as he stomped out of the room.

I retreated quickly to the basement to finish my radio contact and, when I went back upstairs a short time later, he had gone to bed. The next morning, however, he caught me at breakfast; he had not forgotten the night before.

"Son ..." he said, obviously trying to conceal his anger, "I checked the electric meter last night and it was going around so fast that the index mark on the wheel was a blur!" Sticking his finger just off the end of my nose and, with an air of doom, he ordered, "From this minute on you will use your radio only one hour each day ... there will be no exceptions. Is that clear?" The next day I moved my antenna to a new location between the rear of the house and the garage.

Horses' Teeth

Headquarters Battery of the 130th Field Artillery, a unit of the Kansas National Guard, was located in Salina. To me and a couple of my buddies who needed the money, enlisting in the guard loomed up as the wave of the future. In addition to being paid for showing up on drill nights, the armory provided the use of a well financed amateur radio station. Joining up, we amateurs continued our self-study of electronics and, working together for the next several years, designed, built, and installed the first mobile two-way radio communication system for the Kansas National Guard.

During my first summer encampment near Ft. Riley, Kansas, the 130th had not as yet become mechanized. Our 75-mm field pieces were drawn by horses, and, of course, they went to camp with us. As the entire company stood at attention during the first morning's muster, the "top kick" gave this green recruit his undivided attention. I was flattered.

"Private Lewis," he barked, "step one pace forward."

"Me, Sir?"

"Yes, you ... "Your name is Lewis, isn't it?"

"Oh, yes, Sir."

"Fine. You will report immediately to Corporal Brown on the picket line."

With that, he handed me a foot-long tooth brush and a quart jar of tooth paste, adding, "The horses' teeth have got to be washed every morning. This will be your personal assignment. Companeee ... dismissed."

Well now ... I'd never even been near horses, let alone wash their teeth, and yet, I had been given a direct order by the top sergeant. I hurried off toward the picket line, trying to figure out how I was going to manage this. Without counting, I guessed there must be at least twenty-five or thirty horses! Most of the company had assembled to watch my act, and, after everyone had enjoyed a good laugh at my expense, I learned that the top kick loved his practical jokes.

Radio KFBI and Wedding Bells

I n August of 1932, an entirely new career opened for me. I cannot remember how it came about, but I auditioned for a job with one of the largest radio stations in Kansas as a fiddle player for Pa Perkins and his Gang, a hillbilly outfit, and they hired me. KFBI was a 5,000 watt, cleared channel station whose main studios were in Abilene, 25 miles east of my parents' home in Salina. Moving to Abilene, I rented a room for seven dollars a month and went to work at the radio station.

"Pa" whose real name was Lynn Butcher, was the group's leader and string bass player. Instrumental support was provided by two guitars, fiddle and accordion, and everyone sang. The program was laced with spontaneous dialogue in the form of hillbilly hi-jinx. Having been a schooled musician, fiddlin' in the backwoods group took considerable getting used to. Filling two thirty-minute spots each weekday for a number of years, we sold vegetable and flower seeds for Interstate Nurseries of Hamburg, Iowa, "The Largest Direct Selling Nursery in the World".

Radio Abilene

One particularly hectic morning at the studio, the station manager ran out into the hall, wild-eyed, looking desperately for someone ... anyone. I happened to be in the wrong place at the right time.

"Here Lewis", he ordered, "get in there to that microphone and read this."

I glanced at the title on a sheaf of papers he had shoved into my hands: "How to Control Coccidiosis in Chickens!" I stared at him in disbelief as he pushed me through the studio door. It was time for the *Farm and Home Hour*, and the agriculture man had not shown up. A few seconds later I had taken the cue from the booth announcer and began to read: "Coccidiosis is any in a series of infectious diseases caused by epithelial protozoan parasites ..." Out of the corner of my eye I could see the manager grinning at my performance through the studio window as I stumbled over the words. From then on they had me doing everything from stock market reports to horse races.

But that was not all ... the station manager learned of another facet of my talents. Summoned to the front office one morning—and curious to know why—I hurried up there. The reason soon became apparent.

"I understand you can read Morse Code," the manager said, "Is that true?" Being young and inexperienced, I proudly admitted that I could.

"Fine", he went on, "I'm subscribing to Transradio Press Services. I want you down here Monday through Saturday at 5 a.m. I've ordered you a short-wave receiver, and you'll have a typewriter."

Beaming with satisfaction, he folded his arms contentedly behind his head and leaned back in his chair. "We'll soon have a fifteen minute edition of the morning news." Then abruptly sobering up, he added, "That will be all for now." Rising, he waved me out of his office.

Directly across the street from the radio station, the new seven-storey Sunflower Hotel was the center of Abilene's social life—the only building in town, in addition to the wheat elevators, with more than two floors. For fifteen years Radio KFBI was the town's biggest attraction, and in 1937, the station branched out with studios in Salina. I was transferred and, with my background in electronics, worked as an announcer and technician there until February, 1940.

Fifty years later, in the spring of 1985, I had traveled east with my wife and, on our way back to the West Coast, made the decision—motivated mostly by nostalgia and curiosity—to swing through Abilene once more. Needing a haircut that particular day, I dropped in at the Sunflower Hotel barber shop. The building had had good care and looked much as it did when I lived there. A large window in the shop afforded an excellent view of the area directly across the street where the KFBI studios had once stood. It was a parking lot now. With a friendly greeting, the barber motioned me to his chair.

"Are you a stranger here?" he began.

"Well ... yes and no." I replied. There was no one else in the shop at the time.

The barber, whom I judged to be in his mid-forties, adjusted the cloth around my neck, and, as he turned to reach for the clippers, I volunteered, "I used to work at the radio station across the street."

He changed his mind about picking up the clippers and instead came around in front of me.

"You must have the wrong town, Sir," he said. "I was born and raised in Abilene; we've never had a radio station here."

"Oh ... but you're mistaken," I countered emphatically, "I'm not in the wrong town!"

My annoyance must have shown as I pointed my finger out the barber shop window.

"Over there where that parking lot is today, stood one of the finest radio stations in all of Kansas. I know because I worked for KFBI for seven years—four and a half of them right there across the street." He appeared incredulous, totally unbelieving.

This little experience really shocked me, as I thought of that time in my life which had been so filled with exciting events. Now, it seemed I was the only one who remembered ... or even cared.

Inquiring around town, I tried to locate someone who might have known Marie Gunzelman. Marie was the station's organist for fifteen years. An accomplished musician, she had been my accompanist during my time at KFBI. Finally someone directed me to a druggist who might be old enough to remember. In the back of his store and still filling prescriptions, he did not remember me, but his tired grey eyes lighted up at the mention of Marie's name.

"Oh, yes, Marie and I were good friends," he recalled, "I still hear from her now and then." He put down the flask he was holding and gazed off at some distant point in reflection. "She married you know ... went to farmin' with her husband on his family's place out west of Salina ..." His eyes lowered to meet mine.

"Chuck—that's her husband—he passed away about a year ago, but Marie stayed on out there. Word is she's got a couple of hired hands, and runs the place by two-way radio from her livin' room ... Marie is pretty well off I imagine."

Pausing briefly, he picked up the flask again and carefully emptied its contents into a nearby bottle.

"Got four or five hundred acres in wheat ... and, from what I hear, her grain storage bins are all full ... Probably holdin' out for higher prices."

I remembered Chuck; he used to come around the radio station when he and Marie were going together. Thanking the druggist, I drove out of Abilene that afternoon in a state of melancholia, holding but one bright thought: no one could take away my memories.

Lawrence Welk

One of the most popular big bands in the Midwest during my KFBI days was Lawrence Welk out of Yankton, South Dakota. While playing at dance pavilions within Radio KFBI's listener range, the bands used the radio station to publicize their appearances. In addition, they played across the street in the coffee shop of the Sunflower Hotel for the lunch crowd, in return for their room and board at the hotel.

Welk's public relations man and booking agent for many years was Vic Schroeder. Handling bookings for six different Midwest dance bands, Schroeder ordered specially built ten-wheel trailer rigs for each band from a company in Sioux City, Iowa. Amenities included small pot-bellied stoves for winter travel, adequate storage space for each band's library, wardrobe, and musical instruments, and seating that could be converted to bunks. The driver of the rig doubled as property manager and librarian.

Welk, who fronted his band personally, was a born showman. Gifted with an uncanny ability to sense the mood of his audiences, he knew how to sell his brand of music. Occasionally he picked up his accordion to play a few bars, all the while smiling benignly at the hoards of happy patrons on the crowded dance floor. Honoring requests, he greeted fans by handing out wrapped sticks of Lawrence Welk chewing gum.

Working through Abilene and KFBI on one such road trip, band leader Welk asked me to join the band for a job in Junction City, twenty-five miles to the east. I agreed. It was the most important decision I would ever make, for I was to meet the girl who would share the rest of my life.

Love At First Sight

Following a dance break that evening, the upcoming set did not require violins. Off the band stand now, I checked along the row of girls seated against the wall for someone who might like to dance. Glancing down the line, my eyes fell on the most attractive brunette I had ever seen, sporting a gorgeous tan, she was slender, and, though I could not be certain, somewhat shorter than I was. Her face, framed exquisitely in a boyish bob, possessed a striking pair of green eyes that were complimented by an expanse of flawless olive skin. A white blouse, open at the neck, accentuated her deep rich tan. Whatever else she may have been wearing that evening seemed unimportant.

Fascinated, I stood there, mentally trying to determine her age. She looked very young—perhaps several years younger than I was. Suddenly I became aware of an older lady sitting at her side. Might this be her chaperone? The two of them must have noticed me staring. Hesitating now, I almost backed away, but it was too late; I was drowning in those eyes. "Courage, don't desert me now," I whispered to myself.

Covering the remaining few steps, I flashed her what I hoped would be a winning smile. "Would you like to dance?" I asked. There was a brief moment of hesitation while both she and the older woman looked me over. Then, smiling faintly, she stood up.

That charmer turned out to be Mina Lily Thomas who, at the time, was just fifteen years old. The lady sitting beside her was her mother. Trying to keep my infatuation a secret around the radio station was like trying to prevent the earth from turning. The news leaked out and I took a lot of ribbing for snatching this "child" from her mother's arms. We were married April 17, 1938, at St. John's Lutheran Church in Salina.

Following the wedding, my days became much busier. Every waking minute, it seemed, was spent studying technical source material on broadcast practices. A Radio Telephone First Class License would qualify me as a radio engineer at any broadcast station and was an essential step before applying for a better job.

In February of 1940, having soaked up as much knowledge as my mind could digest, I rode the train to Kansas City, Missouri, where I took the two-day examination in the federal Communications Commission's offices. My license, a certificate of competency, followed me home a short while later, confirming my new status as a member of the broadcast engineer's fraternity.

Yuma

No time was lost in submitting letters of application to a number of radio stations in areas we thought might appeal to us. An immediate response came from KYUM in Yuma, Arizona, a brand new station with NBC affiliation. An opening existed there for an announcer/engineer at a salary of $110 per month—a twenty dollar increase in pay. We would be rich! I wired Mr. Akers, the station's manager, accepting the job, then suddenly realized that we did not own an automobile.

Signing a note for the loan of a hundred dollars from my father, we bought a used Model A Ford sedan. Mr. Akers had said to come as soon as possible, so we loaded our meager belongings into the "new" ten-year-old car, said goodbye to our parents and friends, and with little more than pocket change in our jeans, headed for Yuma.

Pulling into this small Southwest desert town three days later, we found an inexpensive motel for the night, and the next morning drove to the radio station. KYUM was a brand new plant from its modern building to its 250-foot vertical transmitting antenna. Taking a seat in the lobby, we waited while the receptionist announced our presence on the intercom to General Manager

Akers. From where we sat, the view into the control room revealed the very latest in RCA equipment from transmitter to control console and turntables.

As we waited in silence, the engineer/announcer on duty was clearly visible behind a big plate glass window. About my age, he seemed suave and sophisticated beyond his years. His deep rich baritone voice issued forth in a steady stream of clever patter from the speaker in the wall opposite us. Exuding self-confidence, he addressed the microphone as he would an old friend. Could I turn in an equally impressive performance? I was beginning to have butterflies as I contemplated my new position. My responsibility for a young wife was a haunting reminder, too. Mina and I were a long way from home with almost no money. My brief reverie was broken now by a voice on the intercom at the receptionist's desk.

"Will you show Mr. Lewis in, please?"

Mr. Akers rose from behind his desk, cheerfully extending his hand in welcome, and began shuffling awkwardly through my papers and letter of application. Then came a moment of embarrassing silence as his expression changed from a warm smile to one of guarded apprehension.

"Mr. and Mrs. Lewis," he finally began, "I'm afraid I've made a terrible mistake!"

He's made a mistake? ... I could not breathe. My heart sank to my toes ... What kind of mistake could he have made? What would we do now? How would we get back to Kansas without money? I felt sure he must have detected the pitiful look of utter despair on my face. Looking at first one then the other of us, he continued apologetically.

"After reviewing your letter of application, I realized that you had said you were married. You won't be able to live here in Yuma and support a wife on $110 a month. I'll have to give you more money ... say $120." He sat down again and made a note of the increase on a scratch pad, then added, "You and your wife can stay right here in the station's bachelor apartment until you find a place to live." My worst fears vanished. We had hit the jackpot.

Late that afternoon we moved in. The little apartment was completely furnished. There was an efficiency kitchen, and everything was brand new. We went to bed that night feeling that we had found the pot of gold at the end of the rainbow.

About daylight the next morning we were awakened by a loud banging at our door, and before we could open our eyes and sit up in bed, in burst the disc jockey for the "Dawn Patrol", who put KYUM on the air each week-day morning at five thirty. The entire record library, it seems, was housed in our closets! From then on, until we could find an apartment of our own, we had to be up and dressed by the time the station went on the air, unless we chose to remain in bed while the staff dashed in and out all morning, unannounced, putting their shows together.

We remained in Yuma all that summer, then, in August, we had a letter from a friend. We will call him Paul ... In March of 1937, in his early twenties, Paul had joined the announcing staff of Radio Station KFBI, where he and I had become good friends.

A genius with words, Paul wrote love letters to Mina while I was courting her—and let me sign them. They were so effusively romantic, however, that she soon saw through the deception. Subsequently, he took a position in Missoula, Montana, where he joined the announcing staff of KGVO.

Shortly afterward, I received a letter from him. "There's an opening here on the engineering staff right now," he had written, "Why don't you apply? These Montana mountains are beautiful; you and Mina would love them."

We talked over Paul's letter and decided to make the move. Four months of unbearable summer heat helped convince us that a change would be welcome. Almost immediately we had a telegram from A.J. Mosby, owner and general manger of KGVO.

WILL PAY $140 PER MONTH FOR FORTY HOUR WEEK. STOP. URGENTLY

NEED TRANSMITTER ENGINEER. STOP. GOOD OPENING FOR RIGHT MAN.

I did not know that anyone paid that much money for my kind of work. Thinking Western Union must have made a mistake, I wired back:

PLEASE CONFIRM $140 SALARY FIGURE.

Mina answered the knock at the door when the delivery boy brought Mr. Mosby's reply. Opening the envelope, she read aloud, "$140 salary firm." She glanced at me, grinning broadly, and I knew what she was thinking: "At long last, we would be able to afford servants!"

We telegraphed our acceptance, said goodbye to our Yuma friends, and once again set off in the Model A, which by this time had also become an old friend, to drive the 1,300 miles to Missoula.

The Rest of the Story

But ... back to Paul. Accompanying him when he moved to Montana was his new bride of a few months, a young lady named Lynne Cooper, whom he lovingly introduced to everyone as his 'Angel'. But Paul and Lynne did not remain in Montana very long. Paul's destiny, still unfulfilled, lay elsewhere.

Paul Harvey, who became one of America's great communicators, poses for my camera on the campus of Montana State University, in Missoula, Montana. Beside him is his bride of just a few weeks, Lynne Cooper. He and "Angel" were married in 1941.

To those who had known and worked with him, this fellow clearly was qualified for stardom in the art of mass communication.

Born with a rare combination of gifts possessed by few, he had a natural feel for the broadcasting medium. Intelligent and articulate, with a keen sense of humor and flawless diction, he romped through his material with a quality of voice that put him head and shoulders above others in his field.

His clean, crisp, staccato-like delivery of folksy newscasts over the ABC Radio Network and his syndicated columns in hundreds of daily newspapers across the country brought him to national prominence and eventually celebrity status.

Some time in 1944 he made an important decision. Believing his last name to be somewhat unwieldy, he opted for one that would be more prounceable by his growing audiences. Replacing 'Aurandt', with his middle name 'Harvey', he became simply ... 'Paul Harvey'.

And now you know the rest of the story.

A Chance to Fly
... and be Paid for It

The move to Montana was my second major one within six months, and once again, all of our personal belongings filled up the back seat of the car. A rolling stone gathers no furniture, they say, and without money we could not have bought any anyway. Having been 'Kansas bound' all our lives, we reveled in the beauty of the ever-changing scenery as we drove along through the mountains. For the first time since we had bought the car, we encountered rain. The Ford sported an electric windshield wiper that worked very well, but that did not help much because the roof leaked ... like a sieve.

Missoula, Here We Come

Our route took us north through Sun Valley, Idaho, over Galena Summit, and down into the spectacular Sawtooth Valley. Here, on the north side of the summit, rises the middle fork of the Salmon River. Winding its way up the valley floor, it starts as a trickle and flows gently northward. Melting snow from the mountains on either side fills the lakes and streams, which in turn swell this crystal-clear river with every advancing mile. The jagged Sawtooths rise precipitously to our left, stretching off into a straight line to disappear in the distance some fifty miles to the north.

It was the fall season and an early dusting of snow had tipped most of the higher peaks, making it easy for the eye to follow the crest of the range. The valley through which we were driving was probably two miles wide and as level as a floor. To our right were the White Clouds, themselves rising to an elevation of over 10,000 feet. The two ranges, on opposite sides of the road, paralleled each other, cradling river and valley in between.

At the northern end of the valley, we stopped briefly at Stanley, Idaho, population 79, to refuel. Returning to the gravel road once again, we veered to the right and paralleled the ever-widening Salmon River, now bordered by thick stands of Douglas fir and Ponderosa pine.

Occasionally, high up on the slopes, we caught glimpses of isolated Aspen groves. Their brilliant yellow leaves shimmering in the bright sunlight bore witness to the nearness of winter. Except for the leaky car roof, we gloried in every minute of the trip north to Missoula.

7 December 1941

The Second World War had been raging in Europe since 1939, and although there was general apprehension that Japan might join the Axis powers, no one suspected what was about to happen. The event that shook the world on December 7, 1941, profoundly affected the lives of every living American and indirectly of half the population of the planet, and those who recall the event today have no trouble remembering their own activities on that fateful Sunday morning.

The KGVO studios were in town, but the transmitter was located on Highway 10, seven miles east. Air time on Sunday mornings was 8 a.m., which allowed me an extra hour's sleep. Snow had fallen quite heavily during the night, and was deep enough by morning to make driving difficult. Plows would have cleared the highway, but I was apprehensive about negotiating the hundred or so yards to the transmitter building itself. It turned out to be no problem, however, and, after clearing drifted snow from the front door, I entered and turned up the thermostat on the oil heater.

The tubes in the linear amplifier, which supplied 5,000 watts to the 200 foot Blaw-Knox vertical radiator, were water cooled, so we maintained room temperature during the night at 50° to prevent the water jackets and cooling system from freezing. Conversely, the heat generated by the transmitter vacuum tubes during daytime operating hours was enough to heat the building on the coldest winter days.

By mid-morning the weather had cleared, and it looked as though we were going to have a beautiful day. At the control console, I had just finished making an entry in the station log, when shortly before noon the CBS network announcer broke into a religious musical performance:

We interrupt this program to bring you a special news bulletin. The Japanese have launched a pre-emptive air strike against Pearl Harbor, Hawaii. The extent of any damage is not known, nor do we have a report of casualties at this time. Stay tuned. We will bring you additional information as it becomes available.

World War II had suddenly become a reality for 134,000,000 Americans. Within sixty days I had registered for the draft, taken a physical exam, and less than a week later was classified 1-A. I fully expected to be called up for military service with my old Kansas National Guard outfit, but the call never came. My 1-A status changed anyway when my job as a radio engineer was designated as essential to the country's communication network. The military promptly erected a large sign in front of the transmitter building that read:

BY ORDER OF THE WAR POWERS ACT THESE PREMISES
ARE OFF LIMITS TO ALL UNAUTHORIZED PERSONNEL

Shacked Up in Utah

With the advent of spring, we decided to upgrade our mode of transportation. Trading the Model A for a 1937 Chevy sedan, we left 'old faithful' in the hands of a dealer. Some time in May, I received a postcard from a radio friend of mine, now a civil service employee at Hill Air Base near Ogden, Utah. The immediate need there, he wrote, was for qualified instructors to teach radio theory to enlisted personnel in the rapidly expanding U.S. Air Force.

In June of 1942, having been accepted for employment at Hill Field, we left Montana for Utah. I was just one of thousands who had been drawn to Hill Air Base with a job offer, but when Mina and I arrived there, we had a problem. There was no place to live. Every nook and cranny in the area was bulging with humanity. Our situation appeared desperate until we finally inquired at the Chamber of Commerce in Clearfield, a small community nearby. We learned of a Mormon lady, a spinster named Nettie Sims who, with her elderly father, lived in a small farm home two miles west of Clearfield. According to the Chamber spokesman, she had a 'one room shack' at the rear of her house that she was willing to rent for eleven dollars a month. Hurrying out there, we found the description of the place to be completely accurate. We took it anyway.

Life soon became distressingly primitive in the 'out back', for not only did we lack conveniences, we did not even have the necessaries. We were allowed to use Nettie's electric refrigerator in the house for our perishables, and she agreed to sell us a tray of ice for a nickel. There was a two-burner coal oil stove for cooking. To use our chemical commode we had to go out the front door, down the steps and around to the side to a small door that led under the building. In spite of its shortcomings, however, the 'shack' reflected Mormon cleanliness which Nettie herself exemplified. Our new landlady, though homely in appearance and plain of dress, always had a cheerful, friendly smile. We had moved in on Friday, and I was to report for work the following Monday morning.

Tired and dirty from our trip, we asked Granddaddy Sims where we might take a bath. "Oh, that's no problem," he replied, "Just follow that path behind your house for a short distance and you'll come to the irrigation ditch. It's a great place for a bath." The idea did not strike me as a particularly good one, but surely he would know what was acceptable in his own neighborhood. The weather was quite warm, so with soap and towels in hand we headed off in the direction he had indicated. The water turned out to be refreshingly cool and swift flowing—not too bad after all, we decided. It became a ritual. Every evening we headed for a relaxing bath in the irrigation ditch.

About a week after we had taken up residence with the Sims, Mina reminded me that our commode would soon need to be emptied. Once again I sought the advice of Granddaddy. "Our chemical toilet is almost full," I said, "How do I take care of that?"

"That's an easy one," he shot back, "Out there behind your house there's a path that leads down to an irrigation ditch ..." The next day we bought a wash tub in which to bathe; our dips in the irrigation ditch were over. Later on, though, as Nettie got to know us better, she allowed us the use of her tub for 25¢ a bath.

Opportunity Knocks at United

Hill Air Base was a giant supply depot and training center that mushroomed almost overnight to a small city of civil service employees and military personnel. Just a few months after the Japanese attack on Pearl Harbor, the number of base workers had swollen to thousands. Towed by special vehicles, trains of four and five canopied flat cars, linked together, were used to transport workers from remote parking lots to their various work places around the base.

One morning in November 1942, as I boarded one of those 'people movers' for the six- or seven-minute ride to my classroom, I noticed that someone had left a newspaper on the seat next to mine. Idly thumbing through its pages, a small article caught my eye:

> United Air Lines announced today that it has signed a one year contract with the Air Transport Command to fly two round trips daily between San Francisco, California, and Brisbane, Australia. The first scheduled flights, however, may have to be postponed until crew personnel can be recruited.

Here, spread before me, was an open invitation to future employment in the airline industry which, but for sheer luck, I might never have seen. They would almost certainly need radio operators, I told myself. Tearing out the article, I stuffed it in my pocket, and after supper that evening, succeeded in persuading Mina that this apparent opportunity should be pursued. Before leaving for work the next morning, I used Nettie's telephone to call United's station manager in Salt Lake City.

"Sir," I began, "I understand United Air Lines is hiring crew members for military contract flights to Australia. Will they need radiomen?"

"I don't know," came the reply, "but if you'll hold on, I'll TWX San Francisco and find out." In a few minutes he was back on the 'phone. "They want to know if you have commercial licenses, the extent of your experience, and your present age."

Obviously they were interested. "Tell them I hold Telephone 1st and Telegraph 2nd licenses, and that I'm thirty years old," I replied.

As I waited, my excitement grew; I was almost certain I could qualify. What a great stroke of luck, I thought, to come across the newspaper article purely by accident. The station manager's voice came back on the line.

"Can you be down here tomorrow morning for the 8:15 flight to San Francisco? They want you out there on the Coast for an interview."

"Oh, yes, sir!" I said, hoping that Mina would agree.

"When you get here," he continued, "I'll have you ticketed for a round trip flight at company expense." I could hardly conceal my exuberance as I answered, "I'll be there."

The next day was Saturday; I did not have to work. Hanging up the telephone, I ran out of Nettie's back door toward our shack, wondering how Mina was going to take this news. We had hardly settled down, and now she would have to put everything back in boxes. She was delighted at the thought, however, that she might once again have her own icebox and indoor bathroom.

Rookie Radio Instructor

Immediately upon arrival at United's San Francisco base, I was interviewed and hired by Superintendent of Communications, H.L. Garrison. That same afternoon, after taking a company physical, I was sent across the Bay to the Oakland Airport for a three-week brush-up course at the Boeing School of Aeronautics. Upon completion of the course, I was to return to fly out of Mills Field which, at that time, was the San Francisco Airport. Mina, now an old hand at packing and unpacking, packed up once more, said goodbye to Nettie and Granddaddy, and flew back to Missoula to visit her mother.

With ground school out of the way, and Mina back in San Francisco, we took an apartment near the airport, in San Mateo. Flight crew members, recruited to fly for the military, were sent to an Air Force clothing depot where each man was issued a fleece-lined leather flight jacket, trench coat, khaki jump suit, two complete officer's uniforms, military head gear, and a B-4 bag. Rounding out the wardrobe were insignia identifying us civilians as officers in the Air Transport Command.

After a day or two more of indoctrination, I was assigned to a flight crew and ordered back to Salt Lake City to train a group of neophyte flight radio operators for the Air Force.

Now ... I think we need to bear in mind that I had been in an airplane only twice in my life: once in Mr. Hidecker's Eaglerock at the age of sixteen, and again just three months back, during my trip out to San Francisco. I found it hard to believe that I was sufficiently qualified to train other FROs, but, after all, there was a war on, and events in everyone's lives were being speeded up. Once again, I deadheaded back to Salt Lake City.

The following morning 'my' crew, consisting of captain, co-pilot, a flight check captain, and me, were driven to the airport. As we walked onto the ramp, the training aircraft, a military Curtiss Commando C-46, was standing nearby, along with my student group of half a dozen would-be flight radio operators. We all climbed aboard, and, while the pilots were taxiing out and running up the two engines, I introduced myself and went over radio procedure with the group, vainly trying to leave the impression that there was absolutely nothing I did not know about flying. The thought that these guys could not have known any more about the subject than I did, bolstered my flagging ego.

We strapped ourselves into the bucket seats, which lined each side of the cabin, and a few minutes later went roaring down the runway. Take-offs are usually noisy enough, but this airplane had no cabin insulation, which added to the uproar. Over the din, as we lifted into the air, we heard the captain yell, "Gear up!" but then a strange thing happened—at least, I thought it was strange. The cockpit door was standing open, and, as we watched, the check pilot, who had been sitting in the jump seat between pilot and copilot, now suddenly vaulted into the left hand pilot's seat as the pilot slunk underneath him and into the jump seat. In other words, they had exchanged places during take-off! Over the racket one of the GIs yelled, "What's going on up there?" Not wishing to appear ignorant, I shouted back, "Don't worry—that's the way they always do it!"

Pratt & Whitney R-2800 radial engines powered the C-46, and this particular craft was equipped with Curtiss electric propellers that were known to have a nasty habit of feathering out unexpectedly at critical times—in this case during take-off. One of the engines had to be cut. Landing three miles down range at an emergency airstrip, we managed to collect a bunch of telephone wires as we came in somewhat short of the runway. The scare shook me up, and I remained tactfully silent all the way back to the hotel. The pilots did all the talking.

Next morning, following a rather fitful night, I joined the three pilots in the hotel lobby, and after a light breakfast in the coffee shop, we headed once again for the airport to start over. In the meantime, the captain had learned that the Air Force was bringing up a different C-46—news that filled me with enormous relief.

My students had arrived at the field ahead of us, and were waiting expectantly on the ramp. Once again we went through the pre-flight procedures. It was a beautiful morning, and the prospects for a better day looked bright.

But that was not to be. We were scarcely airborne once more, when an excited voice from the cockpit shouted, "I don't have any rudder control!" I think it was about that time that I remembered how enjoyable my life had been while working in broadcast radio ... on the ground.

"My God!" I thought, "I'm supposed to go through this war flying? Two emergencies in the first two days? I'll never live long enough!"

In spite of the handicap of a locked rudder, however, the captain managed to maneuver the aircraft around to the other end of the field using rudder trim tabs and ailerons to make his turns, and landed. The problem: ground crews had removed the chocks from the ailerons and elevator, but had overlooked the rudder chock.

Usually painted a bright yellow or red for easy visibility, a chock is a wooden, V-shaped device with a bungee cord attached to one end. It is used to lock aircraft control surfaces in a fixed position to prevent them from flapping in a high wind while the aircraft is parked on the ground. Although not mandatory in those days, a challenge and response cockpit check would have turned up the locked rudder. It seems incredible that a pilot could reach take-off position without first making sure his controls were free.

I was pretty naïve about professional airline pilots at the time. They epitomized perfection to me; the cream of the species. Awed by their exalted position in life, I deemed it a privilege to touch the hems of their garments. Now, all of a sudden, there was reason to question their infallibility. I was to

(Above) UAL/ATC crew members along the Mackenzie Highway near Fort Simpson, Northwest Territories, Canada. During free time between flights, someone lent us a jeep. (Below) On the apron at Fort Nelson, B.C., this flight of Curtiss P-40s, bearing British markings, was in transit to Fort Franklin, Northwest Territories. 1943.

learn down through the years that pilots, too, were made of flesh and blood, just like the rest of us.

Northern Lights

We finally completed our program with no further problems and were returned to San Francisco where I was reassigned with another crew, this time to Edmonton, Alberta, for work in DC-3s, hauling oil-drilling supplies and personnel to the Canol Project in the Northwest Territories. This was an exploration project north of the Arctic Circle, based at Fort Norman Wells. Over the next couple of weeks we completed a number of trips through Ft. Simpson to this Mackenzie River outpost.

On one of these flights we overnighted at Ft. Nelson, and after dinner, as I stepped out of the mess hall into the night, I was treated to a dazzling display of Northern Lights. Suspended from a sky hook up there somewhere, they hung down like draperies, rippling from horizon to horizon, their delicate translucent shades subtly alternating from ice blue to pink. I stood, transfixed, watching this spectacular show for several minutes, convinced now that the stories I had heard as a boy about the Northern Lights were really true. Running for camera and tripod, I snapped three or four photos of the phenomenon.

Again reassigned, this time to Seattle, we shuttled through Anchorage, Alaska, and out along the Aleutian chain as far as Shemya. I remember seeing Russian pilots strutting around Ladd Field in Fairbanks, where they had come to ferry lend-lease aircraft back to the Soviet Union. They were big fellows, with their uniformed chests covered with medals. U.S. Air Force officers told us the Russians were picking up half a dozen fighter aircraft every day.

All these various assignments were interspersed with trips back to San Francisco, then home to Mina in San Mateo for a day or two. For us, gasoline rationing had now become a problem. With our six-cylinder Chevy, we barely had enough gas stamps to take me to and from the San Francisco airport. We decided to sell the car and go in search of more economical transportation. The four cylinder Model A, I remembered, had given us excellent gas mileage, so we headed for the city where used car dealers along Van Ness Avenue lined both sides of the street. Winding up at 'Horse Trader Ed's' lot, we closed a deal for a 1931 Model A Ford Coupe, the horse trader himself calling after us as we drove away, "You don't get much these days for $175, folks!"

Living eight miles from Mills Field, we now occupied the nicest apartment we had had since our marriage, but, predictably, Mina was not entirely happy with my new flying job. I had been away much of the time, but at least an icebox and indoor bathroom made her life much more pleasant.

The Douglas DC-3:
A Remarkable Flying
Machine

Something should be said here about the remarkable flying machine that Donald Douglas called the DC-3—C-47 or R4-D in military parlance. This twin-engined iron maiden, though made of aluminum, was as unyielding as a tank, and undoubtedly one of the safest and most dependable air transport 'planes ever to leave an assembly line. Compared to today's sophisticated aircraft, it was rugged simplicity itself. Yet, while in the air, it could withstand unbelievable punishment from the elements.

One pilot flew a C-47 over the 'Hump' from China to India with 72 people aboard. Originally designed to carry no more than 21 passengers, the C-47 was overloaded so often that it got used to it. The DC-3 made its first flight in December, 1935. By 1940, this work horse was carrying 80% of all airline traffic in the U.S., and, by 1945, about the same percentage of the traffic throughout the world. When Douglas stopped making them that year, more than 11,000 had been built, plus 6,500 under license in the Soviet Union and Japan; DC-3s were flying under the flags of at least thirty foreign air lines. A hundred or so are still active today.

Aleutian Flying

Consisting of captain, first officer, and radio operator, United Air Lines' crews, flying C-47s in the Aleutians for the military during the winter of 1942-43, had their work cut out. Ceilings of 300 to 500 feet, with a quarter to half a mile visibility, were commonplace, and we found ourselves flying 'in the soup' much of the time. Other than a compass, our only guideposts were the 'highways' of the sky: electronic radio ranges and homing beacons.

Icing, to one degree or another, was a constant threat, so in addition to carburetor heaters, our C-47s were equipped with de-icing boots on the

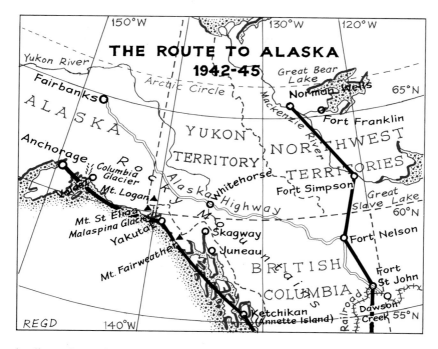

leading edges of the stabilizer, fin, and wings. Alcohol was pulsed to the propellers and windshield. Wing or prop ice could be very scary. A fifteen or twenty second burst of ice could reduce air speed from 180 to 140 mph.

More than one such brief episode could so seriously disrupt the wing's aerofoil surface that the airplane could no longer fly. With boots operating, clear ice pulsed off the leading edges of the wings rather easily, causing chunks of the stuff to strike the fuselage with such force that crew members thought they were being bombarded with croquet balls.

Rime ice was the hardest to dislodge because of its characteristically porous composition, but when ice of either variety formed on wing surfaces, only warm temperatures could remove it. When this happened, the pilot landed as quickly as possible and sought shelter in a hangar to allow the ice to melt. With all three crewmen working, every square inch of the wing's surfaces had to be dried by hand with rags before taking off again.

Weather signals were transmitted in Morse code in groups of five-digit numbers and were coded differently each day to prevent weather data from being deciphered by the Japanese. In Aleutian flying it was necessary to monitor weather reports continuously for fifteen or twenty landing facilities at a time, then decode the reports into usable information immediately. It was a demanding routine. I should have been concerned about the conditions under which we were flying, but I was far too busy to take much notice. (Incidentally, after years of sending and receiving signals using the Morse code, the combination of dots and dashes become so firmly imprinted in the mind that they are still easily read, even after five decades of retirement)

Ceiling and visibility at our destinations might be suitable for a landing approach one minute and be zero-zero the next, so the earphones never left my head during these flights. I seem to recall that those C-47s had water boilers of some kind that supplied heat to the cockpit, and of paramount importance—to the captain at least—was my responsibility in keeping that boiler at fever pitch. "Hey, radio operator, it's getting cold up here again," he would yell at me, "Let's keep that damn boiler fired up back there!"

Keith Murray, a co-pilot with Colonial Airlines at the time, wrote what he titled, 'The Co-pilot's Lament.'

> I am a co-pilot, I sit on the right.
> It's up to me to be quick and bright.
> I never talk back, to prevent regrets,
> >   but I must remember what the captain forgets!
> I make out the flight plan,
> >   and study the weather.
> I pull up the gear,
> >   and stand by to feather.
> All in all, I'm a general stooge,
> >   as I sit on the right of the man I call Scrooge.
> I guess that you think that it's past understanding,
> >   but maybe some day he'll give me a landing!

When United Air Lines was awarded military contracts at the beginning of the war, the cockpit jobs were put up for bid according to seniority. The 'prima donnas' of the air line—the company's senior pilots who had been flying routine domestic runs—were highly competitive in the rush to bid on the military flights. The spirit of adventure and the promise of change were the lure. They wanted excitement, and excitement they were to have, in good measure.

Beating Up on Bears and Glaciers

The constant stress of instrument flying in the Aleutians would be broken on rare occasions by a bright, sunny day. In the springtime it was just plain fun

(Top left) Minutes into our C-47 climb-out from Yakutat, southeastern Alaska, heading north, we cross Malaspina Glacier. From an altitude of 2,000 feet, its very size makes the slowly moving ice and earth appear much closer. (Bottom left) 15,300 foot Mount Fairweather is the highest point in British Columbia. Massive Fairweather Glacier, issuing from the range, spreads out to the ocean below. (Above) This awesome view of Columbia Glacier, on the route between Seattle, Washington, and Anchorage, Alaska, is one of the most impressive along the entire Alaskan Coast. During the winter months the atmosphere is seldom this clear, and even in the summer months, solid overcasts along the route are common.

to drop down to within a hundred feet of the ground, fly along the level beaches, and chase the bear packs as they munched away on berries.

As we came thundering down on them, they would turn to run, then realizing the futility of running, they would stop, whirl around, and rear up on their hind legs, clawing at us as we passed overhead. The DC-3 used a 200-foot trailing wire antenna that could be reeled in and out while in flight. We were so close to the ground on one occasion that the lead weight on its end struck something on the ground, ripping the antenna from the airplane. One of those bears perhaps?

Some of the most spectacular mountain scenery in the world lies in an almost direct line between Vancouver, Canada, and Anchorage, Alaska. On rare days when it is exceptionally clear, the unending views of glaciers and mountains from ten thousand feet up are awesome. The Fairweather Range and Icy Bay, Melaspina Glacier, 18,000-foot Mr. Saint Elias, and Columbia Glacier: these wonders parade before the eye in a dazzling display of nature's monuments.

The sheer faces of glaciers provided great sport for pilots. 'Gunning' the engines in a near fly-by could set up enough vibration to loosen tons of ice, sending it cascading off the glacier wall and into the sea. The impact, as it struck the surface, sent huge plumes of water hundreds of feet into the air. This happened on such a massive scale that the entire scene unfolded as if in slow motion.

Out along the chain, the bone-chilling wind blew incessantly, and grasses grew three feet high in the lowlands. For protection against unrelenting wind and penetrating cold, the military placed metal quonset huts half way underground, In clusters near the air fields, as many as ten or twelve variously sized buildings were connected together by half sunken tunnels. Steam heat throughout the entire complex kept its occupants comfortable. Those whose presence was not required on the flight line could, without leaving the shelter of the tunnels, visit the mess hall, library, barbershop, PX, movie theater, barracks, and general living quarters. It rains and rains out there, but it seldom snows, except in the higher elevations along the chain's backbone.

Until the outbreak of war, the Aleutian island chain was as remote from mainstream America as the craters of the Moon, and almost as inaccessible. But by the end of 1942, names of places such as Umnak, Adak, Unimak, Attu, Agattu, Kiska, and Dutch Harbor became thoroughly familiar (see map, page 157).

Based now in Edmonton, Alberta, with over three months and 250 hours of Alaskan flying behind me, I fancied myself a veteran. I was beginning to wonder, though, what had become of the trips to Australia that I had been promised when applying for the job. Then one day the order came returning me to San Francisco. I was being scheduled for a familiarization trip to Brisbane.

Armed to the
Teeth in C-87s

United eventually hired 75 crews to fly the military shuttles in the Pacific Theater for the Air Transport Command. Almost all these trips terminated in Australia, first at Brisbane, and later, as the war moved north, at Townsville. An occasional flight ended up at Auckland, New Zealand, and a series of trips late in 1943 through the Society and Cook Islands terminated at Pago Pago, Samoa.

Individuals were assigned to fly together as a crew. The co-pilot, navigator, radio operator, and flight engineer remained with the same captain until the contract ended late in 1946, nearly four years later. Performing as a team, we got along famously together. In all that time, I cannot recall a single incident in which a cross word passed between any of us. We slept and ate with the branch of the service that controlled the airfield at which we landed—sometimes in quonset huts and sometimes in tents. The military along our routes serviced the aircraft.

The captain with whom I was to fly for the duration was a gentleman named Fenton L. Brown—'Brownie' to everyone who knew him. He was a likable, easy-going man of rather slight build, with thinning, reddish brown hair, a ruddy complexion, and enough laugh lines in his face to make a wonderful smile. Probably in his mid-fifties, he was like a father to the rest of us, who were many years younger. When emergencies arose during the course of a flight, his calm, unruffled approach to the problem instilled confidence in us all. Along with several other pilots, Brownie had come up from Pan Am Ferries in Miami to fly the Pacific with United. Before WW-II, the Navy had a squadron of enlisted men who were navy qualified pilots, and Captain Brown had been one of those. Our crew's first officer, Harry Orlady, had just received his commercial license and multi-engine rating when United took him on. After the war, he was promoted to captain and flew with United until his retirement. Navigator Howard Keller took pilot training at the end of the military contract and also became a United captain.

William "Del" Dalleske, flight engineer, eventually went back to his old job in the San Francisco hangar as an inspector. Although Del was a couple of years older than I was, both Harry and Howard were in their middle twenties during the war years.

"Pop" Skinner, United's chief radio operator, was my immediate boss. He always kept a thermos of hot coffee in his desk drawer and a full cup constantly in front of him. Handling the scheduling for seventy-five radio operators, he made up the code packets, kept our communications manuals updated, and did occasional route checks.

We were supposed to have begun service using four-engined C-54s, the military version of the Douglas DC-4, but they were not immediately available, so the military provided us with a dozen or so C-87s, Consolidated-Vultee B-24 bombers that had been modified to transport passengers and cargo. C-54s did not begin coming on line until late 1943, and some of the C-87s were in service until the end of 1944. At that time the United Air Lines base at Mills Field in San Francisco had only two large hangars for aircraft service and maintenance. The Ad Building, adjacent to the hangars, housed administration, accounting, communications, sales, flight operations, and the medical department for United's entire Western Division. 'Pacific Operations' were conducted from the second floor of this building.

United's Pacific Network

To avoid confrontation with the enemy, we were given a route that took us far south of the battle zones. Crews were staged at Honolulu; Canton Island; Nandi, in the Fiji Islands; and Plaines Des Guyac, New Caledonia. The terminus was at Brisbane, Australia.

Scattered along this route were any number of small islands and atolls on which the American military had established weather reconnaissance stations. We brought them mail, priority supplies, and replacement personnel. Over the next three and a half years, we must have landed on every airfield in the South and Western Pacific that had a landing strip but was not in enemy hands. Later on, as the tide of battle turned and moved farther to the north, we were able to use new stepping stones to our Far East destinations.

An average of two United flights left San Francisco's Mills Field each day. Ferrying up to Hamilton Air Force Base in the North Bay, we picked up military payloads that consisted of everything from truck tires and electronic equipment to passengers and mail. Flying time to Hickam Field, Hawaii, in a C-54 was eleven to thirteen hours, depending on winds aloft. Our airplanes

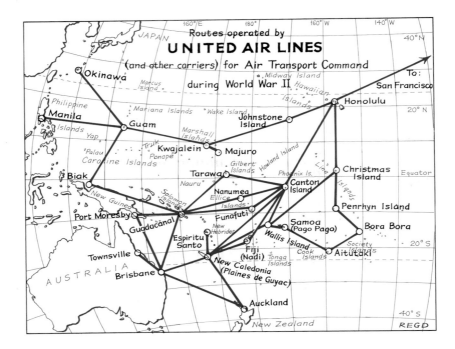

were not pressurized, and although we had oxygen for emergency use, flight levels seldom exceeded 13,000 feet.

To aid in guiding aircraft across the 2,398-mile stretch of water, the U.S. Coast Guard maintained three air/sea rescue vessels on track, in equidistant positions, between San Francisco and Honolulu. Later reduced to two, these ships were equipped with homing and communications facilities, and were prepared to assist any aircraft that might be lost or forced to ditch at sea.

Wartime Hawaii

Before the war, almost all tourists traveling to Hawaii from the mainland booked passage on the *Lurline,* pride of the Matson Lines passenger fleet. Necessitating five days travel time in each direction, ship excursions to the islands were enjoyed mostly by those who were wealthy enough to take extended vacations.

Commercial air travel in the Pacific before 1942 had been limited to Pan American Airways' trans-Pacific Clipper service, begun in 1936 with Martin 130s. These flying boats could transport a maximum of 32 passengers,

(Above) My United crew in front of the Outrigger Canoe Club on Waikiki Beach shortly after the beginning of United's ATC operation in the South Pacific. The barbed wire was not because the crew was incarcerated, but was hastily placed in anticipation of a Japanese invasion. From left: Flight Engineer Bill Dalleske; purser, unknown; Radio Operator Ralph Lewis; First Officer Harry Orlady; Flight Navigator Howard Keller; and Captain Fenton L. Brown. 1943. (Below) Waikiki and Diamond Head area as it appeared in 1953—a place of much beauty ... then. Clearly visible near the center of the photo is the Moana Hotel— at that time the largest structure along the entire beach front.

but the segment between California and Hawaii was limited to nine passengers because, at a range of 2,100 nautical miles, the Martin could not carry enough fuel and still handle a full passenger load. Its cruising speed was a sluggish 120 knots, often requiring in excess of eighteen hours to traverse this stretch of Pacific Ocean. In 1939 the Martin boats were replaced by the larger and longer-ranged Boeing 314s.

Travel by air to and from Hawaii was only for those who could afford the high fare. The big boom in tourism to the Islands began after the War, when larger and faster landplanes offered lower fares with more comfort and convenience.

Approaching Oahu from the Mainland in a DC-4 after a twelve hour flight, then letting down to round Diamond Head at about 2,000 feet, all of Waikiki came into view. The Moana Hotel, painted a gleaming white, was easily the most visible object along the entire five mile stretch of beach front.

United Air Lines' lay-over crews stayed at the Moana, one of only two hotels of major importance in Waikiki at that time. Hawaii was a relaxed, beautiful, and uncrowded paradise when we first landed there in early 1942. On the beaches, sun-tanned Hawaiian men, with plumeria blossoms tucked behind their ears, wore brightly printed shirts and shorts—their faces shielded from the tropical sun by palm frond hats. On the sidewalks along Kalakaua Avenue, native women, in colorful muumuus, their long black hair adorned with hibiscus, worked at their flower stands stringing leis in a happy, light-hearted spirit of friendly competition.

The Moana

The Moana hotel, a six-story, U-shaped wooden structure, was meticulously maintained: a prestigious old hostelry of world-wide fame, comparable to the Raffles in Singapore or Shephard's in Cairo. Its courtyard, which faced the ocean at the rear of the hotel, possessed one of the largest and most impressive banyan trees in all Hawaii. Following the war, the shady Banyan Court was a pleasant place during afternoon hours to sip mint juleps with friends while listening to the weekly Mutual Network broadcasts of 'Hawaii Calls'.

Directly across the street from the hotel were the Moana Garden Cottages. Scattered at random through two or three acres of spacious lawn, they provided a palm tree setting for hibiscus, plumeria, frangipani, pikake, and many other sweet-scented tropical flowers and shrubs. Amid all this languid fragrance and charm were the ever-present staccato notes of Mynah birds, which seem to be everywhere in Hawaii. Standing today, where those

The famous King Sisters perform in the Banyan Court of the Moana Hotel during a radio network performance of 'Hawaii Calls'. Honolulu, Hawaii, August 14, 1954.

Moana cottages used to be, is the fourteen-story Princess Kaiulani Hotel, itself now dwarfed by a jungle of still larger hotels and high rises.

Adjacent to the lobby, the spacious Moana dining room, supported on wooden pilings, extended beyond the water's edge. Surrounded by glass on three of its sides, guests were able to sit at a table beside an open window, look out over the blue Pacific to the horizon, and listen to the intermittent sound of the waves as they rolled lazily up on the sandy beach below.

The waiters were all men in those days. Diners were served with dignity and professional pride in a pleasant, unhurried atmosphere. Cordoned off in a corner of the dining room, stood a very large round table that seated a dozen crew members: the exclusive domain of Pan American flight personnel. The memorable old hotel dining room was torn down sometime around 1948.

To reflect that Waikiki, after just forty years, has been choked by hundreds of thousands of tourists is a sobering thought. The quiet charm of a lost era will never again return.

During the war years when nightfall came, all Honolulu was blacked out. Tiny shaded lights around the bases of the columns in the Moana Hotel lobby and hallways were carefully placed, enabling guests to find their way in the dark. The 'Blackout Room', which occupied the entire south wing of the hotel on the first floor, had all its outside windows painted black. After dark, this popular well-lighted room became the center of hotel social life, which usually extended well into the wee hours. Although most of the time there was standing room only, it was a place where GIs from off the street could meet to play cards or just visit the night away.

Steel rails, still in place in the center of Kalakaua Avenue, had at one time carried streetcars from downtown Honolulu to Waikiki's beach hotels, but in more recent years, the steel-wheeled cars had been replaced by electric trolley buses. Automobile traffic was subdued because gasoline was strictly rationed during the war.

All the civilian airline flight crews, under contract to the Air Transport Command, stayed at the Moana; USO troupes, traveling to and from the Pacific Theatre, were also transient guests. Many evenings, USO performers gathered around the grand piano in the blackout room, providing impromptu entertainment for all those who cared to listen.

Wartime Exigencies

A stark reminder of the nearness of war was the barbed wire barricade, hastily thrown up along the entire beach front from Kapiolani Park, past Ft. De Russy, and nearly to Kewalo Basin, in preparation for what just about everyone believed likely: a Japanese invasion attempt.

Narrow removable sections were taken out during the daytime so that swimmers and sunbathers would have access to the beaches. A hundred yards to the north of the Moana was the crown jewel of hotels in Hawaii, the Royal Hawaiian. Taken over by the U.S. Navy as a rest and relaxation facility, it became a temporary home to war-weary submariners, causing its facade to take on the appearance of a navy barracks. Strung between window ledges across the entire front of the hotel hung an assortment of white sailor suits, skivvies and navy hats, hung out to dry on makeshift clotheslines. Even the 'Royal' was forced to suffer such indignities on behalf of the war effort. The rapidly expanding military presence in the area reminded everyone that our nation was at war.

Social drinking among flight crew members, though common, was rarely done to excess. The twelve-hour rule, forbidding air crews to drink alcoholic beverages within twelve hours of flight time, was religiously adhered to, although there was a story going around that a United pilot, having imbibed too freely, was fired when his crew refused to fly with him.

Barbed wire stretches past Kuhio Beach in Waikiki to thwart a possible landing attempt by the Japanese enemy—an attempt that was never made. 1943.

One incident involving liquor, to which I can attest, created quite a stir one night in the Moana lobby. Members of a Pan Am flight crew were partying on the second floor when someone decided it would be fun to test the room's sprinkling system. Climbing up on the bed, they held a lighted match under the sprinkling head on the ceiling long enough to learn that it worked only too well. Water damage to the room and the gift shop in the lobby beneath, ran to several thousand dollars.

Call To Arms

In the attic area on the sixth floor was a section used by the hotel for storage. Contract crews were allowed to use the space to view and study silhouette slides of enemy aircraft and surface vessels. We were not supposed to be flying through battle zones, but the Air Transport Command felt that we should be able to identify hostile military forces, just in case. Someone must have suspected that sightings might be possible, and we soon realized that if this were to happen, we would be sitting ducks. Back at Mills Field a few days later, this point was brought out in a conversation with United's Operations Department, which in turn notified Hamilton Air Force Base of our concern.

On the very next trip through Hamilton, the refueling, cargo loading, and tie-down took considerably longer than usual—until nearly three in the morning—and we were anxious to start. Finally clearing the blocks, we taxied out to the end of the runway and were waiting for take-off clearance when the tower radioed, "Operations has asked that we hold you; they're sending a jeep out with something."

Del went to the rear of the cabin and held the door open while two GIs, standing on the hood of the jeep, hoisted a machine gun up and onto the cabin floor, then waved us off from below and drove away. No ammunition, mind you, just the gun, and no way to mount it. Each of our other airplanes, in its turn through Hamilton Air Base, received one of these weapons with the same careful, but somewhat limited, attention to detail that had been accorded to ours. I suppose we could have thrown the gun at the enemy, but that idea did not seem too practical. Our 'protection' rattled around on the floor in the rear of those C-54s throughout the war.

A Close Encounter
of the Worst Kind

Ever since Matthew Brady experimented with the daguerreotype process in the 1840s, the art of photography has provided the world with a window on itself. Unsurpassed by any of the other graphic arts, its successful use requires only a sharp eye, an artistic nature, and a healthy imagination. A camera lens instantaneously captures and preserves, in exacting detail, a thin slice of time which otherwise would instantly recede into the abyss of fading memory and be lost forever.

My fascination with the magic of cameras began early in life, as Mother gathered us children around the kitchen table after dark, to develop and print pictures of family groups. I could not have remembered so many of life's experiences without the prompting of images captured by my cameras through the years. When Mina and I were married, friends gave us a 'box brownie' as a wedding gift, and from that moment on, my serious involvement in photography was off and running.

Through A Lens—Lightly

By the time my flying career with United had begun, I had acquired a $2^1/_4$" x $2^1/_4$", single lens, Korelle Reflex camera and was taking pictures of everything I saw. Life for this Kansas boy, who in twenty-five years had scarcely left his home town, was now moving along so rapidly that every sight and sound was new and interesting. Accompanying me everywhere I went, camera and tripod became part of my being. Flying in Alaska and the South Pacific provided picture opportunities of an unlimited variety, and I lost no time in putting it all on film.

I think that when our surroundings remain unchanged year in and year out, we take a casual, even superficial, approach to the beauty around us, simply because it has become so familiar. A stranger can visit and notice all kinds of marvels which have never aroused our interest because, to us, the same things have become commonplace.

A few years ago, Mina and I spent nearly two months in Greece and Yugoslavia with Greek neighbors who had a number of close relatives in Athens. These Athenians had lived their entire lives in the shadow of one of the most famous landmarks in the world, yet had never climbed the hill in the center of the city to visit the Acropolis. In the same vein, many Londoners have never been in the Tower or visited St. Paul's Cathedral or Westminster Abbey.

After flying in the Pacific for about a year and having accumulated hundreds of photographs, the thought occurred to me one day that a book of photographs taken along our routes might have commercial possibilities. After selecting about 30 of my best negatives and talking Ed Harris, a good friend of mine, into doing some caricature illustrations, I set up a temporary photolab in the bathroom of our San Mateo apartment and, over Mina's mild protest, went into business.

Turning out a sample book, I titled it *Pacific Landfall* and began taking orders from fellow crew members. Before I knew it, the whole situation was well out of control. I collected 125 orders almost overnight, which meant that nearly 4,000 5"x7" pictures had to be printed in our bathroom. Counter space was at a premium, so the enlarger had to repose on top of the toilet stool lid, the only place left to put it. Of course, all those photographs had to be washed—in the bathtub—then dried on bed sheets spread out all over the living room floor, making the room almost inaccessible. Mina had to bathe in the kitchen sink, and the enlarger had to be moved every time we needed the toilet.

Our apartment was in shambles, but the book was a big success. President Patterson of United Air Lines wrote asking for one, and United's Captain E.B. Jeppesen, publisher of a pilot's route facilities manual, placed an order. My reputation as a photographer had been established, at least among United's flight crews.

Tree Contact

Driving to Mills Field very early one morning, for my second or third flight to Australia, I parked in United's lot and went up to flight operations to join Brownie and the rest of the crew for briefing. Del Dalleske was already out on the flight line checking the fuel load and preflighting the aircraft. While Brownie and Harry Orlady filed a flight plan, Howard and I checked the weather, ran down the list on the Notams bulletin, and signed for our sealed code briefings.

Picking up our personal gear, the four of us descended the stairway to the first floor and headed toward the ramp in front of the hangars. As we left the Ad Building and stepped out into the night, I checked my watch; it was 3:30 a.m. Walking toward the airplane, the beam from Del's flashlight was visible off in the distance as he scoured the ground beneath the engines checking for possible oil leaks.

"How are things lookin', Del?" Brownie asked as we approached. Del's light swung up into the left wheel well momentarily. Apparently satisfied with what he saw, he turned toward us and wiped his hands with a rag that hung from his waist.

"We'll be ready to go as soon as I pick up the log book."

Boarding the airplane a few minutes later, the pilots started the four engines while the flight engineer stood by with the fire bottle on the ramp below. After pulling the nose and main gear pins, Del climbed the ladder, bringing it up behind him, closed and locked the cabin door, and headed for the flight deck.

We had already begun to roll as Co-Pilot Harry Orlady asked the tower for taxi instructions. There was no traffic at this time of the morning, and we were soon positioned at the end of the runway. During the four-engined run-up for mag checks, the tower advised, "United 456 ... you're cleared for take-off." With minimum fuel and no payload, the C-54 literally leaped into the air. Leveling off at 1,500 feet, a heading of 018° would take us to Hamilton Air Force Base, 75 miles north of San Francisco.

Hamilton Field itself is almost at sea level, but just off the north end of the runway is a wooded ridge of hills that is perhaps a few hundred feet in elevation. On that particular night there was no moon. No physical features on the ground were visible, just a few scattered lights below us here and there. As we came abreast of Hamilton, Harry reported us on the down-wind leg, and asked for landing instructions. Brownie, who was at the controls, made a 180° left turn for final approach to the runway and was descending when he called for gear down and first stage flaps. Harry dropped the gear and echoed Brownie's order, "Gear down!"

Not more than ten seconds later, we were all startled by a sudden jarring jolt. Almost simultaneously, the left inboard engine went into severe vibration. No mistaking the feeling. We all knew that we had struck something. No time now to feather, Brownie had just called for full flaps. Within seconds, we were over the end of the runway, wheels on the ground.

Brownie did not taxi right in to the terminal. Instead, after feathering the number two engine and allowing the airplane to complete its roll, he pulled up in a taxiway and asked Del to climb down the ladder to have a look around. Things had suddenly become very quiet in the cockpit now, as Brownie slid back the window on his left, waiting for Del's report from below. Could we have hit a large bird or possibly a seagull? Not likely at night.

As the beam from Del's flashlight fell on the main landing gear, what we had hit became immediately apparent ... There, wedged into the left wheel strut, was a broken-off six-foot section of a tree limb with the leaves still on it. Del shouted something unintelligible up to Brownie who could not make him out over the noise of the three idling engines. Managing to free the limb, Del wrestled it up the ladder and into the airplane, putting it with some difficulty into the rear toilet area.

The responsibility for this near fatal accident had to rest with the captain. His approach had obviously been too low. Then and there, Brownie called the crew together in the cockpit.

"What can I say to you!" he agonized, "If you choose never to fly with me again, I couldn't blame any of you." He shook his head in a helpless gesture of resignation. None of us knew Captain Brown that well at the time, but it was Del, who broke the momentary silence.

"We're your crew, Captain, and we'll stand by you till the end of this war."

Somehow, Del said what we all had wanted so say. We were young and youth has a way of forgiving. Our arms went up in unison and, with a resounding yell from each of us, the incident was over; we had had a very narrow squeak. We all knew the risks we were facing and were fully aware that something like this might happen again.

At Brownie's suggestion, Del went down the ladder a second time to have a closer look at the damaged propeller. Although obviously out of balance, a careful examination of the prop with his flashlight revealed no physical evidence of impairment. Upon his return to the flight deck however, we all shared the belief that the number two fan had struck and severed the tree limb, throwing it into the landing gear.

As we taxied in toward the terminal ramp, Del's entry in the log book complained of the vibrations experienced in the left inboard engine, but the whole truth was never reported. Three hours later, army mechanics had replaced the propeller, fuel had been loaded and cargo tied down. Poised at the end of the runway and anxious to go, we took off and climbed out over the Farallon Islands just as the sun topped the horizon behind us.

Many years later, I had occasion to visit Del in his San Bruno home, and there, polished and mounted over the fireplace mantle in the living room, was that tree limb, a chilling reminder of the incident which had nearly ended our lives that early September morning in 1942.

All in a Day's Work

Continuing westbound to Canton Island the following day, our crew had asked for a 4:30 a.m. wake-up call at the desk of the Moana Hotel. I was still not used to getting up in the middle of the night, but that's the way it is in the flying business: breakfasts at two in the morning and dinners at midnight. Half asleep, I hassled my B-4 bag, brief case, and camera gear down the hall toward one of the two elevators in the hotel. Both of them, tantalizingly slow, emerged below on opposite sides of the veranda-like lobby. The dining room, of course, was not open this time of the morning, and the festivities in the 'Blackout Room', from the night before, had long since ended. Except for the desk clerk, who appeared to be sorting through some mail, and a bell boy, who was asleep on a luggage rack near the gift shop entrance, the lobby was empty. The only sound to be heard came from the ocean side of the darkened Banyan Court as small waves, broken by shallowing coral, whooshed halfheartedly upon the beach.

The tiny foot-lamps, scattered around the lobby, provided enough illumination to identify other members of the crew standing outside the open-fronted exit to Kalakaua Avenue. First Officer Orlady and the male flight attendant, who was to be part of our crew this day, apparently had not come down yet. Crossing the lobby, I joined my companions in time to hear Brownie suggest that we eat breakfast at the airport coffee shop. We chatted until the other two fellows emerged from the elevator a few minutes later, checked out, and joined us on the hotel porch.

Our crew car was right on time as it entered the crescent-shaped driveway from the street and stopped under the high wooden portico in front of the steps at the hotel entrance. Loading our luggage, we climbed into the army carry-all for the thirty-minute ride to the airport. As we drove along in silence through the balmy, night-scented Hawaiian air enjoying this peaceful place, the war seemed remote indeed. It was difficult to believe that, just a short distance away, half the U.S. Pacific fleet lay destroyed and useless, sunk to the bottom in the mud at Pearl Harbor.

Take-Off to Canton Island

We usually flew out of Hickam field with cargo, but this particular morning our load was military passengers. Bound for Townsville, Australia, they were in transit at nearby John Rogers Airport. The trip had originated at Hamilton Air Force Base in California, and our crew was to fly it on to Canton Island (now renamed Abiriringa), in the Phoenix Group (now part of the republic of Kiribati), about a ten-hour flight in a DC-4.

Pulling up in front of the terminal building at John Rogers (later renamed Honolulu International) the crew entered and split up. Navigator Keller and I headed slowly up the long flight of stairs to the CAA communication center on the second floor. This seemingly endless succession of steps severely tested our endurance. Climbing them was a reminder that on the day when we could no longer make it to the top without resting halfway up, we would have to give up flying. It probably was not the steepness or length of the treads that exhausted us, but rather the hour. We always seemed to be tackling this stairway in the middle of the night.

The master clock on the wall up there was kept accurate to within a couple of seconds. Howard checked his hack watch while I set my Hamilton wrist watch. ('Hack watch' was the slang name applied to a pocket or wrist-type watch whose second hand could be set precisely to the correct time. Probably derived from the expression 'hack the time,' meaning to set exactly, the term was commonly used by commercial airline and air force navigators during WWII when referring to a navigation time-piece.) Correct time is important in celestial navigation because, at the Equator, a one second error in time can result in a quarter mile error in the airplane's position. We walked together down the hall to meteorology for weather briefing. The 700-millibar chart in the weather folder forecast a nine-knot tail wind at our proposed flight level, with no appreciable weather en route other than scattered cumulus at 3-4,000 feet.

Dropping in at the KVM Radio Control Center, I chatted for a few minutes with the operators who would provide us with telegraphic contact halfway to Canton. Voice communication with aircraft over long stretches of water was not practical at that time. Consequently, all en route reports were transmitted by CW (dots and dashes). Air-to-ground voice contact was used only with airport towers and area approach controls.

Harry had already gone to operations to do his weight and balance when Howard joined him to work the flight plan and figure the fuel load. A short while later, the three of us went downstairs together to meet Brownie and the purser in the coffee shop for breakfast.

The first light of day was beginning to show in the east as we walked to the airplane. Passengers were boarded, and we departed from John Rogers on schedule. Climbing up through a broken stratus deck, we emerged into bright sunlight at 6,000 feet and leveled off at 10,000 feet, our assigned cruising altitude. After engaging the auto pilot and synchronizing the four propellers, the two pilots had little else to do for the next nine or ten hours. Brownie, the only smoker in the crew, lit a cigarette and reached for the Sunday paper he had picked up at the terminal gift shop. Our purser had come to the flight deck with coffee and rolls. It was a beautiful morning; there was time to relax.

Beneath us, scattered to the horizon against a backdrop of deep blue ocean, small patches of billowy white cumulus clouds now stretched out to infinity in all directions. Here and there a white cap on the water below gave evidence of an occasional wind gust on the surface. The four engines were singing their favorite song, and the exhilaration experienced from being a flyer seemed to make everything right with the world.

It was time now for the rest of the crew to go to work. Contact was established with KVM, and an hourly position reporting time scheduled. Del, the flight engineer, would keep an eye on the oil quantity gauges, monitor cylinder-head temperatures and manifold pressures, record fuel flow to the engines, transfer gas when necessary, and occasionally check the sight gauges on the two cabin fuel tanks.

Dead Reckoning

The busiest man on the flight deck was the navigator. Updating his position, he was constantly at his chart table. Howard's flight plan for this leg to Canton called for 10 hrs. 18m. During WWII, the U.S. invented and developed a revolutionary navigation system based on radio waves that travel at the speed of light. A master station triggers a nearby slave station and a vessel receiving these radio signals can plot a line of position by reading microsecond time differences on a cathode ray scope. Known as Loran (long range navigation), it was accurate, fast, and relatively simple to use, but was not deployed in the Pacific Theater until late in 1944.

Although military aircraft had radar at that time, none of the airplanes in use by contract carriers was so equipped. Airline navigators had to rely entirely on celestial navigation, dead reckoning, and the few radio beacons that existed in the South Pacific.

At night, if there was no cloud cover, celestial worked very well, but during daylight flights, when all the navigator had was the sun, and sometimes the Moon and Venus for 'lines of position,' it was another matter entirely. The Moon and Venus are often too close to the sun to obtain good cuts, and Venus, if it was to be seen at all, had to be precomputed with the octant to locate in broad daylight. To locate Venus during daylight hours, the airline navigator assumes a DR (dead reckon) position, then for that position, consults his almanac and star tables to extract the azimuth and elevation of the planet for the correct time and date. He then positions the octant for those coordinates. Assuming his aircraft is somewhere near his DR position, and there is no haze in the upper atmosphere, he should be able to spot Venus somewhere within the range of the eyepiece on the octant. Trying to find the planet in the daytime without precomputing is nearly impossible. Once it has been located, he takes a two-minute sighting to arrive at the body's true elevation.

To complicate matters, there was no alternate for Canton Island, which is only seven miles long and three miles wide, so Howard, as required, had flight-planned three hours holding fuel. Running down a small dot in the vast Pacific Ocean during the day, after flying over water for ten or more hours,

The navigator takes a two-minute sighting on the sun. He wears a watch on each wrist ... one for local time, and the other for Greenwich time. The aircraft, a C-87, was one of several flown by United at the beginning of its military contract, until C-54s became available. Note the plastic cover across feathering buttons (upper right) to prevent accidental feathering. 1943.

can be very risky. If the island happens to be covered by any one of hundreds of small cumulus clouds, it can be missed entirely. This is where the sun line comes in. A 'line of position' is arrived at by 'shooting' the sun with an octant, a device that measures the angle between the sun and the horizon, and, when plotted on the navigator's chart, represents the body's sub-stellar point.

If you are traveling west and the sun is somewhere in the sky directly in front of you, or directly behind you, a plotted sun line will lie on the chart at right angles to your direction of travel; this is called a speed line. Your position is somewhere along this line, but without a cross bearing from some other source, there is no way to pinpoint your exact location on that line.

Positions based on dead reckoning are derived from forecast winds and ground speed only, so if the forecast is in error, there is an excellent possibility that the airplane will drift away from the desired course line. Nine hours into this trip, the outside air had been so smooth it was like sitting in an arm chair at home, which prompted Brownie to comment, "Routine flights ... that's the way I like 'em!"

But hour upon hour of position reports are terribly dull when there is nothing out there to look at but huge expanses of ocean in all directions. In many areas of the Western Pacific, we had only hourly sun lines, forecast winds, and educated guesses to use in determining our position during the daytime. This particular day wore on until our latest DR position placed us just an hour or so from Canton Island. Howard jotted down his best estimate for time of arrival (ETA) on a slip of paper and with a piece of masking tape, stuck it to the pedestal in front of the pilots. He would have to make a sun line approach.

As we near our destination, we must know which side of the island we are going to be on as we come abreast of it. To be absolutely certain, the navigator introduces a slight error by changing the aircraft's heading enough to be sure he will be well to the right ... or to the left. It makes no difference which, just as long as he knows. Now he plots sun lines, one after another, each one advancing down his track as he goes. When he finally plots a line of position that passes through his destination, he instructs the pilot to make a turn to the right or left, depending on which side of the island he knows himself to be.

Posting a heading that will carry the aircraft down that line of position, he continues to make two-minute observations of the sun. What had been speed lines now become course lines. He must be certain that each succeeding line he plots falls across his destination. Several such approaches were made to Canton Island before the military located a truck there that emitted homing signals from a whip antenna, but sun line approaches were always a tense experience. Night-time navigation was much easier because sightings could

Barren Canton Island—almost on the equator— had but a couple of trees, the tallest of which was used as an observation post. There is no earth here, only bleached fossils of tiny sea organisms, but a coconut tree will grow in coral. The sign over the officer's quarters (in foreground) reads "Hotel Astor".

be made on three stars evenly distributed around the airplane's azimuth, which yielded excellent fixes.

If all goes well and the crew keeps a sharp lookout, the island will be spotted. If not ... the flight could end up as Amelia Earhart and her navigator, Frank Noonan, did: lost and in the water. (All other speculations as to Amelia's fate are products of wild imagination or commercial avarice. We found the problem difficult enough in a technically advanced, almost brand new, C-54. Fred Noonan was on his own in a 1938 twin-engined Lockheed 14).

Gear Down—Eventually

This day we were just three minutes behind flight plan when a sun line put us abreast of Canton. Howard changed the aircraft's heading to parallel the sun line, and Brownie began his letdown. Ten or twelve minutes later we leveled off at 2,000 feet, with all eyes straining to catch a glimpse of the island, which should be somewhere up ahead of us. Over water, low clouds in the distance can play tricks on you; you swear you have landfall in sight, but upon closing in, what you thought was land turns out to be just another cloud.

On our very first trip through Canton Island, a refreshing dip in the lagoon seemed like a good idea. We paid dearly for the pleasure ... with second and third degree burns, our skin peeled off in chunks. Copilot Harry Orlady reads a book, as Captain 'Finnie' Brown, Navigator Howard Keller, and our purser take the water. 1942.

Temperature and humidity are quite comfortable at cruising altitude, but we were approaching Canton Island, which lies two degrees south of the equator. In this latitude, and at low elevation, the cabin becomes hot and humid. Body heat, generated by a full load of passengers, only exacerbates the problem. We had no air conditioning.

For eleven more unpleasant and anxious minutes we flew down a succession of sun lines. Finally ... we all experienced a sense of relief when the island was positively identified away in the distance.

"Wanna take her in Harry?" Brownie asked. Harry's answer came with a nod of his head as he slid his seat forward a couple of notches and checked the buckle on his seat belt.

"Canton tower, this is United Two Five Three" Brownie called. "We have the island in sight ... five miles out on long final ... landing instructions please."

"Roger, United, you're cleared straight in. Altimeter 29.95."

The Canton archipelago comprises a string of narrow coral islands, pear shaped, with a lagoon in the center. No point on the island is more than six or eight feet above the level of the surrounding ocean. There is no earth, as we know it, just blinding white coral. In 1942, the island sported one well known tree, a thirty foot coconut palm. American GIs built a lookout platform at its top.

For the first time since the crew had been together, Harry had been offered a landing and he was understandably nervous.

On short final now, he called for 15° flaps, but in concentrating on his approach, he forgot to call for gear. Brownie waited as long as he dared, then finally had to remind him.

"I think you're gonna need wheels to land this thing, Harry!"

The airplane came down smoothly on the coral runway, just twenty-one minutes more than estimated flight time. We taxied to the terminal behind a 'follow me' jeep. The engines were shut down, gust lock set, and the nose and main gear pins dropped to the ground crew. I entered flight and block times in the ship's log book; we had had a good day.

The Truth Was Never Told

The southeastern part of New Guinea with its main port, Port Moresby, was never in the hands of the Japanese. After the Allied occupation of the Solomons in 1943, and the securing of New Britain and Bougainville islands in March of 1944, the civilian airlines flying for the Air Transport Command (A.T.C.) began serving these areas. At that same time, March 1944, our Australian terminus was moved 680 miles north, from Brisbane to Townsville, further up the Queensland Coast.

The war took another step farther north and west when the Japanese defense of Guam collapsed in September of 1944. Tinian and Saipan also fell, and soon after, the Mariana island group became an armed camp from which American bombers could strike the Philippines and Japan. Then, early in 1945, Iwo Jima gave way to a bloody onslaught by U.S. Marines, bringing American air power even closer to the Japanese homeland.

Kwajalein, as it appeared in 1945. The airstrip is located on the largest of a circular string of coral islets with a giant lagoon in the center. Today the island is the site of a U.S. missile tracking and testing facility.

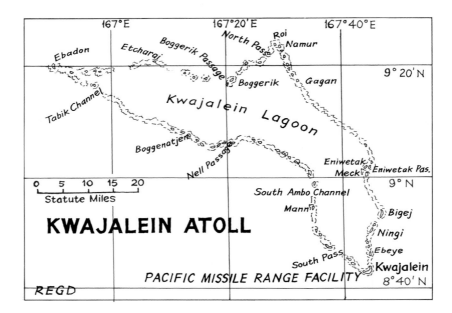

Kwajalein atoll was wrested from the enemy in 1944, and soon replaced barren Canton Island as a lay-over point for us. 'Kwaj,' too, was almost entirely devoid of trees, but not for lack of soil. Trees and shrubs had been shredded away by shellfire during intense fighting when the Americans stormed and took the island. Dead Japanese were buried in mass graves, and I recall seeing human bones as they washed ashore on the incoming tide. By the time I had made my last flight through Kwajalein in 1962, the ravages of war had disappeared and Nature's rejuvenation process had completely restored the island's thick mantle of coconut trees.

Pacific Island Life

By the middle of 1945, several hundred thousand American GIs were serving in the military throughout the Pacific Basin. During this island-hopping process, the Navy's construction battalions moved in with heavy equipment, leveling out dozens of airstrips on as many coral islands. Crushed and packed coral made excellent runways, and in areas where coral was not available, sectional steel matting, which was able to withstand heavy military traffic, was used.

(Left) Best buddies, these happy Fiji Island debutantes are seen cooling their feet in the river near Nandi, Fiji. 1943. (Right) Need a shower? Fred Gentner, UAL navigator, had only to step outside his tent in the downpour with a bar of soap. Henderson Field, Guadalcanal. 1943.

For over two years, Nandi (Nadi), Fiji, was a layover point for A.T.C. contract crews, who usually averaged stays of only 24 hours—not much time to explore the surroundings. There were wild horses in the Fiji Islands then, and GIs went into the hills, caught and broke them, and kept them tethered to their squad tents for personal transportation. Occasionally, if we had sufficient layover time, we were able to borrow a horse or two and ride from the airfield to Nandi, or even Lautoka, a good-sized town some distance farther away.

We were overnighting at Guadalcanal within a few months of the American Marines takeover there, and although the fighting had stopped, the GIs were living a pretty miserable existence. Most of Guadalcanal was a tropical jungle which had to be cleared for landing fields and living space. The Seabees were still laying steel matting at Henderson Field when we flew in for the first time. We lived in tents, tolerated field kitchens and mess kits, and suffered mosquitoes; malaria was a constant threat.

Wash bowls were inverted helmets set in a waist-high plank and diversions of any kind were non-existent; certainly no Carole Lombard or Betty Grable movies. Cigarettes and beer seemed to be even more precious to the GIs than food . Always in plentiful supply, these items were among the first to be brought ashore by landing vessels.

Night and day on Guadalcanal was like living in a perpetual steam bath. We could almost wring water out of our bed sheets. Because of the humidity, there was no way to dry them. Warm rain fell incessantly and hard, so we had no problem taking a shower. With no women around yet, we just stepped out of our eight-man pyramidal tent into the downpour naked with a bar of soap. The problem came when we tried to dry ourselves.

A favorite prank to play on our fellow travelers was to catch a toad or frog, both of which were plentiful; and, after the victim had tucked his mosquito netting under his mattress in the early evening, slip the creature under the netting and onto the uninitiated victim's bed. This little trick generated considerable excitement in the middle of the night, until everyone learned to check his bed very carefully with a flashlight before climbing in.

During the New Guinea layovers we often saw bands of highland natives from the interior of the island as they wandered down into the camps selling handmade souvenirs. Formidable looking groups armed with eight-foot spears, they tramped in from the jungle trails. If you happened to be downwind from these aborigines, you smelt them before you saw them. Their painted faces, distorted by bones through their noses and crude brass rings through their ear lobes, could make John Wayne himself run for cover!

Now and then a crew left the States with a substitute crew member. On one such trip, Howard, our regular navigator, had developed a bad cold, so United's navigation department assigned a replacement. A company check pilot was also aboard to give Captain Brown a route check. We were scheduled to leave Nadzab, New Guinea, at midnight on a four hour flight south to Townsville, Australia, a distance of 680 miles. In light of the departure time, we had all hit the sack right after an early dinner, all of us, that is, except this pinch-hitting navigator who, having run into some old Aussie friends of his, decided to party right up to the last minute.

Airborne on schedule, we climbed to level off; it was always a relief to reach cruising altitude when flying in the tropics. On the ground, the moisture-saturated atmosphere caused clothing to cling to our bodies, and constant sweating, no matter how clean we were, made us feel dirty. One hour at flight altitude, though, and we all dried out. This particular night was remarkably clear. A full moon mirrored itself on a glassy sea, lighting up the night sky with its reflection. Winds aloft were forecast to be light and variable, with no en route weather of any kind. Our Townsville destination was forecast to be clear, with unlimited visibility.

Feeling somewhat weary from his evening with friends, our substitute navigator scribbled a heading of 185° on a scrap of paper and taped it to the magnetic compass in the center of the cockpit windshield. Then, handing me prepared DR (dead reckoned) positions to report for the next couple of hours, he headed for the rear of the airplane where he could stretch out on a stack of military mail sacks for a little nap time.

All four fans were churning away normally as we settled down for a short but boring flight. The three pilots: Brownie, with one foot cocked up on the throttle pedestal, had lit a cigarette; the check captain stood behind him, chatting over his shoulder, and Harry, having removed his shoes, relaxed in the right hand seat. Del, the flight engineer, occupied the jump seat.

The four of them whiled away the night drinking coffee, telling stories, and otherwise making small talk about flying, as pilots are inclined to do, pausing only to correct a slightly precessing auto-pilot now and then, or jockeying the props for synchronization. The air was as smooth as glass, and each hour I reported our position based on the DR forecast, which the now sleeping navigator had given me.

As the night and the chit-chat wore on, so did time, which seems to pass more quickly when no one is paying attention. Suddenly, Harry leaned forward, peering intently through the cockpit windshield.

"I thought I saw a light down there" was his surprised comment.

Brownie reached down, dimmed the cockpit lights, and, shading his eyes with his hands, also leaned into the window. Sure enough ... just ahead, stretched the Australian coast, clearly outlined and visible in the bright moonlight. Straining a bit harder now, he was able to make out the lights of a city thirty-five or forty miles in front of and to the right of us.

"Hey! That's Townsville out there!" Brownie's sudden confirmation brought everyone alive. Hurriedly disengaging the autopilot, he eased forward on the yoke and readjusted the throttles, sending the nose down slightly. The rate-of-climb indicator soon steadied at 500 feet descent per minute. Townsville had apparently slipped up on us.

"There must have been a light unforecast tail wind," Brownie guessed out loud—more in question than statement. Turning around, he called to me. "Where's that navigator?"

Without bothering to answer, I headed back to the cabin to wake the guy up; he had slept through the entire leg. Upon returning to the flight deck, the altimeter at the navigator's station had wound down through 5,000 ft., and the pilots were trying to raise someone on the ground.

Townsville, Here We (Don't) Come

"United Air Lines 891 calling Townsville tower ... do you read?" ... Several seconds passed; no response. Harry, who was doing the calling, thought we might still be too far away to be heard. Hanging up the mike, he bent over to put his shoes back on, as the lights in the distance grew steadily nearer. "Better give 'em another blast, Harry." Brownie ordered.

Again Harry took the microphone from its hook, repeated the call, then reached down to turn up the volume on the receiver, but his only audible reward was the monotonous crackling of background noise. The second try was as fruitless as the first. Could he be using the wrong frequency? Route information from his briefcase quickly confirmed that he was not.

Crossing through 3,000 feet, the runway lights, quite visible now, twinkled brightly across the night sky in front of us. Glancing at his watch, the check pilot, who up to this point had said nothing, speculated, "The tower operators are probably all asleep. It's just a bit after three in the morning down there."

At 2,000 feet, and still three miles out on long final, Harry made still another attempt to raise the tower.

"Townsville Tower ... Townsville Tower ... United 891, on final approach ... we need landing instructions, please."

It was no use, they were not answering. Gear and flaps came down and we were soon on the ground. Turning into a taxiway, we had begun rolling toward a distant lighted area before it finally dawned on any of us that something was wrong.

"They must have moved the operations area," Brownie was saying. "I don't seem to recognize anything."

After all, we had just been in Townsville the month before. They could not have rearranged the entire field in that time. Brownie paused out there on the taxi strip, confused, wondering where to go next, when out of the darkness a pair of headlights appeared, moving in our direction. Someone was coming out to intercept us.

As the vehicle pulled up on the tarmac in front of the airplane and stopped, Brownie poked his head out the window. A man had stepped from a 'follow me' jeep down below, and a beam from his flashlight caught Brownie's face as he yelled up, "Who are you blokes?"

Cupping his hands around his mouth in an effort to make himself heard over the noise of the running engines, Brownie shouted back, "We're United Air Lines, flying for the Air Transport Command ... We've got a load of mail for you" There was a brief pause from down under. Then, "Where do you think you are?" ...

By this time, of course, Brownie realized that we must not have landed at Townsville, but where we might be, he hadn't the foggiest notion. The man on the ground stood waiting for a reply but none was forthcoming.

"This is Cairns Municipal Airport" finally came the answer.

"Where do you think you are?"

No wonder we could not raise the tower on the radio. Cairns did not have a tower. We had mistakenly landed seventy-five miles short of our destination. Turning around, Brownie poured the coals to 891, and we left there in a hurry. No one back in San Francisco ever learned of this incident. The route check captain could not write it up because he, of all people, should have been familiar with the route. During the last thirty minutes of the flight on down to Townsville, everyone remained wide awake—especially the navigator.

Guam

As the American invasion forces gained strength and advanced north, so, too, did the contract operations of the Air Transport Command. Guam then became a major stop for us. There were three large airfields on the island: Anderson Air Force Base on the north end, Harmon Field, also an Air Force Base, mid-island, and Agana Naval Air Station, situated on top of a hill above Harmon. ATC flights shared Harmon Field with hoards of B-17 and B-29 bombers which, in conjunction with squadrons based on Saipan and Tinian, began their bombing runs very early each morning.

*Gear down and locked, this DC-4 is on final approach to Harmon Field,
Guam. 1948.*

Every few minutes for three or four hours, one of these giants thundered
into the air, bound for Japanese targets. Loaded beyond maximum gross
weight with bombs and gasoline, they struggled to gain flying speed, barely
able to drag out over the palm trees and transient crew quarters which fringed
the end of the runway.

Billeted with the Air Force, our United crews were assigned to these
quarters, where a little sleep was possible early in the evening. But shortly
after midnight, as the great exodus got under way, our cots began jumping up
and down beneath us. Unable to sleep, we dressed, headed for the mess hall,
and drank coffee till dawn.

The island of Guam has a forested ridge of mountains that extends from
its southernmost point, gradually flattening out to a high plateau on the north
end, which is bounded by steep cliffs that drop precipitously into the ocean.
Hundreds of Japanese soldiers committed suicide by jumping off these bluffs
rather than surrender to the Americans. Late in 1944, the southwestern section
of the island was packed with army installations of all kinds: military car
pools, acres of armaments, and thousands of quonset huts and tents. Outdoor
movie theaters, giving the GIs a choice, were everywhere, but you needed to
carry rain gear because showers in the tropics, though brief, were heavy and
frequent, sending movie-goers scurrying for cover.

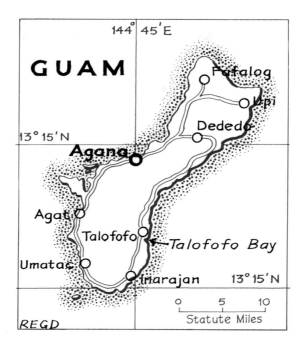

In 1944-45, Guamanians were a small minority—most of them living in and around Agana, the main town on the island. A heavily traveled highway ran down the west side and around the southern end and back up the east side, where there was no military activity at all, just a few peaceful villages scattered along the ocean shore amid banana groves and coconut trees.

I Was Only Picking Flowers

We had learned of a popular Guamanian eating place which overlooked the ocean at Telefofo Bay, directly across the island from us, so the entire crew opted to 'dine out' one evening rather than eat at the Air Force mess. Borrowing a carry-all from a company mechanic, we drove out to the main road, where we asked a local Guamanian for directions to Telefofo Bay.

"Yes ... I show you," he said. "You take main highway around end of island, but ... very long way ... maybe thirty-five miles" He stopped, scratched his head and turned, pointing toward a ridge in the hills behind us. "I know way to make short distance ... Only eight miles across mountain." Our eyes followed the line indicated by his finger. Using the imagination, faint segments of a red dirt road could be seen winding up a ridge not far away, finally disappearing into a heavily forested area that was visible some distance farther up the mountainside.

"Kapu?" we asked. "No kapu!", he replied. ("Kapu is Hawaiian for "Keep out", and Guamanians knew what it meant.)

Dropping off the pavement, we were soon climbing up the one-lane road, leaving a cloud of red volcanic dust in our wake. The route was not well traveled, disappearing almost altogether at times. Working our way up the ridge for three or four miles, we reached an open promontory, where we stopped the car and got out to look back. From this elevated vantage point we had a sweeping view of the entire west side of the island. Along the ocean shoreline to our right lay the town of Agana, while still farther to the north we could see curving Tumon Bay, one of the most striking crescent-shaped beaches I have ever seen. Rising abruptly as a backdrop to the bay, and following its contour, was a picturesque vertical cliff, perhaps three hundred feet in height. We stood for a while, taking in the beauty of the scene, before driving on.

The faint tire tracks of other vehicles were hard to follow now, and dense vegetation was closing in around us. The temperature was at least ten degrees cooler than back at sea level and we were enjoying our little outing into the hills, when one of the fellows spotted what looked like flowers growing high in this dense forest of forty-foot trees. Harry, who was driving, again pulled up and we all had a stretch and a better look at the large pink and white blossoms overhead.

"They look like orchids, but I didn't know orchids grew in trees," he observed, shading his eyes against the sun that filtered through the branches above. What we saw were too high to be reached from the ground, so I was elected to go up and bring down a few. My one-hundred-thirty-pound frame, the smallest in the group, made it easy for the other fellows to boost me to a limb where I could begin my climb. About twenty feet up, I managed to pick a half dozen blossoms, dropping them, one by one, to the ground.

They were not orchids. We learned later that they were, in fact, blooms from a forest of breadfruit trees that covered the mountainside at higher elevations on the islands. As I climbed back down, one of the crew members was showing off a mess kit that he had kicked up in the brush near the car; it bore Japanese inscriptions.

Daylight was fading now, and we preferred not to be out there on that glorified cow path after dark, so, placing the flowers on the front seat, we climbed back in the carry-all and resumed the trip. The highest point on Guam is something over 1,300 feet and we were not much below that level when we started down the other side. With darkness approaching, we guessed that we still had four or five miles to go. Dense trees and undergrowth had so reduced visibility now that Harry needed headlights to make his way along the curving road.

About three miles farther down the slope, we broke out into a clearing ... and got the shock of our lives. A battery of flood lights instantaneously illuminated the entire area with a brilliance that turned night into high noon. Momentarily blinded, we could see nothing, and before we had time to realize what might be happening, a rifle shot rang out directly in front of us.

"Stop the vehicle, or you'll get a free ticket to hell!" came an ominous command from a bull horn somewhere up ahead. Harry slammed on the brakes, catapulting everyone forward. Then, silhouetted against the intense light, two figures emerged from the darkness, and advanced cautiously toward us. We found ourselves looking down the barrels of automatic weapons aimed menacingly at our heads.

There was no top on the vehicle and Brownie, who was in front, jumped up yelling, "Don't shoot! Don't shoot! We're unarmed." Then, as a nervous afterthought ... "We're Americans!" Ignoring Brownie's frantic appeal, they continued closing in on us.

"..... free ticket to hell!"

"On your feet! All of you! Hands above your heads!" commanded the taller of the two.

We must have presented quite a sight ... all five of us standing up in blinding floodlight with arms high in the air, feeling very stupid and scared. The two were upon us now. Surely they must have realized that we were not Japanese.

Lowering their weapons somewhat, the one who appeared to be in charge ordered, "You in front there ... step out of the vehicle!" He jerked his head to emphasize his point. "The rest of you keep those hands up where we can see 'em!" Harry was out first.

"Where's your I.D.?" The voice was belligerent.

During the examination of Harry's passport and A.T.C. identification, Brownie, with hands still stretched high above his head, tried to explain to our interrogators that we were civilians in military uniform. They did not seem impressed. Not until after they had checked the last of us did the two appear satisfied and lower their rifles, apparently convinced that we were harmless. The tension finally relaxed and they seemed just about as relieved as we were.

Our eyes had become accustomed to the bright light now, and we could see our inquisitors clearly. A tall three-striper had done the questioning.

"Every military unit on the island has been warned to stay off that road," he lectured, "What on earth are you idiots doing up there?" Handing back our papers, he continued dressing us down.

"We send three patrols a day up that very road to flush out Japs, and we bring in three or four a week. We estimate there are a couple of hundred still hiding out up in that area and they're well armed. You people are lucky we aren't hauling you out in body bags!" His eyes then fell on the colorful blossoms on the front seat.

"Don't tell me you're up there picking flowers! My gawd!"

We found our restaurant and took a table out on the deck overlooking Telefofo Bay. The moon had topped the horizon in the east and its reflection rippled across the water in a long slender yellow ribbon.

After each of us had put away a couple of San Miguel beers, we enjoyed an excellent dinner. Leaving Telefofo a short while later, we all agreed that taking the long way back to Harmon Field would not be a problem.

Adventures in Paradise

To most of us, the very mention of the words "South Pacific" conjures up visions of white encrusted coral atolls, floating in a deep blue ocean. We can imagine azure lagoons, pristine sandy beaches, and the rustle of coconut palms swaying gently in a languid tropical breeze. Of all the thousands of islands out there which fit that description, none can radiate romance more eloquently than Bora Bora, the most idyllic tropical island I have ever known.

Island Paradise

One of the Society Islands, it lies in the southern hemisphere, 17° south of the equator, and 2,700 statue miles due south of Honolulu. Entirely surrounded by a lagoon, it is ringed by a coral reef, much of which is above

4,000 feet and descending, this enchanting view of distant Bora Bora greets us through the cockpit window. A small coral atoll, Motou Iti, glides by beneath us on our left.

sea level with enough surface area to support an adequate runway. The island itself is densely covered with vegetation up to an elevation of about 2,000 feet. Its upward slope increases quickly from the water's edge, then abruptly becomes a vertical cliff, ending in a small, slanting plateau on top at 2,680 feet.

In approaching Bora Bora by air, the panorama from the cockpit window epitomizes what every romanticist imagines a south sea island paradise to be. Under the bright tropical noonday sun, the water around it presents a tapestry of changing colors that is breathtaking.

The water becomes shallow as it stretches in toward the encircling reef from the endless depths of the ocean, creating a kaleidoscope of color near the fringes of the reef. As the coral rises under the water to meet the shore, the hues change subtly from a deep blue to lavender, then to a deep green and finally a pale green as gentle waves ripple lazily upon the sun bleached coral sand. Bora Bora is an incredibly beautiful and enchanting place.

The officers and men who manned such remote outposts during the second world war looked forward to our weekly flights from the States because we brought mail from home, so we were welcomed with open arms.

For reasons which will soon become apparent, we generally chose to stay with the Navy, who happily met us at the airfield, out on the reef, and took us by launch across the lagoon, a distance of about a mile, where we were put ashore at the pier in front of the Navy Officers Club.

This large, rambling, open-sided structure on the edge of the lagoon had been superbly built by native craftsmen. The frame, constructed of bamboo poles lashed together with coconut tree fibers, supported walls woven from palm fronds. Its steeply thatched roof hung well out over the edge of the eaves to prevent occasional heavy tropical downpours from blowing into the club house. It had an open-sided but covered veranda on the lagoon side where tropical drinks were served from the bar. The view of the club from the lagoon was a travel agent's dream.

Lying on our stomachs at the end of the Navy pier, we could easily distinguish intricate details in the sea anemones and coral formations 20 feet down on the bottom. Swimming before our eyes was a natural aquarium of multi-hued tropical fish in all shapes and sizes. Guppy Swordtails and Angel Fish mingled with darting schools of semitransparent, minnow-sized, Neon-Tetras, radiating iridescence in blue and green. Still other species were striped in yellow and white, trailing feather-like antennae; a spellbinding vista in Nature's own aquarium.

Adjacent to the Club was the Officer's Mess, which sported linen table cloths and sterling silver place settings. The Air Force out on the reef was having to rough it compared to the Navy's luxurious quarters on the island. Nonetheless, those GIs fortunate enough to serve in this area of the Pacific Theater considered it good duty indeed.

In 1945, Bora Bora became a layover point on a series of special trips which United Air Lines' crews dubbed the 'milk run'. Scheduled once weekly, flying only daylight hours, we island-hopped from Honolulu through Christmas, Penrhyn, Bora Bora, and Aitutaki to Samoa, overnighting at Bora Bora and Pago Pago before returning over the same route to Honolulu.

This was indeed the gentleman aviator's way to fly, and everyone on Pacific Operations hoped that the next rotation would set his crew up on the 'milk run'. All these islands maintained weather observation posts and airstrip maintenance personnel comprising from fifty to a hundred technicians, But Bora Bora not only had the Air Force, which occupied the reef, but the Navy, which maintained marine refueling facilities on the island proper.

French is the official language and is widely spoken in the Societies, a French colony since 1843. The islanders of Bora Bora maintain close ties with Tahiti, less than 200 miles away. Koa, breadfruit, monkey pod, and other hard woods are native to the island, and the Polynesians are skilled wood carvers. Some of my most prized possessions today are the work of these artisans.

Aitutaki Laid Bare

Five hundred and sixty miles due west of Bora Bora is Aitutaki Atoll; for us, by far the most intriguing stop on the milk run. A New Zealand mandated territory, alluring Aitutaki is part of the lower Cook Islands group. Its schools were staffed originally by English speaking teachers, and although the two thousand Polynesians on the island at that time used their native tongue, most of the young people spoke English as well, with a pronounced British accent. Because the island is of volcanic origin, houses are built of local stone, with layers of coconut fronds providing roof thatching. The climate is ideal, the soil fertile, and almost any fruit or vegetable can be grown on the island. There were no cars, so roads were unnecessary. The half dozen or so vehicles brought ashore by the military drove along the sandy beaches to traverse the five-mile length of the island.

Aitutaki was unique for two reasons, both of which readily come to mind. First, the island enjoyed a wide-spread reputation for its exceptionally attractive Polynesian women. Secondly, there was a pronounced shortage of young men on the island. As soon as the native boys were old enough to earn a living, they left home to follow the sea on the New Zealand sailing vessels.

This practice created an imbalance so severe that women outnumbered men five to one.

Christian missionaries, arriving on Aitutaki in the mid-1800s, had taught the islanders that grass skirts were immoral, preferring instead to see the native women in 'Mother Hubbards.' With not a care in the world, the mood of these Polynesians was quite upbeat. Their child-like friendliness and good will, sprinkled with lots of laughter, seemed pervasive. Inhibitions, if any, were certainly not in evidence either. The island girls needed only to be asked, and, giggling at the suggestion, would happily shed their clothing in favor of shell-ornamented grass skirts so that we could take their pictures.

So it was that, on our first trip through Aitutaki, the commanding officer called us together and laid out his rules for visitors.

"Now, I know you boys would like to take a look around our island here, so I'm going to assign a transport vehicle with a driver to take you along the beach to one of the villages, but we do have one cardinal rule: no one goes out of sight of the vehicle. There will be no exceptions. If you violate this order, I'll have to stop these sightseeing excursions. Are there any questions?" He paused to let his words sink in, then commented with a grin, "Actually, it's quite easy to keep my men in line here. I simply tell them that anyone who messes up will be sent back to the States."

A few months later we were overnighting in Honolulu, scheduled to continue westbound the following day, when Brownie received a call from UAL dispatch, advising us that we were being re-routed southbound for another trip to Pago Pago. During the course of a discussion that followed and knowing that we would again be landing at Aitutaki, one of the fellows hit on what we all thought was a brilliant idea. The island girls down there would be delirious with joy, we agreed, were we to bring them an assortment of brightly colored yard goods material in flower prints from the local dime store.

The following morning, the entire crew took the trolley from Waikiki to Woolworth's uptown, where we found exactly what we were looking for—a wide assortment of cotton prints available by the bolt. Making the necessary purchases, we returned to the beach armed with several rolls of elegantly designed cloth. Our offerings, we were smugly satisfied, would create an immediate sensation in those Aitutaki villages, and result in a dazzling improvement over the flour sacks that the missionary boards had been supplying them.

After the first visit, news of our impending arrival seemed to precede us, and the result was, as we had anticipated, a veritable mob scene. The island maidens, jabbering merrily away, ran out to meet us as our vehicle approached, clamoring up on the truck bed while the vehicle was still moving,

Kato and Kairoki are Polynesian girls of Aitutaki, an island in the Cook Archipelago. At 18° south latitude, it lies 700 miles due west of Tahiti. Navigator Keller snapped the photo of me and the girls with my Rolleiflex. November 13, 1943.

just to get at that enticing muumuu material; we had hit them where their hearts were.

As I remember it today, our crew made the milk run three times during the time when United crews flew down there, and on each of these trips, we spent an hour or so in one village or another, enjoying our visit, in English, with the villagers. We could go anywhere we chose, as long as we remained within sight of our eagle-eyed truck driver.

During our third and last visit to one of these villages, we met two young island girls whose names were Kairoki and Kato. I remember them because their names are written on the back of an old photograph which Howard had taken with my camera. The two are posing in grass skirts, with me standing between them: pretty heady stuff for this Kansas boy!

I guess we all lose track of time when things get exciting. Our truck driver finally had to remind us that it was time to leave the village and return to the airstrip. Back aboard the weapons carrier, we drove off down the beach, leaving a clutch of a dozen girls standing at the edge of the village, displaying their new 'lava-lavas' and waving to us until we were out of sight. They loved us, we knew, for our gifts from the ten-cent store in Honolulu. We must have revolutionized the pattern of fashion on Aitutaki forever.

As we rode back through the sand at the edge of the lagoon, we all fell silent, knowing that we would never again return to this fabulous place. There was no mistaking the let-down feeling we all felt. I guess, in a way, we were envious of these free-spirited people and the simple but happy lives they led.

For some time, no one spoke as we reflected on our Paradise Lost until, finally, Howard broke the spell with a remark which set us all laughing once again.

"Ooh ...," he said wistfully, "for just one hour away from that miserable truck!"

Other islands in this area of the Pacific which we had occasion to service from time to time included Tarawa, Funafuti, Wallis and Nanomea, but Aitutaki would always have a very special place in our hearts.

Islands Queer and Quaint

Islands come in all shapes and sizes. Crossing and crisscrossing the Pacific Ocean over an extended period of time made us familiar enough with many archipelagos, atolls, and small islands to be able to identify them on sight from the air. The islands were often useful as navigational aids in negotiating the trackless Pacific. Thousands of specks of land, many without names, poke their various shapes above the ocean level in that vast expanse of water. Most have no human inhabitants; many are not even habitable. At flight levels of

A typical coral atoll, Hull Island is part of the Phoenix Group. It lies just south of the equator, near the international date line. In 1938, because of overcrowding in the Gilbert islands, Gilbertese colonists settled here. The island abounds in coconut trees and produces commercial quantities of copra.

8,000 to 12,000 feet, surface features such as trees, anchorages and topography were easily distinguishable. There are atolls with strange sounding names: Rongerik and Rongelap, Ujai and Ujelang, Ailinglapalap, Ogasawara Gunto and Prece Vela.

The Pacific Island Yearbook describes diminutive Mejit Island as a 'jewel floating on a field of blue'. Leaving Kwajalein, east-bound, we often saw it gliding beneath us about the time we reached top of climb. There it would be, basking beneath the tropical sun, its virginal sandy beaches beckoning to us from below. Of course, no airplane had ever landed here. There was no runway, not even space for one. Too small to sustain life for very long, it was uninhabited, but, if you wanted an island to call your own, this would be it: yours for the asking.

A closer look revealed that its surface was blanketed by a mantle of coconut trees. A low prominence near the center of the island sloped gently away toward its broad, smooth beaches. Surrounded by a shallow encircling reef, broken by narrow channels between the coral heads, small sailing vessels would have easy passage to a safe haven. Lost in fantasy, as the scene unfolded, I wondered what it would be like to play Robinson Crusoe for a while.

There would be an abundance of fish, with occasional rain showers to provide fresh water. Coconuts and probably other tropical fruits would be

Tiny Johnston Island—four hours flying time west of Honolulu in a DC-4—could almost be mistaken for a large aircraft carrier. It is now the site for the disposal unit of Agent Orange.

plentiful, and the remote atmosphere would sparkle in the absence of air pollution. The sounds of radios, television sets, automobiles, and even human voices would be replaced by the rustle of palm fronds, and the intermittent whoosh of the surf splashing in puffs of froth against the beach. Most of all, however, there would be profound solitude and endless days. As Mejit gradually slipped away behind us, I realized that no matter how enticing the thought, two weeks in this idyllic environment would lead to boredom, and two months would almost certainly lead to madness.

Johnston Island, about the size of a large aircraft carrier, actually resembles one from the air. Seven hundred miles WSW of Honolulu, its runway occupies the entire length and most of the breadth of the land area. At that time, it was the exclusive domain of the U.S. Navy. The officer's mess here was unforgettable. In typical Navy style, table service was impeccable with sterling silver service and dining attendants attired in white jackets.

Japan deserted the League of Nations in 1937, and promptly claimed absolute sovereignty over the mandated territories of the Marshall, Caroline, and Mariana Islands. Among others, Wotje Atoll in the Marshalls was, during the next several years, developed militarily with construction of a major fighter base. In 1944, with supply lines cut and the island bypassed by American forces, the occupying garrison was quickly reduced to impotence. Before the war ended, American bombers were using Wotje for target practice (see the cover of this book). We 'feather merchants,' flying C-54s for the Air Transport Command, were warned not to fly too close to the island because the defenders down there had guns and ammunition and knew how to use them.

Of considerable value to the Japanese during the War, triangular-shaped Marcus Island was approximately mid-distant and slightly off track between Wake Island and Tokyo, Japan. Barely large enough to accommodate a runway and a weather reporting station, it served as a visual fix for those who flew overhead.

Nauru and Ocean islands, lying just south of the equator, are 160 miles apart, have no lagoons, are cone-shaped with vertical development and are one and two miles in diameter, respectively. Ocean Island, at its center, reaches an elevation of 460 feet. Both islands, rising steeply from the water's edge, are covered with coconut trees and are encircled by shallow reefs with no anchorages inside. Nauru is rich in high-grade phosphates, the result of countless bird-droppings, or guano, which since the beginning of time have covered parts of the island to a depth of several feet.

An interesting topographical feature of Tanna Island in the New Hebrides is its continuously active volcano. Belching smoke and steam by day and fire by night, it is highly visible around the clock from any direction.

Baby Gooney birds (black-footed albatrosses) are shaped like bowling pins.
Unafraid of humans, they may be approached, and when young, even picked up.

Sticking up out of the ocean about half way between Kauai and Midway Island in the Hawaiian Chain, are the Gardner Pinnacles, a striking oddity of nature. Were you to stand a wiener on end in a sand pile, you would have a model of one of these pinnacles, the tallest of which rises skyward to the height of a seventeen storey building.

*Heat and smoke rising from the
crater of Tanna volcano in the
New Hebrides, causes
condensation high in the upper
atmosphere, making its plume
visible over great distances.*

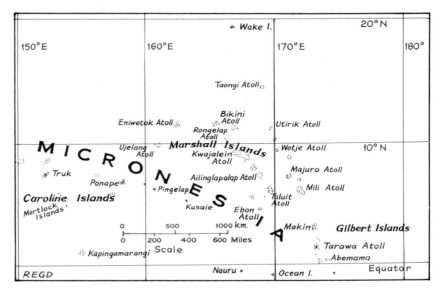

The End of United's Military Involvement

From the middle of 1942 until late in 1946, United Air Lines crews serviced U.S. Military installations throughout the Pacific and Alaskan theaters while under contract to the Air Transport Command. We flew military cargo, mail, and personnel as far south as Auckland, New Zealand, and as far north as Fort Norman Wells in the Yukon. Before World War II, there had been almost no flying in the Southwestern Pacific. So little, in fact, that in hopping from one island to another, we pioneered routes that had never been flown before.

Alone, Alone

At times we were out of radio contact for two or three hours at a time because of long distances and the use of radio frequencies that were vulnerable to atmospheric conditions. In 1942, electronic navigational aids capable of fixing an aircraft's position while flying over large bodies of water did not exist. Early versions of aircraft octants, with which we made celestial observations, were primitive at best, and star tables requiring a knowledge of advanced mathematics were difficult, time consuming, and cumbersome to use.

The radar altimeter could have been used in conjunction with a pressure altimeter to help determine drift, but only fighting units of the military had radar at that time. To accomplish the same thing, we dropped smoke bombs through a chute in the floor of the airplane, then took angular readings by sighting through a drift meter. This was almost impossible at night, and equally so in the daytime if we were flying over a stratus deck and were unable to see the ocean surface.

Often we were not lucky enough to pinpoint the smoke rising from the water below nor to see the red flare marker on the surface at night. Our airplanes were equipped with dual automatic direction finders which, however, were unreliable in areas of heavy atmospherics during the times when we needed them most; and Loran, already in use in the Atlantic, had not yet been deployed in the Pacific.

Meteorological forecasts were not always accurate either and sometimes were not available at all. The C-54 service ceiling, using high blowers, was about 18,000 feet, but we did not fly above 14,000 because, although oxygen was available in the cockpit for crew members, there was no such provision for the passengers. In tropical latitudes, towering cumulus and line squalls were standard fare, with build-ups to heights in excess of 40,000 feet. We could not fly high enough to top them, so we had no alternative but to tackle them head on. At night, if we saw lightning up ahead, we were sometimes able to dog-leg around the area. Heavy rain and turbulence were not uncommon.

Our United C-54s had two large round auxiliary fuel tanks, one on each side of the aisle just aft of the crew compartment, and crew members were in the habit of throwing their B-4 bags on top of those tanks during flight. Occasionally, after a ten or fifteen minute bout with moderate turbulence, we would need to clear that aisle of baggage before we could reach the rear of the airplane.

United's War Casualties

Australian trips, taking about two weeks to complete, were balanced by similar periods at home, and, except for occasional ground school sessions, my time off was my own. My brother Carol had joined the U.S. Navy and was serving in the Pacific Theater as a ship's lieutenant aboard an ammunition vessel. He brought his young wife to San Mateo where she took an apartment near Mina and me. During our days on the San Francisco peninsula, Mina made friends with a number of people and somehow managed to keep busy while I was away.

VJ Day—Victory over Japan—stands out clearly in my mind for a special reason. Mina and I had gone on a picnic in the woods a few days before a scheduled trip, and when it came time to fly, my body was a mass of poison oak. Eating too many strawberries on the picnic the day before added to my undoing, and by departure time big blotches of hives were telling the poison oak blisters to move over. Thoroughly miserable, I spent the night trying to sleep while standing in a corner of our San Mateo apartment.

As I look back over that period of my life, I suppose I was lucky to have lived through it. Three of United's crews were not so lucky. To this day, eight crew members lie buried where they died, five on Canton Island, and three near Auckland, New Zealand. All of these accidents involved C-87s and

When this picture was taken on September 4, 1944, the small fenced cemetary on Canton Island held only the remains of Flight Engineer, William Henderson, and Flight Navigator, Ronald Ellis, two United Air Lines crew members. Others were to join them.

occurred in the early part of United's military contract with the Air Transport Command.

Captain Chris Pickup, during a moonless night approach at Canton Island, landed short of the runway and in the water. First Officer Hoot Moninger, the only survivor among the crew, was knocked out on impact but regained consciousness in time to scramble out of the sinking airplane through a broken cockpit window. He swam for three hours before reaching shore. No official determination as to the cause of the accident was ever made, but the consensus blamed an asymmetric deployment of the flaps when turning from base leg to final approach. Weather was not a factor. Copilot Moninger writes:

> I understood that our passengers were staff members of the U.S. Army's General Kreuger, sixteen in all. Two of them were evidently thrown from the aircraft on impact and managed to find one of the wing rafts which was partially inflated. Clinging to the raft through the night, they were picked up the next morning some twenty miles offshore. All the others went down with the aircraft in several thousand feet of water. The date was February 7, 1943.

Flight Engineer Bill Henderson and a close navigator friend of mine, George Ellis, perished when Eddie Eshleman's C-87 blew a nose wheel tire during a take-off attempt at Canton Island on May 3, 1944. The bodies of these two men still lie buried in the island's coral, their final resting place marked only by wooden crosses.

In my collection are photographs of two United grave sites. It was wartime and the remains of these crew members were never brought home.

Miracle Survival

Radio Operator Hank Prochaska, another friend, and Flight Engineer George Allen died with Captain Hersch Laughlin in New Zealand. For First Officer John Wisda, who survived that accident, the passage of fifty years has not dimmed his memory of the ordeal. In answer to a recent query, he wrote the following graphic account of the accident:

The UAL-ATC crash in Auckland, New Zealand, involved a C-87 aircraft (Nr. 027) and occurred about 1 a.m. on the morning of August 2, 1943, killing three of the five crew members and half of the passengers. Aboard were about 24 Japanese prisoners of war, their wives and children. They had been trapped on the outer islands when the war started. We were to fly these captives to New Guinea where they were to have been exchanged for American prisoners held by the Japanese.

Our crew had flown 123 hours during the previous 26 days and were coming off a two-day rest when, at 8 p.m. on the night of the third day, we were ordered to the airport for a flight to parts unknown. The captain had the envelope with the orders which he shared as sparingly as possible with the navigator. I was never told where we were going, and not until we climbed aboard the airplane and saw the Japanese did we understand the reason for security.

The weather was at a minimum with light rain. I was in contact with Whenuapai Tower as we taxied out, made a short run-up, and took off. We did not go through a 'challenge and response' check list because at that time there was no such thing.

The captain's gyro-horizon had a knob with which the instrument could be caged; the aux-horizon, in the center of the instrument panel, had no such knob. The airplane ended up in a steep left turn. The aux-horizon had given a true indication.

The captain called for full power on engines #1 and #2. To accomplish this, I had to unfasten my seat belt. Leaning forward, I gave the engines the called-for settings just as we struck the ground. Props #3 and #4 snapped off ... the engines were out of control. Maybe the same thing was happening on the left side. We bounced. I hit the switches and became a free flying body out through the top of the cockpit.

I was told later that I rolled, end over end, through a marsh about the length of a football field, blasting a trail through one-inch thick reeds. On the third bounce the aircraft blew up, spewing blobs of burning fuel all over the place. The tower saw the explosion and sent ambulances to the scene.

When the emergency vehicles had picked up the dead and wounded, they left an ambulance and one driver with instructions to have one last look around. That ambulance attendant noticed a man standing over a burning tire trying to keep warm. He mistook this person for one of the rescuers. He was wrong. He was the rescuer ... I was the rescuee!

I lay unconscious for five days. Burns, cuts and bruises all over my body. Didn't break a single bone. Slight concussion. Eight months later I passed all required physicals and returned to flying on 24 March 1944. Likely causes of the crash were fatigue and lack of a pre-flight check list which would have turned up the caged gyro.

Consairway

Among other civilian carriers flying in the Pacific Theater for the Air Transport Command at that time was one operated by Consolidated Aircraft called 'Consairway.' This company paralleled United's routes flying four engined LB-30s. On a trip into Biak Island off the New Guinea coast in March of 1945, a Consairway crew was eating lunch at the Air Force mess when a Japanese aircraft came in at roof top level and dropped a bomb on the building. Lloyd Herring, the crew's navigator, was killed; the other crew members were not seriously injured.

A lot of good natured kidding went on between Consairway and United crews during the early days of WW-II. Consairway's LB-30s were faster than United's C-87s although both aircraft had the B-24 airframe and Pratt & Whitney 1200 hp engines. Bill Keating, a Consairway pilot at the time, says that the LB-30 was lighter than the C-87. Utilizing flush rivets and aerodynamically superior engine cowling design allowed the LB-30s to overtake and pass United's C-87s.

Palm Trees Ahead

Dale Cavanagh, another United pilot who worked those A.T.C. flights in 1945-46, remembers a dark moonless night during a take-off from Harmon Field on Guam Island. Following run-up, the captain sang out, "Ready?" After each crew member had echoed the word, he yelled, "Hold onto your hats ... here we go!" With that he advanced the throttles for take-off. No sooner were the wheels off the ground than he called out, "Gear up, flaps up, climb power" in rapid succession. Just barely flying, he held the nose down to gain climb speed. This 'procedure' was commonly followed by most United captains. They were 'saving the engines.'

Suddenly, looming up through the windshield, co-pilot Cavanagh spotted the silhouette of a palm tree dead ahead. "My God ... we're below the trees!", he shouted and shoved the props and throttles forward as the captain simultaneously hauled back on the yoke. After that episode the pilots agreed to retract the flaps and set climb power in a much more deliberate manner and only when they thought it was safe. A great deal has changed since the 1940s. Caging knobs on artificial horizons are long gone, and soon after this experience check lists were mandatory.

The War Winds Down

With the Japanese surrender in September of 1945, the war in the Pacific came to an end. Desiring to remain competitive in the home market, United was anxious to return its crews and facilities to domestic service. Though substantially reduced, its role in military flying continued through much of 1946.

According to my log book, my final trip as a United crew member left Mills Field, San Francisco, for Guam Island on December 13, 1945. Mina and I had hoped to be able to spend Christmas with her mother and stepfather in Missoula, but our crew did not return home until the 27th.

Realizing that United would no longer need radio operators, I dropped in at personnel to ask if the company had plans to use my services in some future capacity. As a matter of fact, they did. I was to be sent to Medford, Oregon, as a ticket clerk trainee and baggage handler—at a commensurate reduction in salary, of course. I had no idea what else they might be willing to offer, but this most certainly was not what I had in mind. We had managed to save a little money and, with severance pay and vacation time coming, decided to leave for a three-week visit with old friends in Montana and Kansas.

Upon returning to the West Coast, a waiting letter asked that I turn in my flight manuals and all military material in my possession: trench coat, flight jacket, khaki uniforms, and one B-4 bag.

While driving to the airport, the gnawing question uppermost in my mind concerned our future. I had not the slightest interest in United's offer. What was I to do now that the war had ended? Mina and I had talked about this at some length while returning from vacation and had drawn a blank. There was always broadcast radio, but the pay would have been dismal compared to the $400 monthly salary we had enjoyed the past four years. Besides, I guess I was hooked on flying, but the likelihood that I might land another job as a flight radio operator certainly seemed remote.

Opportunity Knocks Again

Parking the car in front of the administration building, I entered and walked down the hall to the stock room where I turned in my military clothing and was given a receipt. Wishing to return my company manuals and say goodbye to 'Pop' Skinner, my boss, I headed up the stairway that led to his office on the second floor.

Coffee in hand, he was sitting at his desk staring out the window. Glancing up as I entered, he swiveled around toward me.

"Hey, Lewis!" ... His expression and tone of voice implied new knowledge of some kind. Resting both elbows on the table, he put the cup to his mouth, blew gently, and looked up at me.

"How'd you like to keep on flying?" His remark caught me off guard, but the question had a pleasant ring; maybe my future was not as bleak as I had thought.

"You have my undivided attention, Pop; whatever you might have, I'm interested."

Putting his coffee down, he leaned lazily back in his chair, obviously savoring any good news he might be ready to impart.

"Captain Nelson—Orvis Nelson - was in here this morning looking for radio operators. He says he's starting a new airline."

Up to this point, I had never heard of Captain Nelson although he had been one of the United captains flying the Pacific. Pop reached for a pad and pencil.

"If you think you're interested, you can call him at this number in San Lorenzo—that's on the other side of the Bay." Writing Nelson's telephone number and street address on a slip of paper, he handed it to me.

"He's working on a commitment from the military for the use of a dozen DC-4s. Orvis and a bunch of his pilot friends want to take over where we've left off."

Leaning forward, Pop opened his top desk drawer, took out a small carton of cream, and poured some into his coffee. Not finding a spoon handy, he stirred the cream in with his finger while he continued, verbally organizing Mr. Nelson's proposed airline.

"Just because United wants out, doesn't mean that the need for military contract flying has ended," he said. "Orvis has been told that he needs to have a couple of these 'planes ready to fly and in the air by the middle of March ... if he can put it all together, that is."

I glanced at a calendar on Pop's desk. "Well ... that's less than two months away." I ventured.

Pop slowly nodded his head in confirmation. "Orvis says he has President Patterson's blessing and United's promise of help, but, believe me, it's a tremendous logistics problem to solve in a very short period of time. Crews have to be recruited and staged, maintenance personnel hired, and fuel supplies arranged. He'll need a staff of competent administrators and the office space to put 'em in ... ."

Pausing to catch his breath, he slowly turned the cup round and round in his hands. For Pop, drinking coffee was a ritual. More from habit than necessity, he would saucer his coffee and blow on it, even though it was half cold. The serious look on his face left me with the feeling that the responsibility for starting this new airline was resting on his shoulders rather than on Captain Nelson's.

"Adequate hangar space at the Oakland Airport has to be found," he went on, "and he'll need experienced aircraft mechanics, not only in Oakland, but out on the island bases, too. Contracts will need to be signed, insurance coverages must be worked out, and literally dozens of other minor ..."

Interrupting the flow of information from Pop's wellspring of knowledge, I asked, "Are you saying that Captain Nelson plans to base his operation at the Oakland Airport?"

"I believe so," came Pop's answer. "He's trying to work out a deal with the Port of Oakland to use the old domestic passenger terminal over there as his headquarters."

Putting his coffee cup aside, he slid his chair back, rose from his desk, and offered to write a letter of recommendation for me. Everyone liked Pop, and I had enjoyed our relationship. Thanking him, I shook his hand in farewell; then, waiting to hear no more, I left.

Downstairs, I checked in at payroll to pick up my final paycheck and stopped to say goodbye to a number of friends I had made in United's offices.

I was anxious to go back to Mina to see how she might feel about this renewed opportunity to continue my flying career. It would mean continued absences from her over relatively long periods of time, but there would also be equal amounts of free days at home when we could do things together.

Tomorrow morning I felt certain I would be driving across the Bay to meet Captain Orvis Nelson. On the way back to the apartment, I was lost in reflection. During nearly four years with United Air Lines, I had logged 2,700 hours. These should certainly add to my credentials.

You're Hired

Over breakfast early the next morning, Mina and I talked about the opportunities and problems we might encounter in signing on with Mr. Nelson's proposed new airline. Were the job to materialize, we would need to move to some community near the Oakland Airport. The Second World War had ended, and like millions of other young people we were faced with major new decisions in our lives; any choice to be made now could shape our entire future. The morning coffee and our conversation ran dry at about the same time. Mina left the ball in my court, saying with a shrug of her shoulders, "You'll just have to do what you think is best for us."

It was fourteen miles from San Mateo to San Lorenzo, seven miles of which were over the old two-lane San Mateo drawbridge and causeway. Driving north on the Oakland side of the bay for three or four miles, I located San Lorenzo Village and soon found Orvis Nelson's address.

Cars were parked in front of the residence and in the driveway, so I pulled to the curb a short distance up the street. Walking back to the house, I took stock of the neighborhood. San Lorenzo Village was a development of modest three-bedroom homes, perhaps three or four years old. There were no attached garages, but space had been purposely provided so they could be added. Trees had been planted and lawns were in. The 'Village' would be a nice place to live, I thought, and was within easy commuting distance of the Oakland Airport.

Mounting the steps of the Nelson home, I was met at the open door by a man who insisted that Mr. Nelson himself was very busy at the moment. A room full of people seemed to be going in all directions at once. The person who greeted me turned out to be Captain Wally Simpton who later became a friend and fellow crew member. Introducing myself, I explained that I was a flight radio operator who was being released by United Air Lines.

"What are your qualifications?" he wanted to know.

After telling him that I held an FCC 2nd Class Radio Telegraph License with aircraft endorsement, he wrote down my telephone number on a scratch pad he was holding, then turned to address someone behind him.

"We're going to need radiomen, aren't we?"

If there was a response to his question, I did not hear it. Turning back toward me, he extended his hand. "You're hired!" There was no room for doubt in his tone of voice. "Be at the old passenger terminal building at the Oakland Airport on the morning of March 13th." Then, as an afterthought, "That's at the southeast end of Earhart Drive." With that he turned away indicating that the conversation was ended.

I stood there ... speechless. I had been among the ranks of the unemployed for less than twenty four hours, then was hired for another job after a ten-second interview while standing in the front doorway of a private residence.

Leaving the porch, I remembered that I had never had to look for a job; opportunity always seemed to be out there in a limitless variety. If I happened to stick my nose out into the street, someone would tap me on the shoulder and ask if I wanted to go to work.

Walking to where the car was parked, two or three doors down from the Nelson home, I wondered where Mina and I could possibly find the downpayment for one of these houses; but then I soon dismissed the idea as being entirely out of the question.

Birth of Transocean

Word that a new airline was in the offing spread quickly with Captain Nelson's first call, and the response was overwhelming. Looking for employment and happy that the war was over, applicants from all branches of the armed services rushed to the Oakland Airport, hoping to land a job with this fledgling airline. I remember seeing the long rag-tag line that stretched away from the International Terminal Building, out the door, down the steps, and all the way back to the airport restaurant, a distance of a hundred yards or more. Many were in civilian clothes but others, still wearing various military uniforms, were trailing duffel bags.

Yes, indeed, those were halcyon days. We were all young and overflowing with enthusiasm for what we saw as a chance to break ground with a new airline. We wanted to have our place in the sun as pioneers and innovators. The romance and promise of commercial flying ... the excitement and exuberance of this bunch of young hopefuls would provide the spirit that was soon to become Transocean Air Lines.

ONAT

This then was the scene that greeted me as I pulled into a parking spot near the terminal building at Oakland's Airport, got out of my car, and slowly made my way toward the crowded doorway. Having already been hired, I reasoned, I should not have to stand in that line. Inside, there was pandemonium. Mr. Simpton was there and, somehow remembering me, directed me to a side room off the lobby where he introduced me to Sherwood Nichols.

"So ... you're over from United, right? Pop sent you, I suppose." Without waiting for an answer, he held out his hand. "I'm Sherwood Nichols ... I don't believe we've met."

'Nick' Nichols had been Captain Nelson's radio operator at United, and a common bond of friendship had sprung up between the two men from their long association as members of the same crew. He explained that he had been asked to serve temporarily as chief radio operator, adding that the new airline did not yet have a name so Captain Nelson had decided, for the time being at least, to call it 'Orvis Nelson Air Transport', ONAT, for short.

"We shall be flying under a sub-contract from United," he explained. "Since you're an experienced hand, you won't need briefing at this time. Perhaps you can take the first flight out ... if you're available.

I nodded my head in assent.

"Your pay will remain the same: four hundred dollars a month, minimum, for up to eighty-five hours of flight time per month, with overtime up to one hundred hours maximum. We haven't established an overtime pay scale yet."

He walked to a connecting doorway and waved to someone in the adjoining room. "We won't be flying under military flight rules now," he said. "Instead, we'll be living with commercial limitations on flight times, a thousand hours a year, maximum." He paused momentarily, as an impatient voice from the next room called out his name.

"Hold on ... I'm coming!"

Addressing me again, he continued. "Let's see; where were we? ... Oh, yes ... I'll need your 'phone number, address, and social security number."

His telephone was ringing now, as he jotted down the information he had requested. "We don't have application forms yet, but that can be done later. You'll hear from me some time tomorrow with a departure date and time." He was obviously very busy so with another nod I left the room. I had hardly spoken a word, but I guess I had heard everything I needed to know.

It would be an amazingly simple transition because the radio equipment and routine were thoroughly familiar to me. I would miss my Air Force B-4 bag though; I had grown comfortable with it through the years. A suitcase with a week's supply of 'civvies' and my shaving kit would have to do. My Rolleiflex camera, a small tripod, and plenty of film would also come along.

By now, Mina was resigned to her life as the wife of a flyer, so she took the new job opportunity in her stride. That evening we again discussed moving to the other side of the Bay, but in the meantime I would have to commute to and from the Oakland Airport.

For the next two days, I stuck pretty close to the telephone, my bag packed, waiting to hear from Sherwood Nichols. At times I wondered if I might be dreaming. Was this new airline for real? After the needs of the military had faded, what then? Could ONAT survive into a strictly commercial era? What about the prestigious competition ... Pan American Airways, a well established, scheduled airline, that had built and operated bases in the Pacific, even before the war.

Late on the afternoon of March 15, the long-awaited call came through. It was Nick.

Inaugural Flight

"We want you at the Matson Hangar here at the Oakland Airport tomorrow morning at 6:00 a.m. for an 8:00 o'clock departure for Honolulu. Your pilots will be Captain Jerry Byrd and First Officer Jack Brissey. We're sending them, along with Flight Engineer Art Bissett, to Mills Field to ferry a C-54 aircraft over from United. You and the navigator will be picked up when they get back here to Oakland. Do you follow me?"

"Yes, I understand. What about expense money?"

"I'll have a check for you in the morning. We've set up an account with the Bank of Hawaii at Hickam. They'll cash it for you. Now then: you'll ferry the plane to Hickam, load your passengers there, and return eastbound to Hamilton Air Force Base." He paused, ending his instructions with, "We'll be out there to see you off".

Transocean Air Lines drew its first breath the following morning, March 16, 1946. A light drizzle was falling and it was overcast, a typical day's beginning at this time of year in the East Bay. Orvis Nelson, President of ONAT, and a small group of his closest associates stood out on the ramp in the chill wind, watching, as we taxied out and rolled down runway 27 Right for take-off. Transocean, as it would become, was born.

Who could even have guessed that from this inauspicious beginning, Transocean Air Lines would, in a few short years, expand to become an operation encompassing 57 bases around the world with some 6,700 employees?

The ferry flight to Hickam was routine, and on the night of 17 March 1946 we left Hawaii for the return trip to the mainland and Hamilton Air Force Base with ONAT's first revenue load. Covered only by army blankets, life vests hanging along the walls of the unlined cabin, the army passengers slept through the night stretched out on bucket seats and the bare metal floor of the airplane.

Upon our return to Oakland from that first flight, the new company had already set up a dispatch office and there was a note from Nick asking me to be at the field the next day to complete my application.

For the first three or four months, Transocean crews flew two Honolulu turnarounds daily and a few trips through Kwajalein to Guam, using military aircraft. Early in 1946, the company managed to purchase two war-surplus C-54s which, when modified to DC-4 configuration, could be used to transport civilian as well as military passengers.

(Left) N74648 boards common carriage passengers at Honolulu Airport for the twelve-hour flight to the Mainland. A mechanic stands by at engine number one with a fire bottle, waiting for a start up signal from the pilot. 1952. (Below) Radio Operator Sherwood Nichols, and flight Engineer Larry Moe, 'pull the props through' on a DC-4. This was done to prevent oil pooling in the bottom cylinders of radial engines. 'Pulling through' also served to build compression prior to startup. Harmon Field, Guam. 1947.

Some time early in May of that year, my parents took the train from Kansas to California to visit us and, by this time, I had made quite a number of commuting trips across the Bay. Clearly, Mina and I should live closer to the Oakland Airport and, in discussing the necessity for the move with Dad, the subject of the houses in San Lorenzo came up. The four of us drove across the Bay, and, with my parents help in the form of a small down payment, we bought one. I seem to remember the purchase price as being about $7,500.

At the end of WWII, the War Assets Administration announced that a number of surplus military C-54s were available for purchase by American veterans. Two ONAT recruits, Captains Ray Elsmore and William Word, purchased one each, providing the nucleus for Transocean Air Lines' commercial fleet. The first of these two aircraft, N66635, was certificated in July 1946; the second, N66644, in October 1946.

On 1 June 1946, ONAT became Transocean Air Lines, known some-times as T.A.L. or Taloa. Fifty percent of the shares had to be held by veterans to qualify for government contracts. By July, Transocean's flight crews were in uniforms and the new airline had acquired and occupied Hangar 5, a major structure at the Oakland Airport. Near the end of July, I obtained my first pass-port. Now possessing a newly certificated DC-4, the company had concluded an agreement with Philippine Air Lines to provide air service between the United States and Manila. Dispatch set me up for one of these trips, so I was sent to the Philippine Consulate in San Francisco for a visa. Five days later, a Transocean crew, with me aboard, flew in over the city of Manila.

The extent of the war's devastation was clearly apparent; to imagine destruction on such a massive scale was difficult. Dozens of city blocks had been leveled. The gridwork of naked streets was plainly visible from the air, and nothing but rubble remained within those grids where buildings and homes had once stood. We landed at Makati Air Base and, on the drive into the heart of the city, passed bombed-out concrete skeletons of what had been stately, multi-storied government buildings. Burned-out and overturned tanks remained scattered about in the streets where they had been destroyed in battle. Wreckage and debris were everywhere. The devastation of the city of Manila has often been overlooked by war historians; but it was severe on the scale of many of the war-ravaged cities of Europe.

We stayed at the Manila Hotel, or rather what was left of it. Before the war, this impressive building had been one of Manila's show places. For years, all the great social functions of the Filipino aristocracy had been held in its grand ballroom. Completely gutted now, with gaping holes in its roof, this room was just a tangled mass of charred remains, leaving little evidence of its former elegance.

(Left) This music academy, though still usable, suffered extensive damage. Note overturned tank in right background. Manila, Philippines. September 2, 1946.

(Below) Massive devastation, in evidence here, was typical throughout Manila after the fighting during WWII had stopped. 1946.

Our 'accommodations' on the second floor had a bomb hole in the outside wall large enough to step through without stooping. Among what had been carefully tended lawns and gardens of the hotel complex were shell fragments, discarded helmets, ammunition casings, and other remnants of the recent conflagration.

Octants

The octant used by United's navigators during the war was the A-10. A rather primitive device, its celluloid disc rotated in conjunction with the prism in the octant, and each time the operator lined up a celestial body in the cross hairs, he actuated a lever causing a short lead pencil to make a vertical mark near the rim of the disc. During a two-minute sighting, perhaps a dozen or so vertical marks might appear on the disc as the navigator continued pressing the lever. The marks were then averaged visually to arrive at the elevation of the body sighted. To prepare the octant for the next observation, the pencil marks were simply erased. The A-14, which followed a short while later, was nicknamed the 'coffee grinder' because of the sound it made while in operation. Quite an improvement over the A-10, the A-14 incorporated a spring-wound actuator that provided automatic averaging.

Another of our crews was in the Manila Hotel at the time, and one of its members was Al Mays, Transocean's newly appointed Chief Navigator. I remember that, along with three or four of us, he drove back out to Makati Field the next day to investigate a rumor that the U.S. Army Air Force had a stockpile of navigation gear stored in a quonset hut there.

As I remember it, Al somehow acquired the key to that hut and we pulled a 'midnight requisition' in the middle of the afternoon as we appropriated a couple of armloads of brand new A-14 octants. They were the most modern of such instruments at the time. The Philippines were wide open during the days following the war, and as far as I know, there were no repercussions as a result of our act. The new octants went into service immediately on Transocean's commercial runs. Until then, we had been using the old A10s.

Returning to Oakland from this trip, I checked at dispatch before arriving home and learned that I was not scheduled out again for nearly two weeks. We were pretty well settled in our new house in San Lorenzo by then and soon learned that many other Transocean people lived in the 'village' as well. In fact, our company president, Orvis Nelson, and his wife lived just around the corner from us.

Company Photographs

During one of my absences, Mina decided that we needed a garage, and upon my return, I agreed, but I knew next to nothing about carpentry and certainly did not have the money to have one built. There had to be a way, and in a rare display of resourcefulness, I took my camera down the street where a new garage was in the process of construction, and carefully photographed every framing detail with close-ups of all the joints. Using the pictures as a guide, I was able to build my own garage. Extending it to the rear an additional eight feet created space for a home darkroom.

By this time I had accumulated the major components of a first class photo lab. All these items were piled up in a corner of one of our bedrooms and, as you might guess, Mina was pleased at the thought of getting the stuff out of the house. To complete my darkroom, however, I needed two large stainless steel sinks, but for me the cost would have been prohibitive. In Transocean's sheet metal shop were large metal 'brakes,' tools that are capable of bending malleable metals such as aluminum and stainless steel into angles ideal for making my sinks. Maybe I could work out a deal with the company in exchange for the sinks.

Sam Wilson, director of operations, was the man I needed to see about this. Having heard that he was interested in photography as a hobby, I decided to seek his help. Seeing him turned out to be a good choice. The company, he agreed, would most assuredly need photographs. In fact, he confided, they had already used an outside photographer on several occasions. He took me to the sheet metal shop, introduced me to the foreman, and instructed him to make up whatever I required. In return, I agreed to be on call as company photographer when I was not flying the line. I was in business.

Throughout the years, Sam Wilson and I were to become good friends. He was a pilot who had come to Transocean from the military with considerable management experience, and through the Transocean years, became executive vice president, and eventually, senior vice president.

Burglars

Right after the war, Manila was a city in mass confusion. Even in the city center, many streets were unpaved. Clouds of dust and dirt billowed into the air under the unrelenting onslaught of heavy military and civilian traffic. Heat and humidity were stifling and, in the outlying suburbs, pigs and chickens roaming the streets seemed to be as numerous as the Filipinos themselves.

Permeating all this was the sickeningly sweet fragrance so characteristic of the Orient.

Public transportation consisted mainly of old worn-out buses augmented by hundreds of 'jeepneys'. These were jeeps which, more often than not, had been stolen from the American military motor pools or sold by hungry GIs to local entrepreneurs. The enterprising Filipinos filed the identification numbers off the engine blocks and rebuilt the bodies to accommodate as many as ten or twelve passengers, then competed with each other in creating elaborate paint jobs and fancy decorative canopies. Many of these conversions were done in back yards in a single night. The next morning, the new owners would have them on the streets as jeepneys. Doubling as taxis or buses, they stopped at both regular points or on demand if it was at all possible to cram another person aboard.

Over the noise created by the utter disarray of unregulated traffic along Manila's main thoroughfare, the Escolta, could be heard the shrill cry of a jeepney driver calling out his destination as he boarded his passengers. "Pasay, Quiapo!" ... "Pasay, Quiapo!"

Philippine Air Lines had rented a two-story villa out on Fernando Rein in South Manila for use as a crew house, and like most other large homes in outlying

He never even broke stride.

Manila, it was completely enclosed by a six foot high stone wall with broken glass set in concrete along its top. The wall and the lockable driveway gate were supposed to keep night prowlers out of the compound, but these precautions did not always work. Many of the larger homes in the area hired armed guards who had orders to shoot intruders on sight. Tire thefts were common. One night a man was surprised while trying to remove a tire from an automobile parked in the street across from us. He was shot and killed by our neighbor's guards.

The sleeping quarters in our house were on the second floor and each of the large upstairs rooms contained five cots. Mosquito netting supported by a wooden framework covered each cot. We were all sleeping peacefully one night when everyone in the room was awakened by a yell.

"Who's there? ... Hey, someone's going through our clothes!"

More asleep than awake, we all groped around in the dark for flashlights, but Jim Helmer, a navigator, was the first to extricate himself from the mosquito netting. He hit the floor just in time to shine his light beam on the figure of a man disappearing through the bedroom door with his watch and wallet.

Without time to put on clothes, he dashed down the stairway in his underwear in hot pursuit of the culprit. Not more than a couple of yards behind, Jim was doing pretty well until his tender feet hit the sharp gravel just beyond the front steps.

Not so with the fleeing Filipino, who was also barefoot. Right at home on the gravel, he never even broke stride. A single leap, and he was over the wall and gone. By the time we got to Jim, he was sitting on the steps nursing his rock-studded soles. The next morning we found a heavy blanket thrown over the glass where the man had crossed the wall during the night.

Little Rosie

Fernando Rein intersected a main thoroughfare just one block down from the crew house, and on a corner of that intersection, we discovered Little Rosie's Liquor Emporium. Rosie's well-stocked shelves lined the entire back wall of the four-by-eight-foot wooden stand which opened for business each day with the removal of panels from both ends and the front. Her sales pitch was carried on two vertical signboards, one on each side facing the street which appeared to serve as corner posts in support of the roof. The hand-painted lettering read:

GET YOUR STATESIDE
WHISKEY, GIN AND RUM HERE!

Little Rosie ... the toast of Fernando Rein—her GI boyfriend did the sign work.

Little Rosie was no ordinary woman. We guessed her age to be some-where in the mid-twenties but, in spite of her tender years and the rigors of a brisk liquor business, she owned and operated her own string of a dozen jeep-neys, managed their drivers, and provided employment for a handful of shoe-shine boys. Her customers' shoes were shined free while they made their purchases. Rosie herself was a petite, attractive Filipino girl with a winning smile and a cheerful greeting for everyone who passed her way, but she was ninety-five pounds of dynamite, ruling her little empire with complete control; there was never any doubt as to who was boss.

Truckloads of American military personnel passed her stand throughout the day and the men, waving enthusiastically, would whistle at her and yell, "Hey, Rosie, how you doin'?" Her infectious personality seemed to endear her to everyone she met. She had only a cigar box from which to make change, but she handled it like a Wall Street banker ... and she was getting rich at it. So, when things got dull around the crew house, we would go down to the corner, have a beer, have our shoes shined, and watch Little Rosie operate.

Subsequently, Philippine Air Lines moved our crews to a new compound nearer Manila Bay on MacArthur Boulevard. Several months passed and one day we decided to drop by Little Rosie's to check up on her. Her stand had vanished. Not a trace remained. Checking around the neighborhood, we were shocked to learn that she had died suddenly of tuberculosis. That corner would never again be the same.

Transocean and P.A.L.

During April and May of 1947, Transocean flew a series of shuttles out of Manila under the Philippine Air Lines banner and, needing visas for these flights, we chased all over Manila obtaining clearances for travel in China, Thailand, Burma, and Hong Kong. Flight assignments in Manila were broken by occasional trips home to San Lorenzo. During those periods I finished the garage and, with installation of the new sinks, completed my darkroom.

Fruit and vegetable merchants peddle their wares to boat people along this canal (locally called a Klong) in Bangkok, Thailand. 1948.

Stark Terror at
Hong Kong

O f all the airports in the Far East during the Forties and Fifties, Kai Tak in Hong Kong was the most hazardous when the weather was down. In the immediate post-war years, ILS (instrument landing system), had not yet been developed. Kai Tak's single runway was located on the mainland side of Hong Kong where it had been constructed on reclaimed land dredged up from a bay to the east of Kowloon.

Prevailing winds near the airport generally made take-offs to the east advisable, and because of limited maneuvering space inside the harbor, a sharp right turn out immediately after take-off was necessary to avoid a collision with high hills. Before the runway was realigned and lengthened some time in the Sixties, it could not accommodate commercial jet aircraft.

She'll Be Coming 'Round the Mountain

The approach route to Kai Tak Airport from the east at that time was through a small break in a precipitous and rocky coastal range known as 'The Gap'. The portion of that range immediately southwest of the Gap is Hong Kong Island itself, rising abruptly to an elevation of over 1,800 feet. Equally high, rugged and steep, the range continues on the northeast side of the Gap. The normal procedure in approaching the area was to fly in through the Gap, which was the entrance to the harbor, and land. When the weather was clear and the visibility good, there was no problem, although maneuvering space near the airport was tight because of the proximity of elevated terrain.

Leaving Manila for Hong Kong one day, we had a flight plan forecast of three hours and forty-two minutes, and before the day ended, we had wound up in one of those "Please God, just let me out of this one and I promise I'll never set foot in one of these contraptions again!" episodes.

Checking in at Makati Meteorology for weather briefing, we learned that a well-organized typhoon, centered approximately 200 miles southwest of Okinawa, was churning things up out there. Packing 120-knot winds and torrential rains, it had spread cloud cover over most of the South China Sea. The prognosis for our track and altitude indicated a solid overcast with occasional heavy rain showers and light turbulence over the entire 700-mile leg. For our time of arrival, Kai Tak was estimating a 3,000-foot ceiling in light rain.

Departing from Makati terminal, we flew northwest on a rhumb-line course of 322°, a heading which would not give us speed lines even if the sun were visible. A rhumb line is a curve on the surface of a sphere, which, when projected on a Mercator chart, is a straight line that crosses all meridians of longitude at the same angle. After passing abeam of the Laoag range near the northern tip of Luzon, Loran yielded only course lines, so we had to rely on dead reckoning and forecast winds. It seemed reasonable to expect the forecast flight time to hold up fairly well throughout this relatively short flight. For three and a half hours in light turbulence and intermittent rain, zero visibility cloaked us like a suffocating shroud. Upon nearing the end of the flight, the captain made the decision to begin his letdown, expecting to break out beneath the cloud cover as we descended. We dropped slowly from 7,500 to 2,000 feet through a solid overcast.

Tension was beginning to mount in the cockpit as I glanced at my watch, realizing that by now we had closed to within fifteen minutes of the Gap area. Course lines from Loran told us we were on track, but just where on that track, we could not be sure. Continuing to descend, our altitude was nearing the 1,500 foot level. Had the forecaster been wrong in predicting winds at our en route altitude, we might well pile up on those rocks which make up the coastal range.

The captain, however, elected to continue his let down as he dialed in an appropriate frequency and reached for the mike.

"Hong Kong Approach Control, this is Philippine Air Lines, Zero Four Eight ... We'd like terminal weather for Kai Tak ... Over."

"Zero Four Eight ... Hong Kong Approach here." The crisp British accent was unmistakable. "1500 Zebra weather for Kai Tak ... Overcast ... Ceiling 1,200 feet ... visibility two miles in light rain. Surface wind out of the Northeast to ten knots. Station pressure, twenty-nine point eight inches of mercury. Over to you, Zero Four Eight."

"Roger Hong Kong ... we're forty miles southeast", advised our captain, "estimating Kai Tak at two nine."

"Roger, Zero Four Eight ... Report crossing Waglan Island."

Ten or twelve miles off the Chinese mainland, on the Hong Kong approach, a cluster of jagged rocks sticks up out of the ocean. The Waglan homer was located on one of them. The pointers of both our ADF's (automatic direction finders), which were tuned to Waglan, were revolving aimlessly

Final Approach to Kai Tak airport used to be from this direction across the city of Kowloon on the mainland of the Hong Kong dependency. (Today's approach at about 90° to this runway is equally formidable.) The metropolis of Victoria lies behind the camera across Hong Kong Harbour, on Victoria Island.

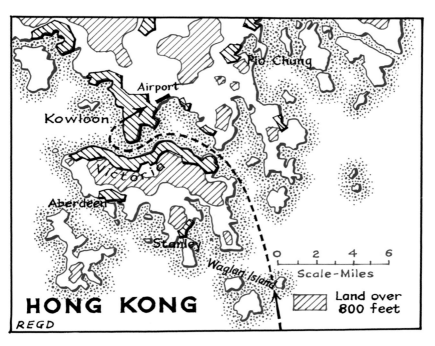

now, the result of heavy atmospherics in the vicinity. Neither of them seemed able to lock on to the signal. I nervously checked the altimeter at the navigator's station ... we were at 800 feet.

It was now critically important to know exactly when we crossed that homer, because at this altitude, and just four minutes after crossing, we would be against those coastal rocks. The ADFs remained stubbornly inconclusive. Guessing blindly that we had indeed passed Waglan Island, the Captain switched VHF frequencies and, reporting us over the homer, requested landing instructions. I found myself wondering what he could have known that I did not.

"Roger, Zero Four Eight," answered the tower, "we have a stratus deck at 1,200 feet ... Overcast ... Two miles visibility in light rain ... Altimeter 29.83 ... There's no reported traffic in the area. Give us a call downwind."

Finding the Gap

Leaning toward the instrument panel, the captain reset his altimeter. Our windshield wipers, though working furiously at top speed, were of little use in heavy rain, but we were finally low enough now to catch an occasional fleeting glimpse below of frothy white caps in a very angry sea. The off-shore rocks were there, too, and, as they flashed past beneath us, I nervously speculated that, at least, we must be somewhere in the ball park.

Descending a couple of hundred feet more with everyone's eyes riveted to the rain-streaked windshield, we were finally able to discern outlined grey areas which appeared to be a mile or so in front of us.

To be certain about distance when you are in rain and fog is difficult, but what we all saw now could only be the coastal hills.

Suddenly the copilot leaned forward, pointing ahead and slightly to the right.

"There's the Gap!" he yelled excitedly.

His pronouncement was countermanded almost simultaneously by the captain, who shouted just as emphatically, "No! ... Look! ... It's over to the left up there," as he pointed off in a different direction.

Returning quickly to the radio operator's position, I fastened my seat belt and waited, heart racing like a turnstile at quitting time. Which one of the pilots was right I never learned, but a minute later we went sailing through the Gap at 400 feet and made a left turn up the harbor past Victoria. Then, doing a one eighty to the right, we came in low over Kowloon and landed at Kai Tak airport. The relief I felt was indescribable. I had been spared once again; it was heaven to be on the ground.

My knees still knocking, I stood at the bottom of the ramp a few minutes later, oblivious to the rain. One by one, I greeted the deplaning passengers with a forced smile. They smiled in return, radiating approval and confidence. My face must have been ashen white, but they seemed not to notice. They knew they were fortunate to have placed their lives safely in the hands of competent, highly skilled professionals who really knew what they were doing. We checked in at the Peninsula Hotel in Kowloon, happy to have survived this day, and thankful that at least one of the professionals had been right.

Shanghai

As a result of the TAL/PAL agreement, I overnighted at Shanghai five times between April 1947 and April 1948. Landing at Lungwha airfield, we stayed in the city at the twenty-storey Park Hotel, the only tall building in Shanghai at the time. I remember it because of a little printed placard that had been placed prominently in our rooms which read: "Please refrain from throwing currency out the window." Foreigners thought it amusing to throw Chinese money from the hotel windows by the handful and, as it fluttered to the thoroughfare below, watch the chaos that resulted as hundreds of Chinese swarmed into the street to scoop it up.

Inflation was rampant in China during the last years of the Nationalist government's regime; an entire armload of Chinese currency could be bought for a few American dollars. Long lines of depositors queued up at bank entrances in an effort to withdraw their savings.

Our agent from B.O.A.C., the British airline, met us at the airport with a black suitcase full of rolls of Chinese dollars, which, by the time we departed the following day, would all have been spent. It was easy to understand why, after choosing breakfast items from the engraved menu in the hotel dining room the next morning. The price of a single egg was $10,000 which, with an accompanying slice of toast and coffee, could run your breakfast tab to $15,000. We paid our check with thousand dollar bills from the black suitcase.

P.A.L. to Madrid

Just one month after my first trip to Shanghai, Philippine Air Lines made its inaugural flight from Manila to Madrid, using Transocean crews and aircraft. Bearing Transocean Air Lines markings and logos on its fuselage, N66635, one of the company's two DC-4s that had just been certificated, arrived in Manila from the States, disembarked its passengers, and taxied to a nearby

Progress of the 'pit stop' paint job is watched by Transocean Air Lines Chief Pilot, Ted Vinson, and TAL Chief Navigator, Al Mays. In 1947, Philippine Air Lines' flights using Transocean DC-4s, flew from Manila to Madrid. Nielson Field, at Makati, was Manila's international airport at that time.

hangar. In a matter of minutes, a crew of Filipino artists and painters had erected scaffolding and were hard at work stripping away vestiges of anything that might indicate Transocean ownership.

Within three hours they had completely repainted the fuselage in big red letters which now read, 'Philippine Air Lines', identifying the aircraft as being of Philippine registry. A final flourish added by the painters as a finishing touch was the name on its nose, 'City of Madrid'.

The scaffolding came down and the airplane was immediately towed to the front of the passenger terminal. With much fanfare, those making the trip were boarded, and N66635, its new paint job still tacky, rose into the air, headed for Madrid, Spain. Total ground time: just over four hours!

These quick change artists stood by, painting and unpainting airplanes every time one went through Manila. The name that went on indicated the direction in which the aircraft was headed.

(Left) The largest of the great pyramids near Cairo, Egypt, is 481 feet high. To grasp its immense size, look for the two camels resting at its base. (Below) Strolling beside the Coliseum in Rome, are Transocean Air Lines' Flight Engineer McCoy, and Captain Vinson. The young lady—our girl in Rome—is Liliano Laudini. Fluent in three languages, she worked our flight plans, did our weight and balance, took charge of our personal luggage, made our hotel reservations, and drove the company bus.

Although I did not make the inaugural flight to Spain for Philippine Air Lines, I was a member of the crew which took the second Madrid trip out of Manila on June 2, 1947. N66644, Transocean's only other C.A.A.-certificated DC-4, flew out with a full load of dignitaries, including Premier Chiang Kai-shek's nieces, the teen-aged Soong sisters. We planned touch-and-go fuel stops at Rangoon and Calcutta, with overnight stays at Karachi, Cairo, and Rome. Our American flight crew had been augmented by the addition of three Filipinos: two stewardesses and a steward making eight crew members in all.

Baluts and Bulls

We were a couple of days into the trip when the cockpit crew discovered that both female flight attendants were carrying "baluts" in their purses for afternoon snacks. What's a 'balut', you ask? Well ... that's a Tagalog word for a

Philippine Air Lines stewardess, Pacita Magtoto, chats with a passenger on an early PAL flight, which appeared to be something of a pilgrimage. Note coffee, tea, and milk thermos bottles on the rear bulkhead. On the unpressurized DC-4, regrettably, there was no way to secure loose overhead storage of pillows, blankets and hand luggage. Circa 1947.

duck egg which has been allowed to develop nearly to the point of hatching, then at the last moment, when the bird inside is completely formed and almost ready to break out of its shell, its progress toward life is arrested by boiling the egg. When cooled, it is ready to be eaten. Sound appetizing? Filipinos think so. We found baluts in bowls on restaurant tables in the Philippines right along with the salt and pepper. Connie Calvento and Matilda Guyoso, our 'stews' for the two week trip, took a lot of good natured ribbing about their gourmet taste.

By today's standards, these early passenger flights were grimly austere. Food for inflight service was iced and packed in Manila and stored aboard the airplane in a well insulated, four-foot-square box, located conveniently beside the main cabin door. To prevent the ice from melting prematurely, the 'food locker' was kept covered with several layers of heavy canvas.

Hot coffee was served from large thermos jugs, as there was no way to heat water aboard. The flight attendants made up cold sandwiches to order for the passengers, who remained on the aircraft almost continuously for more than twenty-four hours without hot food or a bed.

Landing at Karachi, everyone wearily checked in at the airport hotel, located on the second floor of the terminal building, and were fed dinner that evening and breakfast the next morning at the B.O.A.C. dining hall just up the street. In some respects our flight crew fared better than the passengers, because we had the luxury of a double-deck bunk located between partitions separating the passenger section from the flight deck. Crew members could take turns enjoying an occasional nap.

We finally landed at Barajas Airport in Madrid on June 6 and found the terminal area jammed by people who had turned out just to see us land. News photographers on the scene asked the crew to pose on the aircraft ramp, and the following morning our pictures appeared on the front page of the Madrid newspaper under the caption, 'Filipinos in Madrid!'

We were accorded V.I.P. treatment by the Spanish government, which made the most of our presence at every opportunity. They wanted us to be visible, so we were asked to wear our airline uniforms throughout the entire eight-day stay. We were treated to a guided tour of El Escorial, a well-known Spanish showplace, and were wined and dined at night spots around the city. For two days in a row, we were escorted to the bull fights at the Plaza de Toros. To my conservative mid-American mind, a bull fight is not a 'fight' at all. I was quickly turned off by this barbaric sport. A 'sport'? Hardly. To me it came across as legalized cruelty to animals—not just the bulls, but the horses as well. The pageantry, however, was spectacular.

Our trip to Madrid had accidentally coincided with a State visit by Madam Peron of Argentina who was being hosted at the fights by Francisco Franco, the Spanish dictator. All Madrid had declared a gala holiday in the visitor's honor; she and Franco were seated in a special box behind and above us. The stadium was packed with aficionados who came dressed in traditional Spanish costumes. The bullring itself had been beautifully sculptured in colored sand featuring the combined shields of Argentina and Spain, but when they brought out a team of horses to drag away the first dead bull, the beauty of the artist's work was trashed, both under foot and in the mind. I left the Plaza de Toros feeling spiritually depressed, but the photo opportunity was rewarding.

Instant Navigator

Upon our return to Oakland, a note in my mail slot in Operations caught my attention. It read, "To those radiomen who might be interested, Transocean Air Lines and Taloa Academy of Aeronautics are offering, at Company expense, a complete course in aircraft navigation. Cross qualification," it continued, "will result in a pay increase for those who complete the course and check out." Never one to pass up an opportunity, I took up the option and, along with five or six others, enrolled at the Academy.

The author—on the town in Kowloon, 1947. The campaign hat was left over from ATC days. Happily the rickshaw is now rarely to be seen, the memories of life-shortening sweated labor now dimmed by time.

A couple of days before the end of the intensive three-week course, Dispatch phoned the school. They needed a navigator in a hurry for a "Honolulu turnaround" and asked the instructor if he would send over one of the trainees. With the call for a volunteer, I guess I was the first to stand up.

"Lewis," the teacher said, "you're excused. Get on over to Dispatch right away. You'll be back tomorrow night and I'll see you here in class the following morning to finish the course."

"Am I ready to go?" I asked.

"We'll have the answer to that," he replied with a chuckle, "if you find your way to Honolulu and back!"

Running across Earhart Drive to the Navigation Department, I picked up an octant, charts, and other necessary equipment, went down to Meteorology for weather briefing, telephoned Mina, and reported back to Dispatch. An hour later, I was navigating a Fresno Chamber of Commerce charter group to Honolulu. Spur-of-the-moment decisions were not uncommon at Transocean.

N79993 rests on the ramp in front of the Transocean Air Lines passenger terminal at Agana, Guam. The facility, built by Transocean, was shared with Philippine Air Lines. 1948.

Sojourn at Wake Island

Wake Island was to play a major role in the life of Transocean Air Lines because of its strategic location in the central Pacific, 2,009 nautical miles west of Hawaii. Kwajalein, which was entirely under military control, was dropped by Transocean as a refueling stop in October of 1947 in favor of Wake, which had been placed under the administration of the U.S. Civil Aeronautics Authority (C.A.A.).

This atoll, about five miles long and two and a half miles across with a lagoon in the center, consists of three islets, Wilkes, Peale, and Wake. The airport as well as all pertinent island services were on Wake, the largest of the three islets, which also housed employees of the C.A.A., the U.S. Coast Guard, Pan American Airways, and Standard Oil which, at the time, was planning the installation of a large tank farm to service increasing numbers of transiting aircraft.

Lying at 20° north latitude, the tropical climate is mildly humid with warm to hot days and very pleasant nights. There is no soil, only white crushed coral, and the only native vegetation is the Scaviola bush which grows to the size of a small tree. There were half a dozen fig trees on the west end of the island, however, which actually produced fruit, and we surmised that the Japanese had brought them in. Rain showers are brief, except during the winter months when there may be two or three days of rainy weather in a row. Mostly, though, blue sky predominates with only scattered white puffs of cloud floating overhead.

Not Exactly the Ritz

Late on the night of October 3, 1947, Transocean 784, loaded with military electronic equipment destined for Guam, made Transocean's first landing on Wake Island. This was my first trip to the island as well. There had been a three-hour delay in leaving Honolulu that morning and now, after a boring flight of over eleven hours, our crew looked forward to a good night's rest. Having concluded an agreement with the C.A.A., the Company was to take over a cluster of military quonset huts which had been abandoned by the U.S. Navy's Seabees some years before.

(Top) Landing toward the east at Wake Island. This speck of coral looked good to us after ten or eleven hours with nothing but water visible beneath us. 1948. (Middle) Approaching Wake Island down-wind at a thousand feet, this tiny dot in the world's largest ocean was of considerable strategic importance during WWII. Modern passenger airliners overfly the island, but traffic is still brisk, with corporate jets flying to and from the Orient. (Bottom) The usual approach to Wake island runway is from the west, which brought aircraft in just a hundred or so feet above the Transocean compound at the west end of the island. January 23, 1957.

Located off the west end of the runway, the area was to become the Transocean Air Lines compound. While waiting for a car and driver to take us out there, we buttoned up the airplane for the night. A C.A.A. carry-all soon pulled up, and throwing our bags in the back of the truck, we headed for the far end of Wake Islet.

According to the driver, the area we were headed for was about three miles from the terminal quonset. Riding along in the open vehicle, we could hear the intermittent roar of the surf crashing through the reef a short distance to our left.

No moon was visible that night, and out there in the middle of the Pacific Ocean, a thousand miles from land in any direction, no haze, smoke or fog were present either. Millions of stars filled the night sky in the vast pristine atmosphere above—all so bright, that to identify the major constellations was nearly impossible. The awesome immensity of space, when viewed from this tiny speck in mid-Pacific, made us aware of Nature's majestic eloquence without its uttering a word.

"My name's Tex", our driver began, in an effort to start a conversation. "This place shore ain't no substitute for Texas!"

No one challenged him as he continued touting the merits of his home in the States. Cooped up in an airplane all day, everyone chose to remain silent, content just to relax a bit and soak up the cool night breeze. A moment or two went by before he tried again.

"T'aint much down there no more," he continued. "Them buildings' is all growed up with scrubs and weeds now since the Navy moved out better'n two years ago. Ain't nobody set foot down there since the GIs pulled out."

Again, none of us spoke; he did not try again. Down the road another half-mile or so, our headlights illuminated two or three quonsets in front of us and we soon came to a stop.

"Wal ... this is it!" the Texan declared with an air of finality.

Allowing the engine to run, he hurriedly jumped out and began tossing our baggage onto the ground, apparently afraid we'd ask to be taken back to the terminal.

What we were able to see in the light of the car's headlamps could only be described as utter desolation. Our first officer, who could not seem to remember people's names, habitually addressed everyone as Ace.

"Hey, Ace?" ... he asked in disbelief as he swung his flashlight across the scene.

"Call me Tex" the driver corrected.

"O.K., Tex, have it your way ... but are you sure this is where we're supposed to spend the night?"

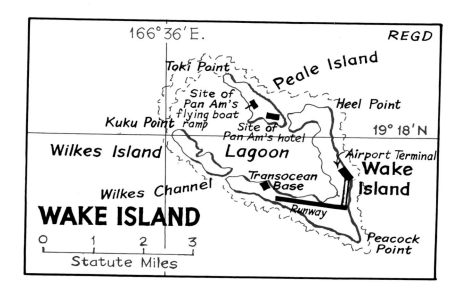

"Yup ... this is where they said to take ya all right!"

As the carryall's tail lights disappeared in the distance, we took out out flashlights to have a look around. It soon became abundantly clear that we were in a mess. Doors to the tin-roofed buildings were scattered around on the ground, with some still clinging by one hinge to their door frames. The roots of errant Scaviola bushes had taken over, shoving support blocks away from building corners, causing them to sag badly. Coral sand had drifted in, covering sections of the walks, the steps, and even the floors in the rooms.

Cobwebs filled every corner, and small lizards scurried across the floor as the beams from our flashlights fell on them. Steel cots with mattresses were there all right, but they too were covered with sand and Scaviola leaves. Debris was everywhere, and, of course, electricity had long ago been disconnected.

In the darkness we found a couple of old brooms and spent the next hour shaking out mattresses, removing trash, and generally trying, with the help of flashlights, to make a couple of rooms habitable enough to use. Frustrated and tired, we slept on bare mattresses that night, in our uniforms.

Such were the beginnings of Transocean Air Lines as a major occupant of Wake Island. Within a few years this compound became the Company's largest overseas base, with 140 employees and a facility capable of servicing half a dozen other airlines as well as transporting, housing, and feeding several hundred passengers and crew members daily.

Taloa Village

Taloa Village, as it soon came to be known, operated its own electric power plant, water stills, car pool, laundry, and even possessed a well-stocked library set up from several large boxes of books that had been packed away, then abandoned by the Seabees. A small store and clubhouse in the village helped make life on the island much more palatable. Operating round the clock, the dining hall, housed in a giant quonset, could seat 200 people at a time. There were rats on Wake Island—which brings to mind a story.

For several years, chief honcho in the mess hall and boss of a crew of fifteen or twenty Filipino kitchen boys was Transocean's head cook, an avowed rat-hater, whom we all knew as Benny. He ran a tight ship and was an excellent cook—when sober; but his performance was seriously flawed on the frequent occasions when he drank too much. Under the influence and imagining himself to be on some sort of safari, Benny would show up at the dining hall brandishing his .45 caliber pistol and indulge in his favorite pastime: shooting at the rats that frolicked high overhead in the ceiling trusses.

Terrified, the kitchen help always took shelter in the walk-in coolers, under the tables, or wherever else they could get out of sight. So far as anyone knew, however, Benny never bagged a single rat, but he did put a lot of holes in the metal roof. Benny never did any real harm, thanks to H. Graham 'Red' Emery. Red was station manager for two or three years at that time. A quiet-spoken individual who enjoyed music from the classics and the creature comforts of life, Red was well liked, yet, to me, he seemed strangely out of place on the Wake Island frontier. A tall and slender man, his appearance and manner were deceiving, but when fortitude was called for, he had the guts to come through in spades.

Gun shots, heard coming from the vicinity of the dining hall, meant but one thing: Benny was at it again. Unflappable Red would drop whatever he was doing, walk calmly to the mess hall, and confront the offender. "All right Benny," he would demand, "give me the gun." Benny would hand it over; there was never an argument. The averted crisis signaled the magical reappearance of the kitchen help, and things soon returned to normal while Red went looking for maintenance man, Axel Sorenson. The new holes in the roof would have to be patched.

An abandoned gun emplacement and scaviola trees frame this 1950 view of the Suwa Maru, *which rusts away on the reef in the background. Exploring the debris left from the war is Randall Levensaler, a radio operator-navigator.*

Because Wake Island became a crew layover point for all trips to and from the Far East, most of us developed a love-hate relationship with this harsh, unyielding patch of coral. With the exception of Hawaii, I spent more time here over a seventeen-year period than on all other foreign bases put together. For a short stay, flight crews could almost enjoy the island, but after waiting three or four days for an incoming flight that would take them out, life did become boring.

Some of my early layovers on Wake were spent exploring the extensive network of slit trenches left by the Japanese occupation forces. Scattered about through the maze of bunkers were makeshift tables and chairs constructed from packing crates. Oil lamps, articles of clothing ... even office equipment, such as Japanese adding machines and typewriters could be found. Strewn across bunker floors and seemingly abandoned in a hurry were a great profusion of personal items necessary for day-to-day living, as well as hundreds of letters and postcards written in Japanese. Even photographs of family and friends at home had been left behind. Two-inch thick cork lined the bunker walls, which the Americans, upon retaking the island, soon stripped out for use in insulating their own houses.

U.S. Forces had blockaded the island, cutting off the Japanese garrison's supply lines. The *Suwa Maru,* a Japanese freighter, had tried to run the

The freighter Suwa Maru, *beached at Wake Island in July, 1943, took hits from two American torpedoes while trying to supply the island's Japanese garrison. 20 members of its crew died, and 30 more were wounded.*

blockade but was struck by an American torpedo as she approached the island. Her skipper managed to hang his ship up on the reef, where her remains continued to deteriorate for more than twenty-five years. Some of our more venturesome crew members swam out through the surf from time to time to suntan on her rusting decks. Ernie Gann, a well known author today and a Transocean captain for a few post-war years, still has in his possession the ship's brass bell, which he and a couple of his friends somehow managed to bring ashore.

The Japanese invaders had been reduced to a diet consisting almost entirely of fish, although, in an effort to grow things from seed, many soldiers had marked off small, individual plots of coral with sticks and string. Incredible as it may seem, cotton plants, which actually produced cotton, seemed to be one of their more successful crops. We could only speculate that they planned to make clothing from it. Dozens of these small garden plots were in evidence around the island.

There were several 'clubs' on Wake, but the favorite one was our own Drifter's Reef. A comfortable bar and lounge, it doubled as a small store where we were able to buy toilet articles, candy bars, cigarettes, and other sundries. The club faced the lagoon where base personnel dredged out a sizable swimming area, brought in sand to make a beach, and installed a diving board.

While I never fell prey to the cigarette habit, I did on occasion enjoy a good cigar during my flying years. Cigar smokers scattered among Transocean's crews preferred to fly with cigar-smoking captains for obvious reasons. These élite groups of social outcasts, upon landing in Manila, invariably made a beeline for the Tabacalera or Alhambra cigar factories where premium hand-crafted cigars were the stock in trade. Works of art they were, and each purchaser left happily with a couple of boxes—enough, at least, to last until the next trip out.

Back on Wake Island, as the day cooled off into evening, we liked to toss a game of horseshoes, then catch the movie bus to the Windy Palace and, while waiting for the show to begin, light up our elegant stogies. Time now to enjoy the camaraderie of our fellow cigar smokers; time to share the supreme contentment that only a good cigar can bring.

Stewardesses, young and single, loved Wake Island. They came prepared for the tropical climate with swimsuits and cut-offs. Greatly outnumbered by single men employed on the island, they never lacked for male companionship. In addition to the Drifter's Reef, there were the Pan Am and Coast Guard clubs, and snorkling equipment and bicycles could be rented on the island. Transocean's stewardesses had their own special quonset. Equipped with additional baffling for privacy, it was aptly dubbed The Iron Girdle.

A channel had been dredged in through the reef near the Standard Oil tank farm, and a small dock lay just inside the lagoon where incoming supplies could be off-loaded.

Adjacent to the channel stood a fifty-foot wooden watch tower with a canopy over the platform on top. We guessed that it had been built by the Japanese. Finding the tower to be a pleasant retreat on hot afternoons, we enjoyed sitting up there in the cool breeze to read, watch the gulls and terns, and enjoy the view out to sea.

Much of the help at Transocean Village was recruited from the Philippines, and Filipinos, devout Catholics, went into the open ocean early every Friday morning to return with a great variety of fish, enough to feed the entire compound as well as the day's transient passengers.

Sometimes, for a little diversion, we talked one of the Filipino cooks out of a chunk of raw beef. Threading it on a foot-long fish hook tied to a rope leader, we threw it into the channel. Buoyed by a piece of two-by-four as a float, the tide soon carried it to the open ocean, and in minutes we had a shark. We hooked into a ten-footer once; the kitchen crew cut it into fillets.

Shown here at C.A.A. Meteorology for weather briefing are pilots Walt O'Brian, and John Russell. The 700 millibar chart will provide Navigator John Searles (middle) with information on weather conditions at the 8,000 foot level, such as wind direction and velocity, cloud cover, and location of any frontal systems which may be present along the route. Wake Island, 1957.

(Above) This view of the Transocean area was taken from the roof of the old quonset dining hall. A new dining facility was constructed after the typhoon of 1953. (Bottom left) Transitting passengers board a Transocean bus for the two-mile ride to TALOA Village for lunch. 1958. (Bottom right) Soon to be reunited with their husbands and fathers in Japan, these military wives and children pause for a lunch break. June, 1953.

(Above) On Wake Island in 1961–62, World Airways crews were housed and fed by Pan American Airways. Pictured here is the PanAm dining hall. Note the Scaviola bush which grows to tree size on the island. (Bottom left) A giant quonset type building served as the Wake Island passenger terminal until approximately 1960, when it was replaced by a new air conditioned facility. Transocean operations was just inside the door behind the jeep. (Bottom right) The Transocean complex on Wake Island as it appeared in 1957. Note Drifter's Reef Club (upper left) in front of the horseshoe shaped swimming area. This mid-ocean watering hole is still open.

If we flew into Wake at eight in the morning and knew that we had to take another flight out at ten that evening, we had no alternative but to sleep through the daylight hours, which, on Wake, was not easy. The heat and humidity after sun-up would generally become oppressive, and the noise of trucks and people passing the louvered walls of our crew quarters only made matters worse. Remember, in those days, air-conditioning in a place as remote as Wake Island was confined only to those buildings where temperature control was essential. On the other hand, night sleep was wonderful. The temperature would have cooled to 65° or 70° and the only sounds might be the soporific roar of the ocean as it crashed through coral heads less than a hundred yards away or a brief but heavy downpour drumming on the metal roof of the quonset. To protect us from sudden squalls, wooden shutters could be lowered to prevent the wind-driven rain from blowing in on us.

A modern new air terminal building was constructed on Wake Island some time in the early Sixties. Its ground floor waiting room was open on three sides and, for a while at least, it sported a small coffee shop. The air-conditioned second floor housed Meteorology, Pan Am operations, and C.A.A. business offices.

Personal telephone traffic out of the island did not exist until a submarine cable was laid in the mid-Sixties, but there were a couple of amateur radio stations, whose operators could put us through to our wives and families. The only cost to us was the phone patch from the amateur station in California to our home telephones. The term 'phone patch' refers to an audio connection between the output of a short wave radio receiver and a telephone line. In this case, the amateur radio operator on Wake Island makes contact with another amateur somewhere in California, who, in turn, dials the home telephone of the resident to whom the person on the Wake end wishes to speak. The California 'ham' operator then 'patches' (connects) the output of his receiver to the telephone line to complete the connection.

The Greany Maru

Wake Island's lagoon is too shallow to accommodate large sea-going vessels, which had to drop sea anchor a thousand yards or so off the island. Oil for the tank farm, therefore, needed to be pumped ashore through large hoses supported on floats.

At the end of World War II, the military abandoned certain materiel on Wake, among which were two shallow draft vessels, LSTs (Landing Ship, Tank) that had been beached, only to rust away inside the lagoon.

The Greany Maru *heads for the channel entrance to the Wake lagoon with supplies that have been off-loaded from a seagoing vessel anchored 1,000 yards offshore. The tower (upper right) was a great place to read or just meditate while catching a cool breeze on a warm afternoon.*

Around 1949, Transocean's Wake station manager was an enterprising young man by the name of Jack Greany. He seized what appeared to him to be an excellent opportunity, and somehow managed to acquire one of the languishing LSTs. Upon examination, the two powerful grey marine diesel engines in the craft appeared to be in a good state of preservation, and with the help of a couple of Transocean aircraft mechanics, and considerable perseverance, Mr. Greany was able to coax them into life.

After a successful trial spin, the new acquisition was promptly christened, *Greany Maru,* and no time was lost in selling Transocean's new lighter service to the other organizations on the island. The venture was a sure-fire money-maker from the start and did very well; but not for long.

The day had been busy and profitable. Having already made several trips out to the supply ship, the 'crew' needed to make one more before dark. A load of mattresses still remained to be brought ashore so, with darkness approaching, they decided to go for it. Loading the mattresses, they headed back in ... but now, daylight was gone.

There were navigation lights at the channel entrance, red on one side and green on the other, but somehow the 'steering committee' mixed up port and starboard, and, alas, by the time they discovered their mistake, it was too late. They piled the flagship of the Transocean Navy up on the reef at the edge of the channel.

The crew managed to get off the boat without injury, but the next morning when everyone went out to survey the damage, the LST had clearly taken such a pounding in the surf that salvage was impossible. Unfortunately, aircraft mechanics and airline station managers do not necessarily make expert seamen. They say that mattresses were seen floating around the Western Pacific for weeks after the incident. Transocean Air Lines' short-lived naval division had come to an ignominious end. Its loss was not recorded in the Lloyds Shipping Register.

Last Days of the Chinese Republic

In the spring of 1948, Transocean landed a contract to ferry 150 Curtiss C-46s to Chiang Kai-shek's nationalist government. At the rate of five per day, all were flown safely to Shanghai in a little more than a month. Each was crewed by a pilot, copilot, and radio operator/navigator, and every four or five days, a DC-4 was dispatched from Oakland to bring back the accumulation of crew members.

At the beginning of 1949, just six months before the Communists overran all of China, a crew to which I had been assigned spent nearly two weeks in Shanghai. We left Oakland believing we were on a Honolulu turn-around, so the only civilian clothing we took with us were shorts and aloha shirts.

Oakland Dispatch, however, changed its mind after we had reached Honolulu, sending us on to Shanghai where we were to pick up a load of White Russian refugees who had long ago fled from Communism in Russia and were now trying desperately to escape from China before another Communist regime took over there. We landed in Shanghai the night of December 31, 1948, New Year's Eve, in the middle of winter.

Shanghai Nights

C.N.A.C. (Chinese National Airlines Corporation), had made reservations for us at the Cathay Hotel, an impressive hostelry adjacent to the Bund. This park-like strip of land separated the hotel from the Huangpu River. Assigned to rooms on one of the upper floors, we had a majestic view of the waterfront that stretched out in front of the hotel in both directions. An American cruiser, riding at anchor just across the Bund from us, fortified our sense of security about being in this troubled country.

Diplomatic snags for the refugees kept us waiting in Shanghai for thirteen days. The weather was bitterly cold during the entire time, and a chill wind made the low temperatures even more unpleasant. Streets were laced with ice, and night-time thermometer readings hovered near zero. Aloha

The Huangpu River forms a waterfront, known as the Bund, for Shanghai, China. The V-shaped building at right center is the Cathay Hotel. The famous Shanghai Racecourse is in the middle distance. Riding at anchor in the river, just months before the communists moved in, is an American cruiser. January 1, 1949.

shirts would definitely not do here. From a haberdasher near the hotel, we bought British long johns, woolen pants and socks, and warm sweaters.

A pair of cotton gloves and Russian-made pull-down stocking caps with eye slits completed our emergency wardrobe. During the coldest weather, hotels and public buildings allowed homeless street people to come inside to sleep. Crews arriving at the hotel in the middle of the night needed flashlights to pick their way through dozens of Chinese sleeping in the hall-ways. I recall seeing 'body wagons' moving along the streets early each morning as the unfortunates who had frozen to death during the night were picked up.

The almost suffocating mass of humanity that was Shanghai's popula-tion of about 10,000,000 was quite a contrast to the wide open spaces of my native Kansas. The inner city seemed strangely quiet, probably because of the absence of large numbers of automobiles. The predominant motorized vehi-cles appeared to be large commercial ones, while lesser merchants made deliveries using three-wheeled pedicabs. The remainder of the citizenry was either afoot or on bicycles, and the unending cacophony created by hundreds of musical handlebar ringers, sounding all at once, almost drowned out the noise of horns and engines.

Thousands of Chinese families lived out their lives on junks, sampans, and barges in the city's waterways. Suchow Creek, which met the Huangpu River about two blocks up from our hotel, was jammed with traffic, leaving barely enough space in the middle of the channel for river travellers to squeeze through.

Shanghai and its environs form the hub of a vast lush plain. From the air, the Huangpu and the Yangtze river deltas appear as a huge mosaic formed by a patchwork of thousands of small farms. Producing in great variety, the area is one huge vegetable garden. Honeycombed by ribbons of canals, the extensive use of boats on these waterways is the cheapest and best way for the farmer to transport his produce to the big city markets. In the 1940s there were no highways, and rural roads were little more than paths, carrying only foot, bicycle, or pedicab traffic. Such is the rate of progress in this largely populated country that the rural areas have not changed much today, half a century later.

As we walked among the Chinese on the streets of Shanghai, we were constantly stared at by whole groups of pedestrians. A dozen pairs of eyes whose bodies stood motionless at intersections, unblinking, gawked holes through us. The Chinese seemed never to have seen occidentals before. The same phenomenon occurred during the late 1970s, after the People's Republic finally ended its long period of isolation with the rest of the world.

Watch For Sale

We were hustled by street vendors, con men, and beggars, not a few of whom understood a little English. At that time I was wearing a Hamilton wrist watch with a stainless steel band that snapped on and off over the wrist; snap-on bands were popular during the war.

Walking along the Bund one morning, I was intrigued by the slow, calculating movements of a few hundred Tai Chi exercisers in the adjacent parkway, when a young boy, about twelve years old, slipped up behind me and tried to tear the watch off my wrist. Managing to put a vice grip on his arm before he could pry it away, I hung on and swung around toward him, changing my grip to his shirt collar. He looked up at me with fear in his eyes.

"You sell?" he asked.

I hesitated ... My wrist watch was the only one I had ever seen with a settable second hand (although all air force pilots had them as standard issue). It was a valuable asset in navigation, and it was more convenient to use than my hack watch. Having purchased it from a Honolulu jewelry store for fifty dollars about four years earlier, it was beginning to show signs of heavy wear. Still.. it had performed well and I was reluctant to part with it.

"One hundred fifty American dollars!" I shot back, believing that the high asking price would send the kid on his way, but then things took a surprising turn. He reached into a side pocket and, with considerable difficulty, pulled out a roll of American one-hundred-dollar bills about the diameter of a baseball bat. Then, digging into another pocket, he came up with a wad of fifties and twenties. Peeling off a hundred and fifty American with the expertise of a G.I. in a high stakes poker game, he jammed it into my hand. Releasing my hold on his shirt, I examined the currency, which certainly appeared to be genuine. With watch in hand now, he whirled around, running, and was soon lost in the crowd. Remembering that Detor Jewelers on King Street in Honolulu had originally sold me the watch, I stopped by on my way home some eight or ten days later and purchased a new one for the same price as the original: fifty dollars.

Meanwhile, Back at the Ranch

Ten years had passed since Mina and I had exchanged marriage vows. In the excitement of a somewhat itinerant lifestyle, those years had slipped away almost imperceptibly, and we began to realize that if we were ever to raise a family, definite plans would need to be made. As with other young couples during those war years, much had happened to us in a short time. We had lived through a period of insecurity and uncertainty and the realization that my war-related occupation could end at any time.

Since coming to Transocean, however, life had been good to us. We had made quite a number of friends among the flying fraternity in San Lorenzo and when we were not socializing, I was usually busy in the darkroom doing photographic work for the various subsidiaries of the rapidly expanding airline.

Now, however, into the postwar period by two years, we needed to make permanent commitments for ourselves. Mina and I had often discussed children. We knew that the addition of a child to our family would restrict our freedoms and bring additional responsibilities. Then, too, a role as a father would not necessarily be compatible with my flying career, which could keep me away from home for two weeks to a month at a time. Nevertheless, we decided to seek the advice and help of a gynecologist to learn why Mina had been unable to conceive. In March of 1949, after a number of tests, we received the joyous news that we were to become parents. Now we would have to begin thinking in three dimensions instead of two.

Throughout 1948 and much of 1949, postwar reconstruction work on several of the larger islands in the Pacific Theater kept Transocean crews busy flying workers of major contractors such as Atkinson-Jones and Brown-Pacific-Maxim to and from Guam and Okinawa. Then, just three months after learning that Mina was indeed pregnant, our hopes were shattered. She miscarried. An outbound crew member friend brought me the news on Wake Island as I was inbound. The date was 29 June 1949. Three more seemingly endless days passed before I was able to get back to be with her, but she had taken the bitter disappointment in her stride.

Let's Talk Turkey

ina had planned a small birthday party for me in September, 1949, but that had to be scratched when I was alerted for a trip which Oakland dispatch said would take me around the world. I was to pack accordingly. By now, the Communist armies had overrun the Chinese mainland and Chiang Kai Shek had retreated to his island stronghold of Formosa (Taiwan). Transocean contracted to fly a load of gunpowder to the Nationalists in Taipei. We were told that the need was immediate and critical because the Nationalists feared a Communist invasion attempt. Purely by accident, we landed in Taipei on an American holiday, Labor Day, and the American attaché, whom we needed to provide a receipt for the shipment, had flown off to Macao for a three-day vacation.

We waited that one out, then headed off with an empty airplane for Bombay, India, where we were to pick up 54 Indian seamen bound for New York City; but because of a problem over landing rights in India, we spent two nights in Bangkok waiting for Bombay clearances. Finally getting out of there, we overnighted in Calcutta and the next day, after a six-hour flight, we flew into Bombay. Early the following morning we boarded the seamen and took off for Nicosia, Cyprus.

Notices to Airmen at the Bombay airport warned that Iraq would not tolerate the presence of foreign aircraft in its airspace and suggested that we avoid flying over any portion of that country, so we decided to refuel at Abadan, Iran, then head north, skirting the Iraqi border. Radio communication was unreliable over much of these segments and, except for three or four homers, there were no radio aids in the area. The flight was by daylight, however, and the U.S. Air Force charts we were using made it possible to track our progress by surface observation of lakes and rivers, railway lines, and other topographical features. We were traversing a high plateau of desert hills, and three hours into the flight, convection currents rising from the desert surfaces were creating choppy, clear-air turbulence which kept us buckled up.

Diversion to Diyarbakir

In another half-hour we sighted 17,000-foot Mt. Ararat. Perpetually snow-capped, it dominates the region on the Russian-Turkish border, and we flew close enough to have a good look at it. Then, turning left, we headed west-south-west and crossed into Turkey. Three and a half hours later we should have landed on the island of Cyprus, but an unexpected emergency changed the entire course of things.

Somewhere over east-central Turkey, while cruising at 12,000 feet, our No. 2 engine registered a sudden drop in oil pressure, and before Captain 'Burr' Hall could react, it sputtered and quit. He reached overhead to feather it, but now the propeller would not oblige. Again and again he activated the feathering button, but to no avail. This sudden turn of events, Burr knew, had the potential for disaster. Disengaging the auto pilot, he turned and called out to navigator Charnley. "Where are we Bill?" There was good reason for concern. The drag created by the windmilling propeller had reduced our airspeed to 150 knots.

Stepping up front, Bill pointed out several airport symbols on the Air Force area chart, the only map we had of the region. A close look revealed the presence of a secondary airstrip at an obscure place called Diyarbakir, perhaps no more than ten or fifteen minutes in front of us. Maybe we would luck out ... Both pilots studied the chart for a few moments and decided that the symbols shown probably represented facilities that were dirt strips of indeterminate length and condition. Looking up, Capt. Hall turned to First Officer Minson.

"See if you can find anything in the route manuals on this place, Roy."

While waiting for a response, Burr cast an anxious glance out the window, scanning the inboard engine for several seconds. Oil was snaking across the side of the cowling to trail off and disappear over the wing's surface. Concern for the passengers suddenly raced through his mind. Neither they nor the crew had Turkish visas, nor did the aircraft have landing rights for Turkey. But now his chain of thought was interrupted by Roy's answer.

"We'll just have to hope that the airport symbol shown at Diyarbakir on the chart means what it says," Roy concluded.

His hurried search through a lap full of reference manuals had produced no evidence of either the city or its landing strip. While Flight Engineer Stearns continued trying to feather the errant propeller, Burr struggled to come up with options that simply did not exist. Like it or not, he would have to find Diyarbakir and its runway. Apprehension was on his face and in his voice.

"Unless we get this bird on the ground, and soon," he warned, "we're going to be in a peck of trouble. We've almost certainly got a blown cylinder out there, and with no oil in that engine, it could seize up and shed the prop ... someone on the ground would have a DC-4 souvenir!"

Leaning forward, Burr groped nervously under his seat for the lever that would allow him to move a notch closer to the yoke. Straightening up, he double-checked his seat belt and, once again, turned to look out the window. The number two nacelle now glistened under the noonday sun as the slip-stream rippled oil across half the surface of the engine's cowling. Burr had a loose cannon to deal with, and he knew it.

Throttles backed off, we started down. No Smoking and Seat Belt signs came on. Burr steadied the airplane to a 500-foot-per-minute descent, then yelled back at me to call the stewardess up front. Questions were now flying back and forth on the flight deck. Could the runway at Diyarbakir support a large transport plane? Would it be of sufficient length? Did it even exist? These and other questions seemed irrelevant now; if there was such a place and we could find it, we would have to use it anyway.

Just another of those times, I told myself. For the past two hours there had been no radio contacts, although I had tried repeatedly to raise Nicosia. Now I sat down to try once again. No response. Daytime communications in this part of the world were poor at best. Minutes ticked by as the propeller continued to windmill. Registering zero now, the No. 2 oil pressure gauge reminded Burr of the danger of fire. The flash of the red fire warning light and the blare of the alarm horn, he knew, could come at any time.

Stewardess Alice Martinez appeared in the cockpit doorway and Captain Hall instructed her to advise the passengers that we would make an emergency landing at Diyarbakir, Turkey.

"Alice," Burr ordered, "collect everyone's passport back there. Have them ready to hand over to local authorities on the ground ... that is ... if we can find a place to set this thing down!"

At 1,500 feet, descending, the situation suddenly worsened. Friction caused by the windmilling propeller snapped the crankshaft, sending the No. 2 fan spinning out of control. In desperation we searched the horizon for signs of habitation; minutes dragged by like hours.

Away in the distance now, partly discernible through haze and dust, a large urban area appeared to be taking shape. We were obviously approaching a major population center. A massive medieval wall, broken at intervals by circular stone turrets, completely surrounded it, and there, not far from the city's edge, was what we had anxiously been looking for: the landing strip at

Diyarbakir, almost inconspicuous against the background of the surrounding desert.

Vibrating all the way to the ground, we held our breaths as we landed straight in on a dirt runway and rolled to a stop near the opposite end of the field, where the three remaining engines were shut down. The agony of our wounded bird was ended; once again, I had escaped the jaws of the dragon.

Our sudden appearance aroused considerable curiosity as several groups of Turkish soldiers, emerging from buildings near the edge of the airstrip, came streaming out to look us over. We learned later that they had never seen a four-engined airplane. There was no ramp, and our passengers were filing down the ship's ladder, when an American jeep pulled up alongside us.

Seated in the rear of the open vehicle was a large, paunchy looking, middle-aged Turkish officer. One look at the man, and we were convinced that he had to be a person of considerable political stature in the region. Later we learned that he was the local commander of the Turkish Air Force with the rank of colonel.

His chauffeur was, incredibly, an American sergeant, without whose ultimate help we would probably still be in Turkey today. The sergeant, we soon learned, was on loan from the American military to provide the Turks with technical assistance in improving their airfield.

Some of the arriving soldiers had now managed to climb the ladder and enter the 'plane's cabin where they helped themselves to the foodstuffs that were aboard. Two or three of them dropped cartons of milk to their buddies on the ground while others came happily down the ladder, their arms full of fresh fruit.

Rifles slung over their shoulders and cartridge belts around their waists convinced us not to try to stop them. Stearns had gone around in front to inspect the damage to the engine and before he could lock the cabin door and stow the ladder in the belly, the food was gone. There had been enough aboard to feed the passengers and crew for three days. In discussing the incident later, we felt sure the colonel must have observed this behavior but made no attempt to stop it.

With the Turkish-speaking sergeant acting as interpreter, our host wanted to know who we were and whence we had come. We in turn needed to know how we could get a message out to our company. According to the colonel, though, there were no communication links whatsoever between Diyarbakir and the outside world. My thoughts drifted off to the possibility that the entire crew might have to throw in with a camel caravan for a six or seven day journey to the Mediterranean Sea. The reality of our predicament returned just as the preliminary conversations between Captain Hall and the sergeant were ending.

The colonel was all smiles now and became quite hospitable. He took complete charge, finding quarters for the Indian passengers, which was fine, but then he assigned Alice to a room in the Officer's Club, leaving her apprehensive to say the least. Taking her aside, we begged her to accept his offer, rationalizing that to displease the base's commanding officer might not be wise.

"Why can't I come and bunk in with you guys?" she asked, apparently convinced that we would have been the lesser of the two evils. We promised to speak to the American sergeant, who was also billeted in the club, to ask him to keep a watchful eye out for her safety. With neither landing rights nor Turkish visas, we certainly did not wish to offend the colonel. Fortunately, Alice was not too obstinate about her room assignment and, with some reluctance, agreed to play the part of the sacrificial lamb.

Turkish Delights

The chauvinistic colonel apparently felt that the male crew members deserved special attention, so he ordered a Turkish family, who lived near the runway, out of their home, and insisted that we move in. Burr tried to protest, but the colonel, with a wave of his hand, made it clear that he was the boss here and would brook no disent.

He topped off his hospitality spectacular by giving us a jeep to drive, furnishing us with an orderly and a houseboy, and finally insisting that we all be his guests at the Officer's Club for dinner that evening. In Turkey, the national drink is an anise-based liqueur called 'Raki', and the colonel made certain there was no shortage of it at our table. He took a special liking to Alice, who was young and pretty, insisting that she grace the dinner table at his right. Directing his attention almost entirely to her during the meal, he proposed toast after toast to her good health and expected her to match him drink for drink.

The poor girl could not have weighed more than 110 lb and was no contest with this heavy weight Lothario. Of course, neither could understand the other, but the colonel gave it his best shot, relying heavily on body language and facial expressions to make his points. While the colonel was romancing our stewardess at one end of the table, the male members of the crew at the other end of the table were giving serious thought as to how we were going to get out of Turkey.

During breakfast in the grape arbor behind the Officer's Club, crew members discuss options with the Turkish speaking American sergeant. Sitting next to Captain Hall (back to camera), is Flight Engineer Bob Stearns. Diyarbekir, Turkey, September 12, 1949.

Dinner over, we rescued Alice from the amorous intent of our host by telling him that she had some duties at the airplane which needed her attention. Taking our leave, we all climbed into the jeep the colonel had lent us and made our way to the airplane. We knew we had to advise Transocean of our whereabouts, so Burr decided to run up an engine while I attempted again to raise someone—anyone—on the aircraft's radio. After several attempts, a successful contact was finally made with a station on the island of Malta.

PLEASE ADVISE TRANSOCEAN AIR LINES IN ROME THAT TAL 644 IS GROUNDED IN DIYARBAKIR, TURKEY, NEED REPLACEMENT ENGINE.

The Malta station acknowledged receipt of the message and assured me that it would reach our Rome office. By this time, we knew we were not going anywhere for several days, so we off-loaded our luggage to the jeep and dropped Alice at the club. Wishing her well, we turned in at our commandeered quarters, where our orderly had made up our beds.

Some time during the night, our newly assigned houseboy polished and shined everyone's shoes; then, at about daybreak, our orderly came through the house, waking us all up with direct orders from the colonel. We were to be served breakfast at the club at seven, and the entire crew was to be in his office promptly at eight o'clock for a conference and briefing. We were beginning to wonder if we were his guests or his prisoners and were somewhat concerned as to what he might have in mind.

Awakened by a knock on her door at the same time, Alice was given the same message. A short while later, rested and freshly groomed, she created a stir as she paraded through a roomful of Turkish officers to join us in the grape arbor annex behind the club. She had slept well, but was relieved to be sitting down with us once again. Breakfast in a pleasant setting, consisted of a local melon of some kind, coarse brown toast with guava jelly, and very black Turkish coffee.

We were a few minutes late in keeping our requested appointment in the colonel's office. Greeting us in dress uniform, complete with a pound of medals pinned to his chest, we were waved to a seat around his conference table. Solicitously inquiring as to our comfort, he began by commenting that if we needed anything at all, to let the orderly know.

Captain Hall reported that we had established radio contact from our aircraft the night before, and that help would soon be on the way. Seated next to the colonel, the American sergeant had a discussion with our pilots concerning the availability of engine stands and hoists that would be needed to change the engine.

The conference ended when the Colonel rose, telling us that we were free to take the jeep into the city if we chose, and remarked that he hoped we had had a comfortable night. We were relieved to know that the conference had been scheduled for the express purpose of exchanging pleasantries. For each of the three days we were there, however, he insisted that the entire crew report to his office at eight each morning for briefing and a conference. Our orderly made it clear that the colonel did not like to be kept waiting, dramatically making his point by drawing his hand rapidly across his throat.

Diyarbakir was on two major camel caravan routes and the entire population seemed to be in the streets. We shared the dusty road to town with a variety of animals, including a string of camels burdened with mountainous bales of hay. Spread out in front of us, a herd of goats slowed our progress to a snail's pace. Behind us, crated chickens, loaded on mules, were thrown from side to side in their cages, in cadence with the animals' stride. Draped from head to toe in black 'abaayas', according to Moslem custom, women rode their donkeys side-saddle and followed us with inquiring eyes as we passed.

(Above) Encircling the ancient city of Diyarbekir, where time seems to have stood still, these basalt walls date from the 4th century A.D. (Below) Desperately poor, but well-fed and cheerful, this family of seven posed for my camera. Diyarbekir, Turkey, 1949.

The wall we had seen from the air had been built under Roman rule in the fourth century A.D., and most of it was still intact. We were looking through a time window at one of the most primitive large cities left on earth.

Passing through a main gate, we found ourselves on rough and narrow cobblestone streets bordered by stone block buildings, centuries old. Streets and alleys led in all directions, opening unexpectedly on squares where crowded merchants in street stalls sold, bartered, and hawked everything from 'eating pigeons' to articles of clothing. Raw meat, displayed on boards along the gutter areas of the street, lay exposed in the hot sun, and when a potential buyer came along, the vendor brushed away the flies with a horse's tail so the purchaser could see what was for sale.

Amid the bedlam and the odors of this ancient world, we were surprised to see a sign in English which advertised Singer sewing machines and another which read, "Kodak Film Sold Here". These people were living their lives as their ancestors had done for centuries, but the western world was really not too far away.

Before starting back to the airstrip, we climbed to the top of the wall for an overview of the city. As we looked out across the skyline, the drab grey of the flat-roofed mud-and-stone buildings was broken here and there by the soaring curved domes of mosques and their accompanying minarets. From these lofty perches the muezzin called faithful Moslems to prayer, reminding us that we were in the heart of Islam. We left the inner city through one of several high stone archways.

A woman sat against the wall on the outside, nursing her infant child. Stopping the jeep, I approached her. Probably in her thirties, she was not young, but character and intelligence, tempered by hardship and privation, shone from her proud yet humble face. Comely though she was, there was something compelling about her bearing that I knew would result in a good photograph. Motioning toward my camera, I recognized a faint smile of acknowledgement and I took my picture.

Skirting the wall through a grove of olive trees, our attention was drawn to what seemed like a nomadic family straggling along the road. Again we stopped the car. Two adults, a man and a woman, had four children in tow; the fifth, and youngest, was still in its mother's arms. The father's feet were wrapped with rags while the mother was barefoot, as were some of their children. Desperately poor they certainly were; but they seemed happy and well fed.

Driving on, we passed adobe dwellings whose yards were stacked eight feet high with dried camel dung. It was late in the month of September and winter would soon come to this high plateau. Looking a little like hay stacks, camel dung served as fuel to heat their sod houses through the winter months. Firewood was scarce; trees were too valuable to be chopped down for fuel.

On long trips, a developing tank and photo chemicals as well as cameras and tripod, were always part of my personal luggage, as an insurance against muffing a shot. All I needed to process film was a darkened hotel room and running water, in case I had to shoot something over again. That evening, back at our borrowed quarters, I developed several rolls of film.

Black and white was my medium in the Forties and Fifties. Color film in those early days was quite slow, and produced only positive transparencies. Negative color film, which could be reproduced in color on paper, had not yet been marketed, and did not come into wide public use until the 1960s. Additionally, extremes in temperature and humidity, encountered while flying around the world, often caused severe color degradation because of chemical instability of film dyes. Luckily, during the war years, I had become friendly with a couple of Air Force photolab technicians on Kwajalein Island in the Pacific, who kept me supplied with positive color film. Used in the large format aerial reconnaissance cameras, this roll film needed only to be cut down for the $2^1/4$" x $3^1/4$" Speed Graphic that I was then using. Although I had good results with it, the inconvenience of having to return it to the Kwaj lab for processing made it impractical.

Revised Flight Plan

The U.S. State Department, through the American Ambassador in Ankara, was able to arrange emergency clearances for our two aircraft and, on the morning of the fourth day, the relief plane and crew located us in the Turkish desert and landed with a replacement engine. Our host, the Colonel, supplied a work detail to help switch the seats from the disabled plane to the good one, and our passengers were boarded once again. Diyarbakir did not have the required grade of gasoline available, so we flight-planned for a fuel stop at Nicosia, Cyprus. The replacement crew stayed behind to wait out the engine change and, I assume, make the eight o'clock muster at the Colonel's mandatory morning conferences.

On the eight-hour flight from Nicosia, Cyprus, to Rome, at 12,500 feet, we could easily identify the boot shape of the Italian peninsula below. In barnstorming style we flew in over Rome and treated our passengers to a sight — seeing run over the city at about 500 feet in a four-engined passenger plane, noless–an act which would be cause for suspension for today's airline pilots.

Circling the Coliseum a few times, we came in low over the ancient Roman Forum and the white marble tomb of Italy's unknown soldier, then headed for St. Peter's Basilica for a few more low circles.

Central Rome, Italy, from an altitude of about 500 feet. The old Roman Forum lies just beyond the Colosseum, while to the right of the Victor Emmanuel Monument is the balconied building from which Benito Mussolini exhorted his followers during WWII.

Sitting in the copilot's seat, with the window rolled back for taking photographs, required caution. Too close to the opening and ... zip! The slip stream could siphon the camera out of the hands and right through the window. A 500th of a second was maximum shutter speed for the Rollei, but the aerial views turned out well anyway.

We landed at Ciampino Airport to refuel and spend the night before continuing on through Shannon, Ireland; Goose Bay, Labrador; and thence to Pennsylvania. In seventeen days, we had flown around the world, and, in spite of the enforced en route stop, our Indian seamen were only three days late in picking up their freighter in Philadelphia.

As for Alice, she held up pretty well considering the rigors encountered along the way. She had not owned a camera, so she borrowed one from a friend before leaving home and had brought six rolls of film in hopes of recording her odyssey. She tackled photography with great enthusiasm, photographing saffron-robed monks against a backdrop of Siamese temples in Bangkok, a funeral procession at the burning ghats in Calcutta, a fight between a mongoose and a cobra in Bombay, and she posed the entire crew in front of the Trevi Fountain in Rome.

Upon returning home, however, she earned the entire crew's sympathy when she took her film to the photo finishers, only to learn that she had snapped six rolls of blanks, having shot every frame without removing the lens cap.

The Miracle of G.C.A.

I n the 1950s, the main runway at the U.S.A.F. Air Force Base near Tokyo at Tachikawa needed lengthening, but when the Japanese government tried to appropriate the required acreage, the neighboring farmers refused to give it up. In Japan, at least at that time, the nation's power to condemn and seize privately-owned land for public works programs was ineffectual (and some years later, it was to confront angry farmers again when trying to open the new international airport at Narita).

By now, Transocean was flying eighteen to twenty trips a month into Japan, almost all of them to Tokyo's two airports. Military cargo and personnel went into Tachikawa, while commercial cargo and civilian passengers were landed at Haneda International, nearer the city.

With the end of the Second World War, the miracle of radar created a whole host of possibilities in aircraft guidance systems. Among the new developments was one known as Ground Controlled Approach or G.C.A., a system in which a controller on the ground, aided by visual reference on a cathode ray tube, is able to guide an airplane on to the end of a runway under near zero-zero conditions. The military airports at Tachikawa, near Tokyo, and Kadena, on Okinawa, were both equipped with this system.

Ground fog, resulting in quarter-mile visibility, was common during the winter months, especially in the Tokyo area, making normal instrument landings dangerous, if not impossible. G.C.A. worked very well, but I was always a little uncomfortable, knowing that the fate of the aircraft, its crew, and its passengers, was solely in the hands of a single ground controller. Our crews, however, made numerous G.C.A. approaches without incident and to monitor the controller's voiced instructions as he 'talked' us down the glide path, was a fascinating experience.

A typical scenario would go something like this. Cruising at 12,000 feet, our airplane has been flying in darkness since leaving Wake Island some six hours earlier. The pre-dawn gray is now gradually giving way to the sun as it tops the horizon behind us, revealing a cloudless morning sky.

Shortly after entering the Tokyo F.I.R. (Flight Information Region), we are advised that our destination is expected to be below minimums for a standard instrument approach at our arrival time. With about an hour remaining

142

on the flight plan, our pilots are instructed to make contact with Tokyo Approach Control when one hundred miles out.

The view from the cockpit windshield now confirms our proximity to the Japanese mainland. Up ahead and somewhat to our left we can make out one of the more famous landmarks in the world, Mt. Fujiyama. The 14,000-foot peak looms up, resplendent in the pinkish glow of the morning sun. Its snow-capped conical mass protrudes well above the dense layer of fog that envelops the mountain's base and spreads out to cover the entire coastline.

A striking scene ... so uncluttered ... just mountain, sky, fog, and sea. The panorama stretches out before us, resembling a simplistic pastel painting, which, once viewed, is hard to forget.

The navigator now notifies the pilot that our aircraft is a hundred miles southeast of Tokyo. Dialing in an approach frequency, the captain reaches for the microphone.

"Tokyo Control ... this is Transocean Nine Nine Zero ... we're a hundred miles southeast, at twelve thousand feet ... Estimate Tateyama at Zero Seven Five Four. Destination Tachikawa ... Over."

"Roger, Nine Nine Zero, read you five by five," comes the immediate reply. "Descend to and maintain four thousand feet ... Report passing Tateyama."

Backing off the throttles, the captain twists the knob on the auto-pilot, sending the nose of the aircraft downward. Every small detail of Mt. Fuji can now be seen. This majestic, symmetrical symbol of Japan appears to grow in size as the coastline and fog bank draw nearer. Its jagged perpendicular furrows, easily visible, stand out in relief in the early morning light.

Nineteen minutes later our captain calls again.

"Tokyo Control ... Nine Nine Zero ... Tateyama at Zero Seven Five Five ... forty-five hundred feet ... descending."

"Roger, Transocean ... contact G.C.A. Approach Control when crossing Kisarazu."

The pilot briefly reviews the Tokyo area approach plate in his Jeppesen manual, then eight minutes later punches in the new frequency on VHF radio.

"G.C.A. Approach Control ... this is Transocean Nine Nine Zero ... Kizarazu at Zero Eight Zero Three ... four thousand feet ... Estimate Tachikawa at One Four ... Request landing instructions ... Over."

"Roger, Niner Niner Zero ... Tokyo altimeter twenty-nine ninety-two ... Terminal weather at Tachi estimated two hundred feet in quarter-mile visibility with patchy ground fog. Wind calm ... You're cleared for a G.C.A. approach ... Stand by one."

A brief pause now while the controller on the ground checks the pattern on his monitor.

"Niner Niner Zero, there's other traffic in the area," he advises, "I'll need a recognition maneuver."

Our captain acknowledges as the voice instructions continue.

"Steer a heading of Two Seven Zero for one minute then turn right to a heading of Three Six Zero ... Please confirm. Over."

Our captain complies.

With the auto-pilot off, and the airplane in level flight, the pilot makes the necessary identification turns so that the controller on the ground can be certain that the blip he is following on his radar screen is Transocean 990.

Shortly after the completion of the requested maneuver, the ground controller is back to us.

"Identification confirmed, Niner Niner Zero ..." comes the voice, "Steer Two One Five degrees and resume descent at four hundred feet per minute. Tachikawa altimeter ... twenty-nine ninety-four ... surface wind at the present time ... light and variable." Still several hundred feet above the overcast now, we continue our let-down. The warming rays of the morning sun stream through the flight deck windows, giving no premonition as to what lies ahead. Suddenly we graze the top layer of the fog bank, skip in and out for a few seconds, then the entire scene passes from view as we plunge deeper into the leaden gray-out of the fog.

Riding in the jump seat, the flight engineer checks cylinder head temperatures, then stretches overhead to switch on the carburetor heaters. A few minutes later tension begins to build as the voice from the ground advises, "Niner Niner Zero, I have you fifteen miles from touchdown at three thousand feet."

The ground controller, in complete charge now, asks that there be no further two-way communication. From here on in, the pilot is instructed to listen only, flying the headings and maintaining the rates of descent that are given him from the ground. Over the earphones we hear an almost continuous monologue.

"Niner Niner Zero, we have you on the glide path at 2,000 feet ... Distance from touchdown ... ten miles ... Take a heading of Two Two Zero and decrease your rate of descent to three hundred feet per minute."

During the brief pause that follows, the captain makes another quick check of his area approach chart. Three minutes later the voice in the headset advises, "Niner Niner Zero ... you're five miles from touchdown. Altitude 950 feet ... You're slightly low on the glide path ... Please correct ... Complete your landing checks."

Here follows a brief exchange of information in the cockpit as the first officer reads off the landing check list. Echoing the words, the captain executes and verifies each item.

"Niner Niner Zero, you're looking good," comes the voice from below.

In zero visibility, we continue our descent. The pilot's concentration is now on the instrument panel, his eyes moving almost continuously between the air speed indicator, altimeter, and gyrocompass.

"Niner Niner Zero ... We have you two miles from touchdown ... altitude four hundred feet. You're still a bit low on the glide path ... You have a twelve knot crosswind from your left. Come five degrees left to Two One Five Degrees ... Check gear down and locked".

"Gear down!" the captain calls out. The flight engineer drops the gear lever, the gear doors open, and the wheels grind to full extension with a jarring 'thunk'.

"Your position now ... one mile from touchdown," the controller advises, "Altitude ... two hundred feet ... glide angle good."

The radar altimeter at the navigator's station confirms.

"Transocean 990 ... Reduce rate of descent to one hundred feet per minute."

The captain quickly checks his rate of descent indicator.

"Niner Niner Zero, check flaps for proper setting ... You're a half mile from touchdown ... Altitude one hundred feet ... I repeat, one-zero-zero feet. Come five degrees left to Two One Zero degrees ... Prepare for flare out."

"Full flaps!" calls out the captain. The flight engineer echoes and sets full flaps.

Up to this point, we still have not seen a thing outside the airplane. Then comes the final words from the controller.

"You're over the end of the runway ... Take over!"

Only now do the pilots see the runway under them. The captain pulls off the power and hauls back firmly on the yoke. The airplane flares out and the wheels skid to the ground. Out of the windows now, in the mist, we see the runway lights flashing past on either side of us and, as we complete our roll, our captain picks up the microphone.

"Good job, controller. Thanks a lot." His voice gives no hint of the relief he must be feeling. His terse, brief comment, though to the point, is vastly understated—in the best tradition of a true airline pilot.

Anything, Anywhere, Any Time

Gold ... 6.6 million dollars encased in aluminum canisters, lay neatly in rows. Fastened securely to the floor with metal tie-downs, precious bars of the yellow stuff covered most of the cabin floor in our airplane to a depth of five inches.

In its role as conqueror, Japan had confiscated the valuable metal from a number of Southeast Asian nations, moving the booty to the Osaka Mint in 1942, where it remained until January, 1950. At that time, the Government of Thailand (Siam), decided to move its share of the impounded cache to the United States to bolster its nation's credit, and Transocean Air Lines was awarded a contract to transport it. This flight from Osaka, Japan, by way of the Aleutians, to Oakland, California, was one of seven which moved a total of more than $46,000,000 in Siamese gold across the Pacific.

Cruising at 10,500 feet, Mt. Fujiyama, dead ahead, looms up through the cockpit window of a DC-4. 1951.

146

Gilt-Edged Shipment

As a company photographer, I was allowed into the vaults of the Osaka Mint, where the gold was stored, to make a photographic record of its removal. Locked entrances to each of several steel-meshed cubicles bore a small wooden sign identifying the owner of the gold stored within. The gold was contained in about ninety canisters, each measuring 12" by 16" by 5". Each one, as it came out of the Thai enclosure, was weighed under the watchful eye of a Thai government official before being trundled out on steel-platformed cars and loaded into waiting U.S. Army trucks. Uniformed American military guards, armed with automatic weapons, were everywhere.

The weighing and loading process took about two hours and when all the gold was safely in the trucks and when all the paperwork was complete, it was time to move out. Seven vehicles, including two jeeps loaded with military police, formed a convoy and, with a motorcycle escort and a dozen heavily armed guards, raced out of the mint compound with the sound of sirens disrupting the morning calm.

The army stood guard at the airport as the canisters were transferred one by one to the airplane. Gold is not only very valuable, it is also very heavy, like lead. Steel rods could be inserted through holes in the end of each canister so that two men, one on each side, could manage the considerable weight. Once inside the aircraft, they were anchored securely to the floor to prevent them from shifting in case we encountered turbulence. Within an hour of the cavalcade's arrival at the airport, we had fired up the four engines and departed for Shemya Island, 2,760 nautical miles up the Aleutian chain.

In an effort to avoid publicity, the Company had probably chosen to route most of these flights north through the Aleutians rather than across the Central Pacific. Had it not been for a forecast tailwind of thirty knots, we would have had to go into Sapporo for fuel, but at 13,000 feet, we made it direct to Shemya, an American military base, in thirteen hours and ten minutes. We turned in for the night, knowing there would be no news media here to alert the world as to our valuable cargo.

Early the next morning we took off on the second leg of the journey with an eight-hour forecast to Anchorage. Favorable winds continued as we flew high above a solid stratus deck almost the entire distance. The monotony beneath us was broken only once when Iliamna volcano poked its snow-covered cone up through the low lying cloud layer. Steam issuing from a vent high on its side turned to water vapor, forming another cloud as it drifted up and across the top of the mountain below us.

Seven hours and forty minutes into the trip we touched down at Elmendorf Air Base at Anchorage. Informing the tower that we were in transit with

Protected by a dozen well-armed American military police, a convoy bearing over six million dollars in gold departs for the ten-mile trip to Osaka International Airport. January 19, 1950.

A million dollars worth of gold sits on the fork lift palette awaiting tie-down crews to move it inside the aircraft.

Under the watchful eye of an American military policeman, the gold-containing canisters are loaded aboard N79991 at the Osaka International Airport.

The DC-4 taxies to the ramp in Oakland, California, with its precious cargo of canisters. Armed crew members stand guard.

With the gold securely aboard, and the aircraft ready to depart, our American military escort poses for its picture.

Grossed out in weight, N79991, with a layer of gold securely fastened to the floor, is about ready to travel. At the price of gold in 1950, the contents of each canister was valued at approximately $75,000.

cargo, we requested and were granted permission to park the airplane out in the boonies. It had been a tiring day and we were all looking forward to a comfortable bed in a warm hotel. The tower would dispatch a car to pick us up and, by the time we had completed the paperwork, our transportation was waiting for us.

Turning the key in the lock on the cabin door, we all climbed down the ladder. The precious bars? We did not give them a second thought, and drove off to town for the night, leaving more than $6,000,000 in gold, unguarded, on the airplane floor—quite a contrast to the security measures taken in Osaka, and an unthinkable indiscretion in today's world.

Back at the airplane the next morning for the final leg to Oakland, every canister was still in its place. Apparently no one had been the wiser. Not until the fourth or fifth trip did an Anchorage newsman finally discover the gold shipments and feed the story to the national press services.

The temperature on this September morning in 1953, at Fairbanks, Alaska, was well below zero, and my camera shutter refused to work. Once inside the terminal building, the shutter thawed, and I snapped this picture through a plate glass window. Note engine heaters in the foreground outside. pilotes are Ed Landwehr, Roy Minson, and George DeJeau.

The vastness of the Alaskan wilderness spreads out before us, as we ride atop a stratus deck in the Valley of the 10,000 Smokes. Directly ahead, a mountain vents steam from its peak in Katmai National Park.

Anything, Anywhere

All through the Fifties, Transocean was heavily engaged in flying passenger charters out of both the U.S. west and east coasts. At the same time, we were transporting American military personnel and their dependents to and from foreign bases, European immigrants to South America, construction workers to the South Pacific and the Middle East, and Moslem pilgrims to Mecca from throughout the Mediterranean area.

We developed a reputation as the airline that would fly anything, anywhere, at any time. Cargo loads through the years included the gold shipments described in this chapter; cattle, coal, and communications equipment; munitions, military mail, and monkeys—in fact, anything that could be squeezed through the main cabin doors. On one occasion it was a Bell helicopter from Oakland to a buyer in Tokyo and, at another time, a complete television station to Hawaii.

Maximum C.A.A. flight time limitations for airline flight personnel during those years was a thousand hours per calendar year. Often completing my statutory time by the end of October, I could not be rescheduled until the following January. Flying in excess of eighty-five hours a month was considered a heavy schedule.

Transporting anything and everything was simply a matter of getting it through the door of the airplane.

The Taj Mahal

A couple of months after the 'gold' trip, I caught a flight that kept me away from home for five weeks. We flew off to Guam with 54 construction workers. Dropping them off, we ferried empty to Hong Kong, where we took on a load of Chinese cedar chests for delivery to Rome. We paused briefly at Calcutta to refuel and were winging our way toward Karachi, when someone in the cockpit suggested that we dogleg over Agra to take a look at the Taj Mahal. The terrain across India along that route is flat and uninteresting, and a view of the famous shrine would break the monotony.

At 8,000 feet, and still a good fifty miles from Agra, we spotted the 'Taj' through a thin layer of ground haze. Reflecting the sun like a mirror, the white marble edifice up ahead stood out clearly against the colorless, bland landscape. As we drew closer it began to take shape and we decided to drop down for a better look, leveling off at 700-800 feet several minutes later.

This incredibly beautiful structure, embraced at its four corners by towering minarets, is a breathtaking sight, especially from the air. Built by Shah Jahan in 1632, the exquisitely graceful Indo-Islamic mausoleum was constructed to express the Shah's love for his wife, who is interred there. The domed white marble tomb, inlaid with gemstones, and its long slender

The Taj Mahal at Agra, India—the most beautiful building in the world and an especially moving site from the air. En route Calcutta to Karachi.

reflecting pool, took sixteen years to complete. Sitting in the co-pilot's seat with the window rolled back, we circled a couple of times while I shot away with my trusty Rolleiflex. Then, climbing back up to cruising altitude for the remainder of the leg, we landed three hours later at Karachi, where we checked in at the airport hotel over night for crew rest.

Arriving in Cairo from Karachi, we did a little aerial sightseeing around the pyramids before refueling at Farouk airport. Eight hours later we arrived at our destination, Rome, Italy, where we off-loaded the Chinese cedar chests.

Hygiene

Dysentery was always a concern when flying around the world like this. Foreign countries have different standards of cleanliness, so we never drank local water, even though the better hotels in these more remote areas kept pitchers of 'pure' drinking water in the rooms. We stuck religiously to Dutch, German, Scandinavian or Filipino beer, all of which were easily available almost everywhere.

While in Karachi, we ate at the B.O.A.C. airport dining room where much of the help ran around barefoot. The first thing one waiter did when he reached our table was to pour water in our glasses from a sparkling glass pitcher. But first, he took a soiled cloth from his waist band and, with a great flourish and an ingratiating smile, carefully wiped the pouring lip of the pitcher 'clean' with the dirty towel to demonstrate his concern for cleanliness; hence our thirst for beer.

We carefully avoided fresh greens of any kind, eating only well-cooked food. Of course, plates and silverware were also suspect, but we very seldom became ill from food. In all of my three and a half million miles of overseas flying, I suffered only one bout with amoebic dysentery ... and once was enough.

SAS flew me from Beirut to Copenhagen, where a doctor made the diagnosis. Sicker than I ever cared to be, I continued on home. It took a seven-day course of Emetin in a San Francisco hospital to rid me of the amoeba, and several more months were to pass before I was once again able to eat fresh vegetables.

Necessity is the Mother of Invention

Consumer commodities were still in short supply worldwide following the war, especially American-made cigarettes and nylon stockings, so before leaving home, we loaded up with these items to use as trading material along the way. Corruption among customs officials at Ciampino Airport in Rome was common, and, of course, they knew what we were doing.

While going through our luggage, they lectured us on the illegality of bringing luxury articles such as these into Italy, then, with a quick glance over their shoulders, propositioned us with the 'One for you, one for me' routine. Of course, we had no choice. It was either that or have it all taken away.

On this particular trip we spent six days in Rome while Oakland operations arranged landing rights for us in Tehran. I seem to remember that we flew machine tools and oil drilling equipment up there and came out with Indian oil field workers who were rotating home to Bombay. Anyway, we flew back through Karachi for an overnight stay and refueling, where Pakistani immigration inspectors, upon examining our passengers' World Health Organization Inoculation records, discovered that none of them had been vaccinated for smallpox. Placing the entire lot under quarantine, our passengers were hauled off to an isolation ward for seven days. With nothing to do but wait it out, we crew members rented a two-masted dhow and spent our afternoons fishing in the Indian Ocean.

Such incidents were typical of Transocean's crew life in the 1950s. Those of us who were fortunate enough to live through the experiences of the early days in the air transport business, look on commercial flying in today's

*In front of the Karachi Airport terminal building, shortly after winning
independence, the Pakistani flag flies overhead, while on the lawn below, a
handful of worshippers go through the various stages of their noonday prayers.
1947.*

world as strictly routine, if not boring. But in the Forties and Fifties, when we
boarded an airplane, we learned to expect the unexpected.

Often forced to improvise, we found ourselves in situations requiring
ingenuity and resourcefulness. And defying Murphy and his Law, luck sometimes favored the brave. Ferrying an empty DC-4 to Tokyo in one such
instance, we were westbound out along the Aleutian chain where the jet
stream, through the winter months, often brings very strong westerly winds
aloft; a hundred knots or more at flight levels are common. During one of
these periods we found ourselves stuck on Shemya Island with insufficient
fuel capacity to buck the existing headwinds to Tokyo.

The crew captain was Joe Stachon, who, when we landed at Shemya,
was aware that we had a deadline to meet, which unless met, could cost us our
return charter. For two days we waited, as the high winds continued unabated.
Realizing that something had to be done, and after making local inquiries,

(Above) First Officer Bob Bunbury and Captain Joe Stachon are about to make a decision concerning the droppable fuel tank found at the Shemya air force dump. (Below) The fuel tank gave our DC-4 the additional fuel storage capacity needed to buck excessive headwinds from Shemya Island, in the Aleutians, to Tokyo, Japan. Joe Stachon and Bob Bunbury finish the job of securing the tank to the cabin floor.

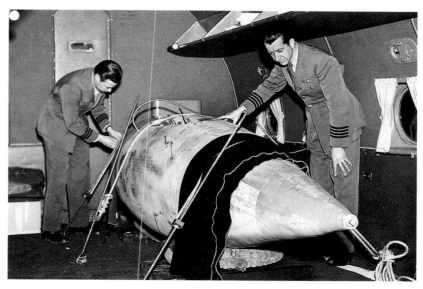

Captain Stachon learned of the presence of an abandoned air force dump not far from the airfield. Could there possibly be an old gas tank out there that might be serviceable?

Borrowing a jeep from the Air Force, Joe and the rest of the crew drove to the dump to have a look around. Would you believe ... half buried in the abandoned rubble of aircraft parts, were a couple of still crated, dropable, fuel tanks. Though showing signs of corrosion from two or three years of exposure to the weather, they still appeared to be serviceable.

Managing to free one, we wrestled it to the jeep, balanced it across the back of the vehicle, and returned to our DC-4. Working against time, we soon had it hoisted up and in through the cabin door. A couple of old tires, also scavenged from the dump, provided support. After lashing the tank securely to the floor, our flight engineer went off to talk the Air Force out of the tubing that would be needed to vent the tank and connect it to the airplane's fuel system. Three hours after rummaging through the debris at the Shemya dump, we were ready for take-off with enough fuel on board to reach our destination, plus alternate, and still land with two hours reserve fuel.

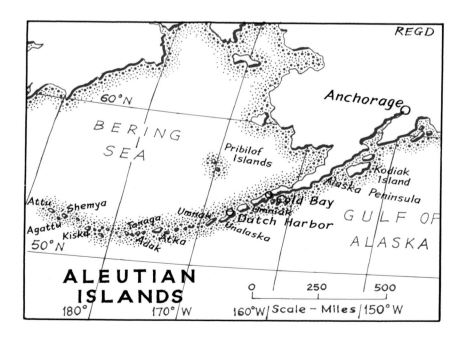

The Blind Fireman

Lining the road just outside the gate to Kadena Air Base on Okinawa were several automobile agencies doing business in small shacks about the size of what kids in my day would call large pop stands. They offered stateside factory delivery of cars by any of half a dozen American manufacturers upon receipt of a four-hundred-dollar cash deposit. In return, the buyer received a purchase order for the car with options of his choice. Upon arrival back in the States, the buyer could pay the balance due when he picked up his automobile at the factory. They were doing a brisk business with returning servicemen.

One day, on my way into Naha (the chief city of Okinawa) during a layover at Kadena, I drifted into one of these agencies out of curiosity, and left with a signed contract for a new 1950 four-door Pontiac sedan. Mina and I had worn out a long string of used cars through twelve years of married life, beginning with the Model A Ford. This would be our first new car. Early in June, I flew back to Pontiac, Michigan, picked up my shiny new sedan, and drove it to Kansas, where Mina had gone to visit and await my return.

While driving back to the West Coast, our conversation turned to the likelihood of another pregnancy. Mina was nearly thirty years old now, and I had just turned thirty eight. A year had passed since her miscarriage, and there had been no indication since then that she might again conceive. We decided to wait no longer, agreeing that as soon as we were back in San Lorenzo, we would look into the adoption process. A couple of weeks later, after discussing the subject with Mina's gynecologist, we filed an application with Alameda County Adoption Services and were told that the demand for adoptive children far exceeded the supply and that a two-to three-year wait was probable. This was disappointing news, but we applied anyway, and fell in at the end of the line.

Indonesian Interlude

Among the growing number of companies spawned and managed by Transocean was the Taloa Academy of Aeronautics which was equipped to train flight personnel for top positions in all categories from commercial pilot

During its lifetime, Transocean's Taloa Academy, located at the Oakland airport, trained over 1,200 American WWII veterans—as well as war veterans from Japan and Germany—for jobs in commercial aviation. March 13, 1953.

down to flight attendant. Located at the Oakland Airport, the school was opened in 1946, and attracted students from a number of foreign countries. Late in 1950, the Indonesian Government elected to send sixty of its brightest young cadets to the Oakland academy to train as military pilots, and the Company made arrangements to pick them up in Jakarta.

Transocean dispatch scheduled a double crew for the trip, to achieve maximum utilization of the aircraft, and I was assigned as one of two radio operators. All our DC-4s at that time were equipped with curtained double bunks, one above the other, located just aft of the crew compartment. While one crew was flying the airplane, the other crew could try to get some sleep.

I say try, because it was not easy. Sleeping fully clothed is not conducive to good bed rest, especially when each person is limited to a couple of hours at a time. If the captain is catching a wink or two in the bunk, and the copilot thinks his boss has been back there long enough, a little jockeying of the engine synchronization up front will bring the sleeping captain wide

*Crew members stand by at Jakarta, Indonesia, waiting to be flown to Bandung,
thirty minutes away in the Indonesian highlands. November, 1950. (Below) These
young Indonesian cadets had no trouble entertaining themselves while en route to
the United States. Here you see them whooping it up while in flight between
Jakarta and Oakland. 1950.*

awake very quickly. The stewardesses, using the bottom bunk, rotated in the sleep schedule along with the male members of the crew.

The double crew system was a good way to move passengers rapidly over routes where there were no layover crews, and although it stretched a crew's ability to perform satisfactorily, it was not too pleasant. Over the long haul, both crews became quite weary and, if no extra seats were available back in the cabin, things got a bit crowded on the flight deck.

Meanwhile, in the Eastern Hemisphere, at six degrees south of the Equator, Jakarta was having a heat wave. The temperature and humidity were almost unbearable. We were supposed to go in and right out again, but our Indonesian hosts requested a three-day delay while their student passengers were being rounded up.

Apologizing for the postponement, they treated us as they would visiting diplomats, offering to fly us to Bali for the three-day stay, but that was ruled out because of political unrest there. Instead, they flew in a DC-3 and took all ten of us up to the Indonesian highlands, where they put us in a resort hotel. At Bandung, elevation 2,400 feet, the air is relatively dry and the climate pleasant. Three days later, they brought us back down to Jakarta where the cadet-trainees were now assembled and ready to go.

The pre-departure festivities turned into a ceremony, as a large crowd of proud parents turned out to see their sons off for training in America. Our captain was asked to address the students and their parents over a loud speaker system and, in a formal ceremony, an Indonesian Air Force official presented each crew member with a beautifully hand-embossed, sterling silver cigarette case. We were overwhelmed by the attention given us. My flight log records that we flew north to Manila for a two-hour stop before heading east through Guam, then home. Our 'plane-load of sixty young cadets would some day be the cream of the Indonesian Air Force.

My workload as company photographer continued to increase during 1951 and most of 1952. I reported to the flightline for only about half my normal schedule. Meanwhile, the quality of Mina's life took a downward turn as she constantly brooded over her seeming inability to bear a child. After one protracted period of disconsolate self-appraisal, she decided something had to be done to occupy her time and thoughts.

About this time, the Korean War was funneling a constant stream of casualties to Oak Knoll Naval Hospital, which was nearby in the Oakland hills, so Mina decided to volunteer for work at the hospital as an American Red Cross Gray Lady. This decision created a problem, however; she would need to drive a car, and she had never learned how to drive. She looked forward to doing volunteer work as a Gray Lady, so she enrolled in a driving course,

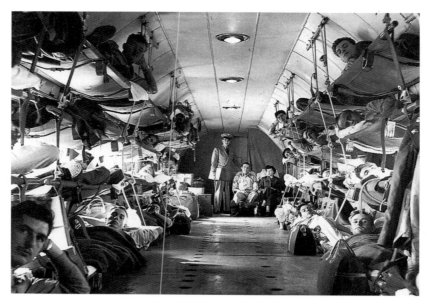

In the first twenty-one months of the Korean War, Transocean flew 7,112 litter patients from pick-up points in the Far East to Travis Air Force Base in California. Seated in the rear are a medical corpsman and flight nurse. The flight's purser stands beside them.

which, she remembers, cost just seventeen dollars. Not long afterward she mastered the exacting art of manipulating an automobile through city traffic.

Transocean Air Lines, among others, became involved in the Korean Air Lift under a civilian contract to transport litter cases back to the States. The military flew the wounded out of Korea to Japan or Okinawa, where the contract carriers picked them up for the trip home. Our DC-4s were converted to accommodate litters, six lengthwise and four high, along each side of the aircraft cabin. In addition to the normal flight crew complement, these trips carried a purser, a military flight nurse, and sometimes a doctor.

Time and technology were moving along now, and the days of radio operators on commercial airliners were numbered. We had seen it coming, as communication by voice through the installation of more sophisticated and powerful airborne radio came into general use.

The C.A.A. had just begun to license navigators, so, upon my return from one of the air-evac trips, I took a two-day written examination in the C.A.A. offices at the Oakland Airport, and received my commercial navigator's license on 7 May 1952.

Up In Smoke and Flames

Our San Lorenzo home had a close brush with a fire in the summer of that year. How could I ever forget? I had installed an electric heater in an outside wall of the darkroom in the back of the garage and had developed a habit of turning it on for an hour or so in the morning to warm the room.

One day, after following this routine, I returned to the house for breakfast and, while sitting at the kitchen table sipping coffee, a glance out the window told me that something was wrong. Steam appeared to be rising from the roof over the darkroom in back of the garage, while none of my neighbor's roofs were exhibiting this disturbing phenomenon. My curiosity aroused, I decided to investigate. Hurrying outside, I burst into the garage, opened the darkroom door, and was swept back by a pall of dense black smoke and searing heat. Slamming the door shut again, I raced out into the yard.

"Fire!" I yelled, with all the lung power I could muster.

Mina came running in answer to my agonizing screams; she always seemed to be at her best in the face of impending disaster. Rushing back inside, she dialed the fire department, then calmly backed the car out of the garage and into the street.

"Ok, Joe ... turn her on ...!"

All the while, I was frantically circling the house in search of the garden hose, which I remembered having seen, sometime, somewhere, only a few days before. Each time I passed the kitchen door, Mina handed me a pail of water which I splashed through the heater vent on the outside of the garage. About the fourth pass around, I remembered that I had coiled up the hose and left it under a thicket at the rear of the yard. By this time, the back corner of my garage was gloriously ablaze.

But now I heard the siren of the approaching fire truck as it lumbered around the corner at the other end of the block. Running into the street as it slowed in front of the house, I pointed frantically down the driveway. The fireman riding on the rear platform jumped off the truck backward and turned toward me.

"Are you the party who reported a fire?"

"Yes, man, yes!" There was terror in my voice; my house was going up in smoke!

"Where?" he said, as he looked around.

My God ... why have they sent me a blind fireman? Again I pointed toward the garage where the flames were now coming out through the roof. The nearest fire hydrant was two blocks down the street, but fortunately, they had come with a water tanker. While I wandered aimlessly about, wringing my hands, the driver of the truck spooled out the hose, and with nozzle in hand, ran toward the rear of the house. It was obvious by now, that my dark-room would soon be a total loss. After what seemed like for ever, the man with the nozzle yelled to the fireman on the tanker.

"OK, Joe ... turn her on ...!"

Seconds passed ... I stared, incredulous, as only a trickle of water dribbled from the end of the hose, falling uselessly to the driveway. My eyes pleaded with the nozzle, but to no avail. Running halfway to the truck, I stopped, deciding to relay messages in case one of these guys could not hear well either.

The hoseman finally called out. "You must have the wrong valve, Joe, try another one."

In desperation now, I echoed, "For God's sake Joe, try a different one! You've got the wrong valve!"

The stubborn hose finally poured forth a torrent of water, and five minutes later the fire was out, but my darkroom was in a shamble. Insurance covered the physical loss, but a precious collection of my films and photographs were irreplaceable. A couple of months later, after cleaning up the mess, I was back in business ... without the benefit of the wall heater.

Command Performance
for an Arabian Monarch

Like most other young married couples, Mina and I dreamed of owning a more spacious home, convinced that we would need it if we were ever to have children; we had already taken positive steps toward adoption. During six years of living in our little San Lorenzo home, we had built a garage, added a room, and with the purchase of a table saw, had made wooden shutters for the front windows. For additional privacy, I built a wooden fence along the edge of the driveway. All dressed up one afternoon, Mina posed beside a lamp post near the front sidewalk. The resultant picture remains one of my all-time favorites of her.

Success in building an attached garage with my own two hands encouraged me in the crazy notion that I might even be able to build an entire house.

After all, time would be no problem, because normally, I was home two weeks out of every month anyway, but could I do it all by myself? I concluded that I could not; professional help would be needed in some areas. Fueling my ego, Mina praised my wood paneling job on the fireplace wall in our living room, but that accomplishment hardly qualified me to tackle an entire house.

Mina Lily Lewis—the woman in my life. San Lorenzo, California, 1948.

Once Again Opportunity.....

Then late in August, 1952, our dream of a new home had to be put on temporary hold. While working in my garage darkroom one morning, my friend, Sam Wilson, company vice-president of operations, called to ask if I would be interested in joining him as radio operator/navigator in the delivery of a custom-crafted Douglas DC-4 to Saudi Arabia. This particular airplane, he pointed out, was something special. Ordered specifically for the personal use of His Majesty, King Adul Aziz Ibn Saud, it was one of five DC-4s being purchased from Transocean Air Lines by the Saudi Arabian government.

We were to ferry the aircraft to Transocean's Bradley Field base near Hartford, Connecticut, for the installation of an elevator that would lift the arthritic King, in his wheelchair, from the ground up to the level of the aircraft floor.

Sam went on to explain that the conversion process was nearing completion on the hangar floor and, when finished, would include a swivel throne, plush lounge, a bedroom with an oversized bed, and a bathroom.

"Louie," he said, "I have some business to take care of with Air Jordan in Amman. I need to go to Asmara for a series of meetings with Air Djibouti people, and I also want to spend a few days in Beirut with John Russell. But first, I plan to deliver this airplane to the King personally. If you'd like to be part of the crew, you and I will squeeze in some time taking pictures. What do you say?"

Of course, I was overjoyed at the offer.

"How long will we be gone?" I asked.

"Oh ... probably six weeks," he answered, "give or take a few days either way."

Sam Wilson was ten years my senior, but we shared a common hobby: the enjoyment of photography. I had just added a larger format camera to my arsenal of photo equipment, augmenting my Rolleiflex with a $3^{1}/_{4}$" x $4^{1}/_{4}$" Speed Graphic. Sam, on the other hand, was not much into stills, but his 16mm Bell and Howell movie camera was always at his side.

Sam served on the board of directors of Transocean Engineering Corporation, one of the airline's subsidiaries. He often took me along on inspection trips to photograph highway and bridge construction, flood control projects, and other engineering jobs. Between the two of us, we lugged tripods, spare lenses, extra film holders, and bags of accessories everywhere we went together. We could have been mistaken for a National Geographic crew on assignment.

Check Elevator

Registered as SAR-4, the King's 'Flying Palace' was wheeled out of Hangar 5 at the Oakland Airport on 13 July 1952, and Captain Wilson, with a crew of four, took off on the first leg of the trip. Landing at Windsor Locks, Connecticut, we checked in at the Bond Hotel in Hartford for what turned out to be almost a week, because problems developed in the installation of the elevator.

Making it work properly was the responsibility of Max Elbaum, a Transocean aeronautical engineer, who needed to make a number of major design

(Above) Jeddah, Saudi Arabia, as it appeared from the King's airplane in 1952. Note the Jeddah airport, which stretches across the upper background. The city has grown out of all recognition to a metropolis of 2,000,000 population today. (Right) No tow vehicle available? No problem—just shove! Jeddah, Saudi Arabia, 1952.

changes in the structure of the cabin floor to accommodate the lift motor, cable, associated gears, and foldable elevator track.

After exhaustive tests, it was finally declared operational and we flew off to Saudi Arabia, via Gander, Shannon, Rome, and Beirut. Landing in Jeddah three days later, we checked in at the Gardens Hotel at the airport. There, we were to await further instructions.

On loan from TransWorld Airlines, Jim Metzger, an American, who, at the time, was operations chief for Saudi Arabian Airlines, had left a message for Sam at the Gardens desk that read as follows:

> SAR-4 must be sitting in front of the Riyadh terminal tomorrow morning at 11 a.m. His Majesty wishes to inspect the aircraft personally at that time. I'll be riding up with you. See you around 7 a.m.
>
> Jim ...

(Left) Installation of King Ibn Saud's 'throne' was done at Transocean's base in Oakland, California. On a raised platform, with swivel base, it could always be turned to face Mecca. (Right) As high-ranking Saudi officials watched, the elevator in a last minute trial at the Jeddah airport performed perfectly. The following day's rendezvous with his Majesty would be the final test. The wheelchair seen here, was empty, and it is not at all certain that anyone ever actually rode the elevator prior to the time the King was placed on it the following day. A large man, Ibn Saud needed a special wheelchair, and because of crippling arthritis in his last years, was confined to it much of the time.

Mid-summer in Arabia brings temperatures which regularly climb to 130° during the daytime, and I remember well how miserably hot it was when we arrived in Jeddah. The air conditioner in our room, set high in the outside wall some eight feet above the floor, was not working, and Sam, my enterprising room-mate, suggested that we bring it down for diagnosis and possible rework.

Feeling that the management might not approve of guests who sought to repair their air conditioning, we considered our options. The alternative to some sort of action meant spending a night of misery in a bake-oven; sleep would have been impossible. On the other hand, we speculated, maybe the thing was fixable. We decided to take the chance—and possibly also to take the consequences.

Cautiously piling up chairs and tables until we could reach the defective unit, we removed it from the wall and managed to wrestle it to the floor. Neither of us knew anything about air conditioners, of course, but as it turned out, we did not need to. After scooping out a paper sack full of accumulated debris and an assortment of strange and exotic looking varmints, we finally replaced it on the wall. Our gamble paid off. It worked.

That night, after the lights were out and we had crawled into bed, enjoying air-conditioned splendor, Sam lay there thinking out loud about the historic morning ahead.

"Louie," he reflected, "we'd better pray that that elevator doesn't dump His Royal Highness on the ground tomorrow. They'd ship us home in empty oil drums."

I must confess that his wry observation made me a bit uneasy, as I recalled the glitches encountered with the elevator mechanism while we were still at Bradley Field; but Sam's concern was not menacing enough to keep either of us awake.

Early the next day, Prince Emir Michaal, Minister of Aviation and Finance in the Saudi Arabian government, and Jim Metzger, the Saudi operations manager, joined us for the two-and-a-half-hour flight between Jeddah and Riyadh. Upon landing at Riyadh, Sam put the elevator through its paces once again; then, satisfied that it was performing properly, took refuge inside the terminal to escape the now rising desert temperature and to await the King's arrival.

About half an hour before the show was to begin, one of the airport guards came running in to report that a Saudi mechanic had tried to operate the elevator and had jammed it. Sam was furious. Hurrying out to the airplane he found the elevator track stuck half in and half out of the airplane. It would not move in any direction.

Framed under the propellers of SAR-4 is the airline passenger terminal at Riyadh in 1952—modest compared to today's air-conditioned facility in the Arabian capital, a thriving commercial and administrative city of 3,000,000 people.

Using hand screw drivers, he and First Officer Jim Mefford worked feverishly to remove a few dozen screws from the floor plate which covered the mechanism, but removal of the plate turned up no tangled cables; everything appeared to be normal. What could have been overlooked? The King's entourage was due any moment now. Lapsing into awkward silence, we stood there staring at each other. Everyone seemed paralyzed, as the prospect of disaster appeared imminent.

Jim Metzger finally thought to ask, "Does anyone have a schematic on this thing? " The ship's pouch, thought Sam. Could there be a schematic diagram in the back of the ship's log book? If there was one, that is where it might be. Still kneeling on the floor, he looked up at me.

"Louie, run up to the cockpit and bring me the log case."

In seconds I was back with the pouch ... Voila! Tucked away in the back of the ship's log was a block diagram of the elevator's electrical system, revealing the location of a fuse block that no one knew had even existed. The problem? A blown fuse.

"Praise be to Allah!", muttered Sam, as everyone heaved a sigh of relief. The fuse was soon replaced and the floor plate screwed back down. This time when Sam pressed the button on the control panel, the elevator responded with a reassuring whirrr, folding itself neatly against the floor inside the cabin. The mechanic had disappeared, fate unknown.

Elevator Up

The heat in the airplane had been stifling. Both Sam and Jim were still mopping the perspiration from their faces when a string of black limousines, preceded by an escort of half a dozen motorcycle police, pulled up on the ramp below. The automobile carrying the King, a custom-built British Daimler, came to a stop just a few feet from the now lowered elevator. Important members of His Majesty's government, including a number of cabinet ministers and a considerable assortment of relatives, probably a hundred or more people, parked their vehicles and clustered around the Flying Palace.

An Arabian Nights scene with modern overtones was about to unfold as the traditional red carpet was placed on the ramp between the King's limousine and the elevator. The entire back half of the royal vehicle now opened out as if on a hinge, carrying the Arabian monarch with it. An attendant pushed a button on the side of the door and the seat slowly descended until the King was able to stand. Badly crippled by arthritis and old war wounds, he was helped to his wheel chair, then trundled across the carpet and on to the elevator platform.

The crowd was quiet now, in hushed expectancy, as Sam stood at the controls in the doorway, waiting for a signal from the ground to bring the elevator up. The button was pushed once more, and, as the king rose slowly above the heads of the spectators, a ripple of applause, then shouts of approval went up from the entire imperial household. The elevator performed flawlessly ... and our Transocean crew had earned a new lease on life.

No other photographers were present that momentous day, so I received a lot of attention from anxious guards as my camera snapped away. The Transocean uniform evidently made me an official. The aged and ailing King never took a real ride in his airplane, but I took my pictures as he rode up on that elevator. He was the George Washington of the modern Arabian kingdom: the powerful ruler who managed to unite the many warring tribes of Arabia under a central government. Shortly after we returned home, he passed away, but the House of Saud still rules the country today. Incidentally, John Wegg, publisher of *Airways* magazine, tells me that Ibn Saud's 'flying palace', SAR-4, changed hands twice after the Saudis sold her. The once

His Royal Highness, King Saud, arrives to inspect his "flying palace". Notice the carpet rolled out beneath the wheel chair.

His Majesty Abdul Aziz Ibn Saud, patriarch of the Saudi Arabian Kingdom, prepares for his first ride on the elevator.

Captain Wilson holds his finger on the elevator control button as the King rises slowly above the heads of his ministers and subjects. Jim Metzger, Saudi Arabian Air Lines' operation manager, watches closely from the open doorway.

proud flagship of the Saudi Arabian air fleet ended her life as a restaurant in Darmstadt, Germany.

When asked by one of the king's emissaries what we would like as a memento of our visit to Saudi Arabia, we decided that a complete dress outfit of Arab clothing would make for interesting conversation back home. Our wish was granted, even to undergarments. The white wool head scarf, worn under the 'camel hobble', was ornately hand-embroidered and the long flowing outer garment was hemmed top to bottom with gold thread. Captain Wilson was presented with a silver dagger and scabbard, both set with gem stones. Some time during the morning, one of the King's wives inspected the airplane. At her gesture, a personal servant handed out gold rials to nearby crew members from a satchel on his waist.

Just a few short months later the world received news of King Ibn Saud's death. I had probably taken the last photographs of the founder of Saudi Arabia.

At the time of the SAR-4 delivery, the entire palace staff had already completed its seasonal move to Taif, the country's summer capital in the higher elevations of southern Arabia. Thus, on the following morning, only two DC-3s were needed to return the King and his closest relatives and advisers to Taif.

Through some previous connection, Sam had become acquainted with the America overseer of the King's palace at Riyadh and had been promised a tour of the complex once the King had departed. I was invited to accompany them. Only a skeleton crew of guards remained in the compound as we were escorted through the palace, its gardens, the concubines' living quarters, and their Olympic-sized swimming pool. It was an unforgettable experience.

Arabian Nights (Camel Class)

Saudi Arabian Airlines flew us back to Jeddah, and on the way, Sam asked if I would mind working just one flight on the Hajj. According to Sam, the operations manager up in Teheran was short of radio operators.

"Just one trip, Louie," he assured me, "as a good-will gesture. I'll go on over to Beirut, then, when you return from Teheran, you can join me at the Palm Beach Hotel there."

At the time, his request seemed reasonable, so we said our goodbyes, and I caught an Air Djibouti C-46 to Teheran later that afternoon. Welcomed by a jubilant project manager, I was promptly scheduled for two weeks of Hajj flights.

I lay there looking up at the starry sky.

"Not me." I protested, "The Executive Vice President of the company told me that I was to make one trip only."

My angry protestations made no impression; he assured me that he was the boss up there. I am somewhat vague in the reconstruction of events at this point, but I seem to recall that I stowed away on the next flight back to Jeddah. However, when I tried to check in again at the Gardens Hotel, the desk clerk insisted there were no rooms available. I was indignant.

"What do you mean, no available rooms," I complained, "I just checked out of this hotel yesterday!" Oblivious to my protest, he blandly thumbed through his desk register for a moment or two, then stopped at one of the pages. Pointing to an entry, he feigned surprise.

"Oh yes ... you were here with Captain Wilson, were you not? Well ...!" He slammed the reservations book shut with the authority of a referee at the count of ten. Then with an icy stare, he added, "You were provided lodging here by order of His Majesty's government; we have no space available for you now."

At that moment, I remembered that Sam and I had repaired his air-conditioner. There's gratitude for you.

Picking up my gear, I walked into the street where a group of five or six hotel porters were socializing near the hotel entrance. Pausing near the doorway with my bags and camera paraphernalia, I stood pondering my next move, when apparently my presence caught the eye of one of the porters. Sensing my dilemma, he walked over and greeted me in English.

"You have trouble, friend?"

A little sympathy at this point was certainly welcome, and this fellow seemed amiable enough. After listening patiently while I detailed my opinion of the uppity hotel clerk, he raised his arms in a gesture of resignation.

"Some of us sleep in the camel yard next door," he volunteered. Then, breaking into a toothless grin, he added, "You are most welcome to come sleep with us." Hesitation was on my mind—but not for long. Maybe, until I had a better offer, I should not burn any bridges.

Temporarily trusting my cameras and baggage to his care, I crossed the street and walked along a row of hangars to Saudi Flight Operations where I hoped to find Jim Metzger, but he had gone off to Bahrain Island on business. I did learn that a once-weekly flight to Beirut had left Jeddah just that morning, but that if I was willing to settle for a flight to Damascus instead, there would be but a two-day wait. I did not relish the idea of spending the next seven nights in a camel yard. Two would be quite sufficient. Although I had no idea as to how I might bridge the distance between Damascus and Beirut, I opted for the shorter stay in Jeddah.

Twilight does not linger in Saudi Arabia. It is either daylight or darkness, and the temperature plummets as rapidly as the sun. As I jockeyed for sleeping space among the camels that night, my porter friend brought me a saddle blanket, saying, "You'll need this before the sun rises." With my flight bag for a pillow and my cameras and tripod anchored securely in my arms, I lay there looking up at the starry sky: a dazzling sight in the clear desert air.

Almost directly overhead, near the constellation of Orion, beamed Sirius, the brightest star in the heavens. Clearly visible nearby were Procyon and Capella. Could these be the same stars that shone so brightly over Wake Island just eight hours earlier? Indeed they are; it's a small world.

My thoughts turned to my recent traveling companion, who was by now, I felt certain, resting comfortably in a luxurious bed at the Palm Beach Hotel in Beirut. I found myself wondering why I had ever agreed to let Sam run off to the comforts of civilization without me. Actually though, the porters and camel drivers turned out to be a pretty good lot, and the camels, though smelly, were not all that bad either.

In my bag I happened to have a copy of the Saturday Evening Post. Its lead story, running in serial form at that time, was *The Daring Young Men of*

Transocean, by Richard Thruelsen, in which some of my pictures appeared. After taking a group photograph of my fellow yardmates looking at the Post article, they were all my friends.

Ah youth! We seemed to have a certain disdain for money in those days. Our crew members often wandered around over the world with as little as ten or fifteen dollars in their wallets, and, of course, credit cards had yet to be invented.

Dawn was just minutes away as I alighted from the Saudi airplane at the Damascus airport. Taking stock now of my spendable assets, a quick check confirmed the fact that precious little cash remained in my jeans. Sam would have access to funds in Beirut, I speculated.

With the cool of the morning a plus, I decided it might be prudent of me to walk the four or five miles to town, carrying my luggage and camera gear. My destination still lay across the Anti-Lebanon mountain range, nearly a hundred kilometers to the west, but upon reaching the Damascus city center, I found no public conveyance that could take me to Beirut. Once again, unable to remember the exact sequence of events which followed, I somehow managed to locate a man with a car who had contracted to take three other passengers across the mountains. I became the fourth, and while examining my passport at the Lebanese border, a customs inspector commented that an American by the name of Wilson had preceded me by a few days.

I found Sam at the Palm Beach Hotel and enjoyed my first bath and good night's sleep in what felt like a month. The other members of our crew had caught an S.A.S. flight to London, then home to California. Sam and I would be gone for yet another four weeks.

Looking more like a fortress, this was King Saud's palace compound at Riyadh, Saudi Arabia, in 1952.

The Jordanian
Connection

Traveling around the Middle East in the 1950s was quite like it is today: tricky business. If we landed in Israel and planned to continue on to an Arab country, we simply tore out the page in our passports that contained the Israeli visa. The only passport never returned to me by the U.S. State Department was one adjudged to be 'mutilated' because I had removed this page during a flight from Lydda, Israel, to Amman, Jordan.

The bitterness between Arab and Jew surfaced one day while I was in the airport control tower in Arab Jerusalem. One of the controllers told me that his ancestral home had been seized when the neighborhood in which he had lived became part of the new state of Israel. His family group of fourteen people was simply told to gather up its personal possessions and move out. Although the family home was in full view from his vantage point in the tower, he would never be able to return to live in his own home.

Sam Wilson, Transocean's Vice President of Operations, had come to the Middle East to assess, personally, the joint operations of Air Djibouti and Air Jordan, both of which were in financial partnerships with Transocean Air Lines at the time. In spite of its name, Air Djibouti headquarters were in Beirut, where we spent several days while Sam conferred with John Russell, Transocean's operations manager in Lebanon.

September, 1952. An Air Jordan DC-3 taxies to a stop in front of the passenger terminal at Amman, Jordan.

177

Jordanian Hospitality

We then flew to Amman, Jordan, the seat of operations for Air Jordan, where we were hosted by Ismail Bilbeisi Pasha, a wealthy and influential Jordanian. In addition to being the owner and president of Air Jordan, he counted among his holdings considerable real estate, the country's Cadillac agency, and most of the government office buildings which, we were told, he leased to the Jordanian Government.

Situated on two or three acres on top of a hill overlooking the city of Amman stood the Pasha's personal residence. Adjacent to it was a three-story palatial structure which he called his guest house. For two days and nights, Sam and I were its sole occupants. The majestic appearance of this stunning edifice, built of marble in alternating shades of pastel-pink and blossom-white, was showcased by a facade of delicate horseshoe arches, supported on

An overview of Amman, Jordan, in 1952. Because minimal taxes were levied against unfinished buildings, dozens of what appeared to be finished structures were left with steel sticking out above their rooftops, thus preserving their unfinished status.

slender pink and white marble columns. The Moorish influence in its design was quite striking and a joy to the eye.

Entry was gained by a series of marble staircases that led to massive double doors, handsomely carved from wood in Islamic designs. In a commanding location near the center of the ballroom-sized foyer, a spot-lighted, glass-enclosed pedestal contained an ancient volume of the Koran. Sam and I were shown to separate bedrooms on the second floor.

The following day Mr. Bilbeisi honored Vice President Wilson with a luncheon in the palace dining room. Invited guests included Air Jordan executives and a number of Jordanian government officials. Also present was the eldest of the Pasha's three sons, Munther Bilbeisi, who worked for Air Jordan as manager of that airline's Beirut office.

In a boyish sort of way he was quite handsome, though somewhat on the portly side for his twenty-eight years. Not the athletic type, easy living had obviously done little for his figure. Speaking passably good English, however, he explained that he had attended American University in Beirut. During the course of our conversation I had the feeling that he was enjoying life on an unlimited budget—a fun-loving young fellow who refused to take life too seriously. Sam had wandered off to talk shop with the Pasha, leaving me to chat with Munther.

The Road to Jericho

"If you and Mr. Wilson can spare the time tomorrow, perhaps you might like to visit Jerusalem. I would be honored to drive you there," he offered, "and it would please me to show you some of my own country at the same time." His enthusiasm seemed to build as he added, "The trip will take us through Jericho and along the shore of the Dead Sea for a short distance, then on through Bethlehem. It's about 160 kilometers there and back, so we'd need to make a day of it. Do you think Captain Wilson would enjoy the ride?"

That evening, Sam decided that his business with the airlines could be put on hold long enough to take advantage of a rare opportunity.

Leaving Amman early the following morning in Munther's bright red Citroen convertible, we passed through desert hills sprinkled with an occasional settlement. The weather was comfortably cool early on, but the dirt road was dusty and barely wide enough for two vehicles to pass. Traffic consisted mostly of occasional flocks of sheep or goats that blocked the road, often bringing us to a complete standstill.

We came upon a small detachment of well-armed Jordanian foot soldiers who smiled and waved us on. With the car-top down, conversation was difficult, but Munther shouted over the road noise.

Near the Dead Sea (with camels in the distance), a shepherd tends his sheep and goats along the Amman/Jerusalem road. The shepherd's dog was there too—out of sight at his master's feet. A split second after this picture was taken, I was in headlong flight.

"Only last month a Jordanian minister was ambushed and killed near here. Now ... because of armed bandits, this road is heavily patrolled." He tossed his head and laughed. "These road police along here all know my car."

Just outside Jericho we drove past mile upon mile of densely packed tents, communal home for thousands of displaced Palestinians, and before long we were skirting the shore of the Dead Sea. Sam, who was riding in the back seat, poked me on the shoulder and pointed toward a half dozen camels up ahead. Grazing along the shore near the water's edge, they were perhaps a hundred yards from the road. As we drew closer, my eyes fell on a seated figure near the camels—a shepherd I guessed. Surrounded by sheep, he was deeply engrossed in mending something with needle and thread; a long crook lay across his lap.

Reaching for my camera, I signaled Munther to pull over. The sea, with camels in the background, would heighten interest in a photograph. With his back to us, the shepherd obviously had not noticed as I stepped from the car and began walking toward him. Treading as gingerly as possible, I moved quietly ahead, realizing that if he were to see me, the spontaneity of the scene

Lethargy seems to have set in for this fellow whose head scarf helps protect him from the blazing noonday sun. The heat in this scene near the Dead Sea can almost be felt. At 1,300 feet below sea level, this is the lowest place on earth.

would be lost. Inching my way to within twenty-five feet of my subject, I stopped, afraid to approach any closer for fear of being discovered. With one eye composing the picture in my viewfinder, and the other eye on the shepherd, I focused the lens and shot.

In the stillness of the moment the shutter went off like an explosion, and instantly, from somewhere near the seated figure, came an ominous growl.

Suddenly there was this large and very unfriendly dog that had apparently been napping at his master's feet. Leaping into the air, the dog hit the ground running, his canine mind obsessed with an intense desire to make me his next meal. The surprised shepherd sprang to his feet, whirled around, and glared at me; it didn't take a clairvoyant to understand that he shared the dog's feelings. "Baksheesh! Baksheesh!" the man shouted angrily, as he stretched his palm out in my direction.

Picture-taking was suddenly relegated to the back of my mind as I turned and lit out for the road. The dog, now being egged on by his master, caught up with me about half way to the relative safety of the car, and with an ugly snarl, began snapping at my legs. Meanwhile, Sam, who had been watching the action from the road, hopped from the back seat and began lobbing rocks—plentiful in that part of the world—at the offending animal. Munther, by now almost doubled up with laughter, enjoyed the entire spectacle as though he were in a box seat at some sort of sporting event. I came away from the encounter with a torn pant leg and a healthy respect for Jordanian dogs.

Air Djibouti

Leaving Amman, we flew by Air Djibouti to Asmara, Eritrea, a province in northern Ethiopia, where we put up at the Ciaao Hotel for three days. Between Sam's conferences, we rented a Fiat automobile and found the time to drive from the comfortable temperature of the high Ethiopian plateau down to Massawa, Asmara's port city on the Red Sea. The 50-mile stretch of surfaced highway, chiseled into the steep mountainside by expert Italian stone masons, dropped us 7,700 feet to sea level, where the sizzling temperature and high humidity were stifling.

Beaming with pride, this Eritrean mother happily posed for this photo as she stood on a street corner holding her child. Asmara, Eritrea.

An Italian colony since 1882, Eritrea was incorporated into Ethiopia in 1936. The colonists constructed a cable car lift designed to haul supplies from the seaport up to Asmara, but it was never successful. The story goes that wild baboons were able to negotiate the cables and raid the foodstuffs on the way up. Dangling cars and rusting supports gave silent evidence of the project's abandonment.

Nearing sea level on the way down, we caught occasional glimpses of monkeys as they swung from tree to tree near the sides of the road. Some had offspring clinging to their backs. During the return trip late in the day, the sound of insects singing in the African jungle was so piercing that conversation was difficult.

Beirut

An Ethiopian Air Lines C-46 flew us from Asmara to Port Sudan, where we paused briefly to refuel. Continuing on to Cairo, we checked in at the Heliopolis House for a couple of days, then caught Air Liban back to Beirut and the Palm Beach Hotel. Beirut was a vibrant and prosperous city in the 1950s, and this elegant hostelry, along with many others on the Mediterranean waterfront, catered to affluent European tourists. It sported dining room waiters who went about their duties in black tie and tails, while a string ensemble performed classical selections from Brahms and Beethoven for hotel dinner guests. The area near the beach was a center of social life for wealthy, oil-rich Arabs, who whiled away their days water-skiing and enjoying their yachts at berth across the street from the hotel.

A few days after our return to Beirut, we again heard from Munther. Having just driven over from Damascus, he dropped by the hotel and was now calling our room from the lobby. He insisted that Sam and I be his guests for dinner that evening at a night spot in the hills west of the city. Young Bilbeisi, it was rumored, had a reputation around the Middle East as a wealthy playboy, and we had heard that he was currently infatuated with a celebrated belly dancer, one of King Farouk's favorite girls, who was performing at this club. We accepted his invitation.

I remember the place as having a rectangular dance floor, surrounded by randomly placed tables. A second floor balcony, sectioned off in booths, ringed the entire room and overlooked the floor below. To allow complete privacy, a set of heavy red velour drapes fronting each cubicle could be raised or lowered by its occupants. From these vantage points, Arab sheiks and their chadar-clothed women, their eyes peering expressionless from behind covered faces, had a commanding view of the musicians and performers on the floor below.

With a roll from a goblet drum, the house lights dimmed, leaving only a single spotlight focused on the dance floor. Then from out of the darkness glided this sensuous female figure, the object of Munther's affections. Radiating charisma throughout her performance, this dusky, Mid-east beauty was a consummate professional whose provocative undulations certainly exemplified the fine art of belly dancing. Following her performance, Munther brought the girl to our table for introductions. There could be no doubt that our young Jordanian friend had developed a discerning eye for attractive women.

Lewis Pasha

After our return to the hotel that night, Sam speculated, "It might be a good political move to invite Munther to visit the U.S. as a guest of Transocean Air Lines. I'll have a talk with his father about that possibility tomorrow. However ..." he hesitated, "if my offer is accepted, I'll have to make it clear to Munther that we don't pay for any women."

Subsequently, he came to America and the Bay Area and, for the next few weeks, the San Francisco newspapers carried daily accounts of his free-wheeling activities on the night club circuit. One day the telephone rang at our home in San Lorenzo; it was Munther. He was calling from Transocean's executive headquarters at the Oakland Airport.

"I will come to visit you this afternoon, Mr. Lewis," he said. "Fine Munther," I replied, "I'll look forward to seeing you."

Remembering my recent gift from King Saud, I decided to surprise him; I would meet him at the door dressed as an Arab. His thirty minute drive to our San Lorenzo home would give me just about enough time to change clothing. The white silk body sheath worn under the brown flowing outer garment was a bit snug, but I managed to wriggle into it. Very carefully, I wrinkled the white woolen kaffiyeh across my brow, and adjusted the black, double-ringed agal at the proper angle over the crown of my head.

After checking my appearance in a mirror, I decided something was still missing. A mustache, I concluded, would enhance my regal bearing, so ... with a little help from Mina's mascara, I 'grew' one. Another critical examination of my reflected image convinced me that I looked the very essence of Arabian authenticity.

Munther was not long in coming. I watched through the living room window as he pulled to the curb in front of the house, stopped, visually checked the address, and got out. He was driving a new, black Cadillac sedan. Not in Arab dress now, he was instead wearing a dark, smartly tailored business suit, pin-striped, with white shirt, conservative necktie, and a western style hat.

Coming up the walk, he reached the front door and knocked. For a brief moment we stood there in the open doorway, staring at each other. Then the comical reversal of traditional dress broke us up.

"Is that really you, Mr. Lewis?"

"Are you the real Munther?" I rejoined.

His hearty laughter was reminiscent of a time not long before when he had taken such delight in my embarrassing encounter with the shepherd's dog.

During his California visit, Mina and I invited him to be our guest at a company Christmas party and, while dancing with Mina, he discovered that other men present, who were dressed in suits, were not wearing vests. Walking Mina to a nearby window, the eccentric Munther removed his coat and vest and tossed the vest out onto the street. Shortly before returning home to Jordan, Herb Caen's column in the *San Francisco Chronicle* reported Munther's final caper. He had set his new Cadillac on fire in a vain attempt to collect the insurance.

"Is that really you, Mr. Lewis?"

Back to the Middle East

Tell ya' what I'm willin' to do ... I'll think about sellin' you the west half of this here three acres, if you're willin' to rent my house on the east half while yore apputin' up yer own place. It'd be real handy for you and the missus, what with you doin' it yerself ... 'course, my house aint' quite ready yet; jist gotta finish her up some on the inside ... what d'ya say to thet?

Thus spoke Everard Forrest, a bachelor in his early eighties. A carpenter all his life, he had bought this property a few years back, intending to build just one more house. No longer young, he walked with a stoop—a legacy, no doubt, of a life of hard work, but he seemed to be a pleasant sort.

Dream Lot

The two of us were standing on a slightly rounded knoll in the hills overlooking the city of Hayward, California. From an elevation of about 1,000 feet, we had a sweeping view of the Bay Area, three of its bridges, and the San Francisco skyline. Lost for a brief moment, caught up in the breathtaking scene spread out before us, I tried to keep my mind on how to approach him.

Neither of us had talked price yet, and I was almost afraid to ask. But, from his affable, friendly manner, I felt that the door might be open; I would try to hold him within reason.

My wife and I are not rich people, Mr. Forrest," I began, "but this location would be ideal for a growing family. How much would you be asking for the west half here?"

"Eh?" He tipped his battered old straw hat backward, revealing a thin line of grey hair, then paused to scratch his ear. I repeated my question.

"Well now ... I'll jist have to think on thet fer awhile," he finally answered. The serious look on his face gave way to a smile as he changed the subject. Reaching into the carpenter's apron which hung loosely from his waist, he withdrew a small object which he held out for my inspection.

"See this?" he said, extending his hand toward me, "It's a square nail. I took it outa thet redwood fence post over there on the property line last week." He pointed a short distance down the slope. "Thet's an ole section line

186

fence ... 'er whatever's left of it! Jist full o' them rusty square nails." He turned the nail slowly between two fingers as he stared intently at it through smudged glasses. "Been there probally a hunerd years 'er more!" There was no point in my pushing him now; he just was not ready to discuss terms.

All along the view side to the north and west, the old fence, marking the property boundary, was far enough down the slope to prevent future structures from cutting off the view. In my mind I could see a long, low ranch-style house, placed to take advantage of the inspiring panorama. Turning in the opposite direction, I contemplated Mr. Forrest's place that was about 100 yards to the east: the one he was just completing. It was small, with only four rooms, but it had a large attached garage that would come in handy as a work-shop.

We stood there in silence a few seconds longer, then Mr. Forrest turned and headed slowly back toward his house with me tagging along behind. In his driveway, I offered him my hand and concluded, "I'll keep in touch with you, Mr. Forrest."

Back on the road, Mina had been waiting patiently in the car while I tried to secure a commitment from the old carpenter. Only the week before, we had gone for a ride in the hills and were awestruck by the possibilities of this particular lot. At the end of a dead-end road, there would be privacy and no through traffic. Although there had been no 'For Sale' sign in evidence, we had decided to investigate anyway. The gentle slope of the lot toward the main road would allow a circular driveway, and we envisioned 'our' house spread along the crest of the knoll above the drive. The kitchen would be in the front for a southern exposure, while the living room at the back would be placed to take advantage of the view ... but who owned the lot? We had noticed an elderly workman painting siding on what appeared to be a new house a short distance away, perhaps he might know the answer, and indeed he did; it belonged to him. Thus we had chanced to meet Everard Forrest, the carpenter.

Rejoining Mina now, I turned the car around and headed out to the nearest paved road about a half mile away. Driving back down the hill, it was all 'house talk'. Mina agreed that Mr. Forrest's place would do very well until we were far enough along to move into our own, but this, our dream lot was on a private unimproved road, located in an unincorporated area with neither city sewer nor natural gas available. Never mind that; we wanted it anyway. How big a house did we need? Would we be able to obtain financing? Would I have sufficient expertise and tenacity to do much of the work myself? Could Mr. Forrest be persuaded to give up half his property at a price we could afford? Our entire future now seemed to depend on these and other questions.

There would certainly not be room for my darkroom in the little rented house, but maybe Sam Wilson and the airline could find space to relocate me at the airport. The demand for record photography was increasing at Transocean's largest subsidiary, Aircraft Engineering and Maintenance Company. Performing on a long term contract with the U.S. Air Force, it had taken over all of the floor space at Hangar 5, and was heavily engaged in the major overhaul of T-33 jet trainers. A company photographic department located at the airfield would have a number of obvious advantages.

While all these new thoughts were buzzing through our heads, another call from dispatch, a couple of days later, once again put our plans of the moment on hold. I was being scheduled back out to the Middle East to fly Hajj shuttles for Air Djibouti. The Hajj season, I knew, would wind up in a couple more weeks; I would not be away too long. Another trip up the hill before I left, to advise Mr. Forrest of my impending absence, evoked only the following comment; "Well ... thet lot'l still be over there when you git back."

The Hajj

Each summer, Transocean Air Lines, along with other contract air carriers, flew thousands of visitors to and from the holiest of Muslim shrines: Mecca,

(Left) Two Hajj pilgrims, Mecca bound, alight from an Air Djibouti C-46 at the Jeddah Airport. Each is carrying two umbrellas. Note the pointed shoe. 1952. (Right) The Hajj season, in full swing, makes for a busy day at the air passenger terminal at Jeddah, Saudi Arabia. 1953.

The parapeted architecture of this Jeddah skyscraper in Saudi Arabia, is typical of that found in Arabian cities in the 1950s.

Saudi Arabia. Flying above, or even near this sacred city at that time, was forbidden by Islamic law, so commercial aircraft used the air terminal at the port city of Jeddah, some forty-five miles from Mecca.

Thousands of other devout pilgrims arrived at the port of Jeddah by ship during the Hajj season, and from here the faithful either took buses or walked to Mecca. Picking them up from points all over Africa and the Middle East, we took them aboard carrying suitcases, bed rolls, cooking pots and portable stoves, prayer rugs, cheeses, and a diverse variety of trading material.

Probably the most important items of all were supplies of drinking water and umbrellas, both of which were needed to ward off the intense heat of the desert. They clamored aboard the airplane, then fought over who was to sit by the window. When disagreements came to blows, the umbrella seemed to be the weapon of choice, until one fellow discovered that the arm rest between the seats could be unplugged, thus giving its

Camels, donkeys, and water wagons ... all wait while their drivers queue up at the watering station in Jeddah. There are many roads leading to Mecca....

This Islamic pilgrim, from Morocco, would do penance by walking the forty-five miles from Jeddah to Mecca. Though trucks and buses were available, large numbers chose to walk—many at night—to avoid the intense heat encountered during the daytime. Summer, 1953.

A typical Hajj traveller—this one from Afghanistan—was persuaded to hold for his portrait as he waited patiently in front of the Jeddah air terminal for a shuttle flight back to Kabul. 1953.

discoverer a distinct advantage in any physical confrontation. The airplane's captain sometimes had to intercede to quell disturbances.

By the time they arrived back at the Jeddah airport for the return trip home, they would have traded away or eaten most of what they had brought with them, and in the religious fervor of the moment, had refilled their suitcases with sacred sand from the holy places. One of the crew had to remain at the bottom of the ramp during boarding, to empty the contents of suitcases and bags, invariably over the owner's loud protests. Now and then it became a tug of war in the effort to remove the bag forcibly from the passenger's grasp as he struggled to wrestle it up and into the airplane. Fifty or sixty pounds of sand in each passenger's luggage would have increased our take-off weight by over a ton and a half; we would have been sand-bound and ground-bound. The Saudi government kept a skip loader at the terminal to remove the piles of accumulating sand.

Fire in Back

Most of these people had led very primitive lives, and their child-like behavior was evident in their quick, and often violent, tempers. Many had never seen a western-style toilet. When confronted with the use of one aboard the airplane, they simply stood on the toilet platform and squatted.

On one occasion we had picked up a load of pilgrims at Tripoli, Libya, and radio'd ahead to Nicosia, Cyprus, requesting lunch for our passengers. But when we landed they refused to eat the food, citing religious beliefs as the reason. Loading them back on the airplane again, we took off, and had no more than reached level flight when the male flight attendant burst through the cockpit door shouting, "Fire! Fire! Fire in the back end of the cabin!"

Fire in an airplane can—to put it mildly—be lethal, especially in flight. The captain flew out of his seat as if possessed, grabbed a fire extinguisher, and made a frantic dash to the rear. Some of the passengers had whittled a pile

Two crew members, with the help of several Afghanis and a giant funnel, refuel a C-46 from a cache of five-gallon tins stacked near the edge of the runway at Kandahar, Afghanistan. 1953.

of shavings from a pair of wooden wheel chocks that hung in a canvas bag near the main cabin door. They were just enough to start a small bonfire on the metal floor. As I remember, they were warming strips of meat. The carpeting had been deliberately removed for these flights, which certainly demonstrated foresight on someone's part. A couple of blasts from the fire extinguisher ended the emergency, not to mention the improvised meal.

Some of the refueling stops around the Middle East were make-shift and dangerous. At Kandahar, Afghanistan, for instance, aviation fuel was stacked in five-gallon tins at the edge of the runway. The cans were then hoisted, one by one, by a chain of airport workers, to the top of the airplane wing and emptied into the fuel tanks through a large funnel.

Still another method of refueling involved the use of a long wooden trough on the ground into which the tins of gasoline were emptied. A pump with a long vertical handle mounted at the end of the trough, was then worked by hand to move the fuel through a hose and up to the wing tanks above. In either case, gas fumes saturated the air during the entire operation, and instant oblivion was just a spark away for the airplane and a dozen or so workers.

A New Home

While I was away in the Middle East, Mina made a couple of trips up the hill to see how Mr. Forrest was coming along with the completion of his house; his progress seemed agonizingly slow. She noted that he worked only when he felt like it. As a bachelor, he had been lonely all his life, and would put down his hammer to talk with anyone who chanced to pass by.

He listened with interest as Mina told him of our application for adoption, which seemed to please him. Our noble gesture impressed him so much, in fact, that he later came by with a twenty-five dollar check for the new baby. Our act may also have accounted for his subsequent benevolent attitude.

One day in October, 1952, shortly after I had returned home again, fortune smiled. Mr. Forrest offered to sell us the front half of his property for only $1,200. We were ecstatic. He must either have liked us or felt sorry for us; we never knew which. We went straightaway to the bank, drew out the money and paid him in cash. In another month we managed to locate a young college graduate who had just earned his degree in architecture. Looking for his first job, he was quite anxious to work with us in designing our new house. Mina and I were to spend many evenings with him over the next six months as our plans took shape.

Meanwhile, photographic requirements were demanding more and more versatility. My Rolleiflex, used so successfully for general purposes in the past, now lacked the flexibility to meet the variety of the work load. Hair-line cracks in aircraft parts, wide angle shots, sharp photos of complicated schematics, and extreme close-ups: all of these called for a larger format camera equipped with an array of lenses of varying focal lengths. Once again I turned to Vice President Wilson for help. On his authority, the accounting department issued a purchase order in the amount of $600 for acquisition of a 4" x 5" Linhof view camera and three interchangeable lenses. Burke and James, a large photographic supply house in Chicago, filled my order by mail, and Transocean's sheet metal shop fabricated stainless steel processing tanks which could handle both roll and sheet film. Two weeks later I was out on the hangar floor, working with the new camera.

Typhoons and
Hail Marys

urbulence encountered in flight, if severe, is a true manifestation of the tremendous power of nature, a humbling experience that very quickly exposes the puniness of man. If you are riding it out, it's great fun—after it's over. I never quite got used to that queasy feeling when the airplane did a little dance of its own as it rippled through a small patch of unstable air. Ninety-eight percent of all flying occurs in air so stable that you have no feeling of motion unless you have a visual reference point. The remaining two percent, however, can be quite another matter.

Caused by rising and falling air currents, turbulence can occur in cloud formations or in spotlessly clear weather. The clear air variety is common during the heat of the day in hilly or mountainous terrain, and although many pilots might characterize convection heating and cooling as light turbulence, it can be violent enough to keep you strapped to your seat, jolting you around hour after hour, while flying over a large land mass.

The tops of towering cumulus, or cumulo-nimbus formations that have attained substantial vertical development, might pack currents severe enough to tear a wing from an airplane, or at the very least, carry you skyward at an alarming rate and drop you like a rock a few seconds later.

During my flying days, the navigator's work table held a chart, dividers, a hack watch, a plotter, a Dalton computer, star tables, an almanac, an octant, and a variety of pencils ... none of them tied down. During an unexpected encounter with moderate turbulence, these paraphernalia could suddenly end up all over the flight deck.

Line squalls were another source of moderate-to-severe turbulence. They could usually be seen, identified, and flown around during daylight hours, but at night we might go roaring into one without warning. Rapidly accelerating and decelerating air currents accompanied by heavy rain characterize these formations, and can scare the pants off you.

Don't Look Now ...

In a DC-4 one dark night, we were nearing Iwo Jima, the half-way point on a track between Guam Island and Tachikawa Air Base, in Japan. Since leaving Guam we had been slogging along at 8,000 feet through occasional heavy rain showers and light turbulence, and because of higher-than-expected head-winds, were nearly 45 minutes behind flight plan. I was somewhat concerned. Were we to lose a like amount of time during the remainder of the leg, we could wind up with a fuel problem. After discussing with the pilots the possibility of falling still further behind, the decision was made to ask Iwo tower for clearance to come in for fuel. Selecting a VHF frequency, the captain called the tower, and explained the problem."Estimate abeam your station in about ten minutes," he radioed.

"Stand by one," came the reply.

A moment later something outside our co-pilot's window caught his attention. Just what it was, he did not know—a flash of lightning off in the distance perhaps—but suddenly he thought he was seeing his own wing light out there. Just as quickly, however he realized that had he been able to see his own wing tip light, it would have been green. In a flash now, he realized that he was seeing the red port light of another craft—not fifty feet away.

Close enough to be dimly visible from the illumination of our own star-board wing light, sat a fighter plane, pacing along beside us, wing tip to wing tip with our DC-4. Its big engine up front and stubby appearance made it easily identifiable as a P-47 Thunderbolt. Pointing excitedly out toward the right wing, the co-pilot let out a yell, "Where the hell did this guy come from?"

Through the navigator's small window, I could make out the U.S. Air Force insignia on its fuselage. Iwo had apparently scrambled the P-47 to look us over. The fighter jockey just sat out there for a couple of minutes, then peeled off and disappeared in the darkness, making us realize how terrifyingly vulnerable our transport plane really was. A few seconds later our attention was diverted once again by a call from Iwo tower.

"Are you declaring an emergency, 416?"

Our captain hesitated ... Iwo Jima was a military base. The sudden appearance of the fighter had confirmed that. With the question just posed by the tower operator, the captain knew that upon his return to Oakland, an exten-sive report would be required to explain the need for such a declaration. Changing his mind about landing, he replied, "Negative, Iwo!"

Obviously, someone outside the tower had been contacted concerning our request. When the answer came, we knew what it would be. "Transocean 416 ... permission to land ... denied!" was the tower's response.

Had we been able to continue the flight at a higher altitude, we might have topped some of the build-ups, but a higher flight level would have resulted in stronger headwinds. We elected to remain at 8,000 feet in the hope that the winds would diminish. A short distance beyond Iwo, the weather cleared, at least temporarily. It was a moonless night but the sky above us now exploded in all its brilliance.

Vega, Deneb and Altair, all first-magnitude stars, were directly overhead, forming a triangle that sparkled against a dazzling background of millions of lesser stars. At night, after plowing through a couple of hours of lousy weather, to break out in the clear and find yourself gazing up at that familiar canopy of planets and stars—the navigator's celestial road map— was always comforting.

Line Squall

The air was remarkably smooth at this particular moment, giving me a chance to climb into the bubble for a three-star fix. The rest of the cockpit crew relaxed for a few minutes while the captain turned in for a little bunk time. Back down from the bubble, I busied myself at the chart table, plotting out lines of position from each star; the result would give us a revised ground speed.

Now, dimming all flight deck lights except for the instrument panel, we peered intently through the cockpit windshield in an effort to determine what might lay ahead. Our eyes had not yet become accustomed to the darkness when suddenly the airplane shuddered, suffered a little sinking spell, then pitched convulsively up on its side. The captain found himself thrown violently from the bunk onto the floor. My navigation table hinged on one side, collapsed, spewing objects in all directions, and the next thing I remembered, the captain was trying to crawl around me to get into the left hand seat up front, yelling all the while at the copilot to throttle back.

The upward acceleration of the aircraft was so overpowering that neither the captain nor I could pry himself from the floor. Acutely aware of the stress on the wings, we could only pray that they stayed on, as our co-pilot struggled to keep the aircraft in level flight. Outside, amid the violence of the wind and rain, the four engines groaned in rebellion. We had blundered into a line squall.

For what seemed to be an eternity, chaos prevailed, as I clung tenaciously to whatever was fastened down. For the remainder of the trip the violence gradually tapered off to intermittent heavy showers and brief bursts of turbulence. Landing at Tachikawa early the next morning, we were grateful for two things: we still had thirty minutes fuel remaining, and our cabin load had been military mail, not passengers.

Typhoon

Among my lingering memories is another DC-4 episode that took place one stormy night during a commercial flight between Wake Island and Tokyo. I remember it well because it involved a typhoon and 53 Catholic nuns: on the one hand natural violence, on the other hand spiritual serenity, an unlikely mix, to say the least.

Walking into the Wake Island terminal one evening to prepare for the flight, our crew was surprised to find a lobby filled with women. The fact that they were all women was not so unusual because we regularly carried military dependents and their families to and from the Orient, but these women's attire set them apart. Dressed in the habit of Catholic sisters, they were a sight not often seen on Wake Island. The duty dispatcher in Transocean Operations greeted us.

"You guys get a look at your passengers out there?"

Then, as if to answer his own question, he tossed a copy of the passenger manifest up on the counter in front of us.

"You're going to have fun tonight," he continued. "Typhoon Beatrice is moving up along the Japanese coast!"

In the C.A.A. meteorological office a few minutes later for weather briefing, we learned that a well-developed typhoon was indeed moving in a northeasterly direction along the Japanese coastline, but was expected to pass through the Tokyo area shortly before our own estimated time of arrival there.

Now ... if you understand pilots—and our Captain Hench was no exception—you will know that most of them would consider a typhoon of this magnitude a challenge; not necessarily something to be avoided but rather an obstacle to be coped with. Anyway, it was supposed to be fifty miles northeast of Haneda International by the time we reached the Tokyo area. Although Nagoya (some 200 miles to the west) was our alternate airfield, we still had the option of holding offshore in the vicinity of Tokyo Bay if the storm was slow in passing through the region. With gross weight to spare on an eight-hour forecast, we loaded out with fuel, boarded the 53 nuns, and headed for Japan and the typhoon.

By the time we reached mid-point, over tiny Marcus Island, we were flying in light-to-moderate rain showers and being shaken up almost continuously. I was never ill from turbulence while riding in the front of an airplane, but riding in the rear of one in rough weather always made me nauseated. The

Out there all by itself—midway between Wake Island and Tokyo—is diminutive, triangular-shaped Marcus Island, the only reference point on track.

stewardesses now reported by intercom that it was even too rough to serve coffee to passengers.

Checking with Tokyo Control while still about an hour out, we reported ourselves at 8,000 feet in intermittent heavy rain, estimating Tateyama intersection (on the tip of Boso Peninsula, 47 miles directly south of Tokyo) at 2 a.m. local time. Upon receiving clearance to descend to, and maintain, 6,000 feet, we were advised that the apex of the storm was now centered over the Tokyo area, and was beginning to pick up speed, moving up along the coast in a northeasterly direction. Surface wind velocities at the time were reported to be gusting to 80 knots. All domestic flights had long since been grounded, and so far as we knew, we were the only inbound traffic.

Over the Tateyama intersection an hour later, we learned that the disturbance was moving on through, so Captain Hench, electing not to proceed to our alternate, requested permission to hold over the Kisarazu homer (midway between Tateyama and Tokyo on the shore of Tokyo Bay), until the winds had subsided enough to permit landing at Haneda International.

This decision had just been made when Tokyo Control reported a total power failure at Haneda: no runway lights, no field communications. For nearly half an hour we flew an elliptical pattern over Kisarazu, in what most pilots would report as 'moderate' turbulence. Just how rough it had to be to earn a 'severe' rating, I did not know, but in thirteen years of flying, I had never experienced anything like this.

Our flight engineer was buckled into the jump seat between the two pilots and I was standing, trying to hang on to a stanchion which ran floor-to-ceiling adjacent to the captain's seat. Suddenly, the plane shot up 500 feet, climbing at 2,000 feet a minute. Hench grabbed the throttle controls, fighting desperately to keep the DC-4 under control.

Several seconds later we hit the ceiling somewhere up there and began to fall, fluttering down like a leaf in a summer breeze, at 2,000 feet a minute. With full throttle, both pilots now struggled to keep us in level flight. Torn away from the stanchion, along with a number of other objects in the cockpit, including the navigator's stool, I was oscillating somewhere between the floor and the ceiling.

Outside the airplane, an ocean of rain forced water through a badly leaking windshield, and the two pilots, strapped in, were getting drenched. Over the din I could hear the two of them yelling for towels. To add to the excitement, an eerie phenomenon known as St. Elmo's Fire (a luminous electric discharge), was creating a halo effect at the tips of the four spinning props, and lightning, as it struck the aircraft, was accompanied by loud explosions, as though someone outside was beating on the fuselage with a baseball bat.

Suddenly I remembered the female clergy back in the cabin. They must have been frightened out of their wits; but, of course, they would be sustained by their faith. The crew, faced with a life-threatening situation, was much too busy to give thought to the ultimate truth: that our earthly lives were entirely in God's hands, no matter our puny efforts. His intervention was the only way out.

Just a few minutes of this can seem like hours. Bob Hench was not a big man physically, but his iron will in the face of this threat from the elements only increased with the violence of the storm. He was completely in charge, playing the controls like a master organist at his keyboard. Mother Nature had thrown down the gauntlet and he picked it up with determination and absolute confidence. In retrospect, I was never able to understand how an airplane could take this kind of punishment and survive.

The Power of Prayer

As the storm gradually subsided, we managed to pick up the cockpit debris and work our way back to the cabin, where 53 pairs of eyes, framed in 53 very white, anxious faces, silently implored us to bring them safely back to earth. Miraculously, no one was hurt, although most of the overhead storage areas in the cabin had coughed up their contents. Blankets, pillows, and hand luggage now littered the aisle.

As for the Sisters, they were virtually—and that, of course, is the operative word—frozen in place under their seat belts. Forcing a smile, I lied, telling them that what we were experiencing was not unusual. Then, hurriedly beating a hasty retreat to the cockpit, I sought the relative safety of my own seat belt.

We held over Kisarazu in heavy rain, and moderate-to-severe turbulence, for another 15 or 20 minutes, but time was running out. If we were to re-file for our alternate, Nagoya, which was now reporting CAVU (clear and visibility unlimited), we could not hold in the Tokyo area much longer. Captain Hench was about to request clearance for a change in destination when we again heard from Tokyo Control with the report that power and communications had been restored at Haneda International.

"Transocean Four One Six, you should be able to raise Haneda now," Tokyo Control radioed. Switching VHF channels, our copilot shouted over the noise of the pounding rain, "Haneda Tower ... Haneda Tower ... this is Transocean Air Lines Four One Six calling ... do you copy?"

"Aircraft calling Haneda Tower, say again ... you're breaking up." The constant jarring motion of the airplane made speech nearly impossible. "Haneda tower ... this is Transocean Four ... One ... Six ... are ... you ... open ... for ... traffic ...? Over."

"Roger, Four One Six." returned the tower. "Haneda is open ... at the present time. Operations has just advised us that there is an inch and a half to two inches of water on the runways ... surface winds gusting to fifty-five knots. Present altimeter 28.72. Ceiling 3,000 feet in continuing rain. Over."

"Roger Haneda, we're coming in."

Both pilots were soaked to the skin from the waist down, victims of the leaky windshield. The area approach chart, clipped to the instrument faring in front of them was blurred and dripping water. Under miserable conditions, Hench fought the airplane from 6,000 feet down to within seconds of landing, when a gusty crosswind carried us completely out of alignment with the runway. "Take off power!" yelled the captain. "Take off power!" echoed the flight engineer. The landing was aborted.

"Haneda tower ... we're going around again" radioed our co-pilot.

On the second approach, the runway stayed under us. We landed softly on a cushion of water, and except for a few seconds of hydroplaning, the braking power of the water on the runway kept our roll to a minimum. God rode with us that night, allowing us a safe return to earth once again. The Lord willing, there would be a quiet time later for prayerful thanks; no one tried to speak. I guess profound gratitude and immense relief adequately expressed the mood on the flight deck. Taxying with difficulty to the terminal apron, the pilots shut down the engines. The euphoria, excitement, and triumph of having beaten the elements was suddenly gone, to be replaced almost instantly by utter exhaustion.

Everyone remained aboard the airplane that terrible night. Wheeling a
ramp up to the door would have been impossible anyway. All of us, including
the passengers, slept in our seats until after daylight, just very thankful to be
on the ground. Could it have been the 'Hail Marys' and fervent prayers of
those 53 Catholic sisters that brought us down safely? I shall never know, but
I would not want to go through that night again without them, just to find out.

Monkey Business

If we were ever to live in Mr. Forrest's house on the hill, we would need to move the airline's darkroom out of the back end of our San Lorenzo garage. So, in August 1953, with the help and encouragement of Vice President Wilson, the major components of the darkroom were loaded into a company truck and hauled to Hangar 5 at the Oakland Airport, where space had been allotted at the east end of the second floor, adjacent to the company's executive offices. After the plumbers, carpenters, and sheet-metal men had left, Transocean and its affiliates had a new photographic department consisting of a small studio and a first-rate processing laboratory.

That problem solved, Mina and I put our first ever home up for sale after having lived in it just seven years. We evidently priced it too low because it sold within a week and we had to vacate. Our landlord-to-be, still puttering around up on the hill, was not ready for us, so we stored our belongings and rented a motel with a kitchen.

Prodded by anxiety to expedite matters, we volunteered to lay oak flooring in the living and dining rooms in the rental house, an offer that our carpenter friend quickly accepted. Mina carried the bundles in from the garage, while I toe-nailed the tongue and groove flooring in place. Mr. Forrest, happy for the free labor, promoted himself to the role of boss and chief inspector, dropping in about every other day to see how we were getting along. Meeting deadlines, it turned out, ranked near the bottom on his list of priorities. Finally, about the middle of October, we were able to move in.

Throughout the following year, flights to Japan were interspersed with work at the airport photo lab, and I was allowed to schedule myself on trips to accommodate the load of picture assignments at home.

Another phase of our lives gained momentum about that time, with receipt of a letter from the adoption agency regarding house visitations by a case worker, giving us reason to believe that our adoption application was now receiving serious consideration. They wanted to see first hand what provisions we were making to care for a new baby. Mina, of course, was beside herself with anticipation,and had converted one end of our bedroom in Mr. Forrest's house to a nursery. What little time I had at home now was spent preparing the newly acquired homesite next door. Down on the road, a culvert

203

had to be installed to provide access. Electric power would be needed on the lot, and soil percolation tests were waiting to be done.

One Saturday afternoon in early summer, I was over there with a garden sprayer trying to stamp out a growth of poison oak that had gained a foothold on the north slope of the property. It was the growing season, and under the day long sun, the earth was warm. Now and then a gopher would pop his head above ground and scamper around, and I found myself wondering what would happen to them when the bulldozer came in and scraped a foot and a half of soil off the crown of the lot. My thoughts were interrupted when Mina shouted across to me to come answer the telephone. Heading toward the house, I had a premonition that it might be a call from the dispatch office. It was. The voice sounded almost desperate.

Off to Delhi

"Lewis, by daylight tomorrow morning we've got to have a navigator on the East Coast who has current visas for Italy, Iran and India. Hoeninger (TAL's chief navigator) tells us you're our man. How long will it take you to pack a bag and get down here?"

I could hear Mina rattling dishes behind me, preparing dinner, as the dispatcher, without waiting for an answer to his question, continued. "By the time you get here, I'll have you ticketed on a United DC-7 flight out of San Francisco International to Philadelphia. We'll helicopter you across the Bay. At Philadelphia you'll join one of our own crews for a working flight to Tehran with a load of Bechtel people." Further detailing my itinerary, he went on. "Your crew will then ferry the empty airplane from Tehran to New Delhi where you'll pick up a load of monkeys for delivery to Eli-Lilly Pharmaceuticals in Indianapolis, Indiana. You should be home in about a week. Oh ... I almost forgot!" he concluded, "Be sure to take along a change of clothing that you can burn when you get back. Them monkeys really stink up an airplane."

"They're dead?" I asked.

"Of course not. That's why they smell so bad. You'll probably wish they were though, before you get back."

"Is that all?" I said, sarcastically.

"That's about it," he answered, ignoring the sarcasm.

"Well ... give me 45 minutes."

"OK, but your United flight departs San Franciscoooo ..." There was a brief pause, "in about an hour and a half!"

"I'll be there," I assured him.

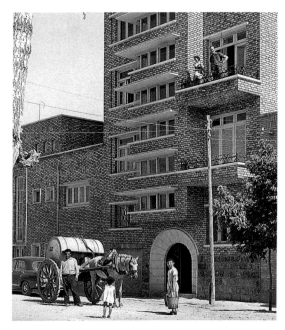

Transocean Captain and Mrs. Bill Piles, stand on the balcony of their fourth floor apartment in Tehran, Iran. Living in Tehran, in 1950, was not easy for the handful of Transocean pilots and their wives, most of whom also lived in this same apartment building. Hot food had to be prepared over a charcoal brazier, and daily rations of water were delivered by bucket from the horse-drawn cart seen here in the street.

About the time my dinner would have been on the table, I rushed out the front door in uniform with camera gear, navigation brief case, and flight bag, which was always kept packed anyway. Through the years, and probably born of resignation, Mina had accepted such emergencies with amazing calm. Following me out to the porch, she kissed me goodbye and, as I climbed into my little 'airporter,' reminded me that when the baby came, I would have to "give up this foolishness of running off on flying trips."

Out of Philadelphia the next morning with construction workers in the cabin of a DC-4, a double crew up front ... and a monkey attendant to care for the animals during the return flight, we paused only long enough to refuel. Down and up again through Gander, Shannon, Rome, and Nicosia, we finally landed in Tehran some 50 hours later.

An Air Djibouti mechanic drove us to the city center, skillfully threading us through flocks of sheep, goats, carts, autos, and a jumbled mass of street people. Needed or not, our horn sounded at regular intervals, joining the chorus already created by many others. The continuous barrage of noise was intended to scare a path through the glut of traffic that lay ahead.

Finally stopping in front of our hotel, the driver handed me a letter and asked me to mail it to his wife when I got back to California. We were tired and hungry, so after refreshing ourselves with baths—there were no showers in the hotel—we gathered in the lobby and walked off in search of a place to eat, anxious to get back to our room for some much-needed sleep.

Iranian Slight of Hand

Darkness was approaching as all nine of us walked along the crowded street three abreast. Two of the other fellows and I brought up the rear. Suddenly, from somewhere behind, a hand wrapped around in front of me and slapped hard against the mechanic's letter that I had put in my shirt pocket. Instinctively my own hands were drawn to the same spot. Then came an awareness that another hand had slipped expertly into and out of my rear pants pocket where there was enough local currency to pay for dinner.

Turning, I saw my attacker hand off the stolen rials (Iranian money) to an accomplice who scooted off on the run and quickly disappeared down the busy thoroughfare. The loose clothing of the man who robbed me, afforded an excellent hand hold as I hollered for help. The rest of the crew whirled around to grapple with the man, and during the process of subduing him, someone spotted a policeman directly across the street. What a stroke of luck! Although my money was gone, we could at least turn one of the thieves over to the law.

With our culprit now pinned against a nearby lamp post, I was free to dash across the street to alert the local cop, but he could not speak English. As I stood there pointing and gesticulating wildly, he just shook his head and refused to budge. A crowd had gathered to see what all the ruckus was about, when one of the onlookers asked, in broken English, if he could help. A further exchange of words followed between the bilingual bystander and the neighborhood constabulary.

Entirely out of the argument now, I watched as the policeman explained to my interpreter, in increasingly understandable body language, that the reported transgression had occurred on the opposite side of the street in another policeman's territory. He concluded his diatribe by insisting that I seek the services of the law man who was assigned to my side of the street. We had no choice but to release our captive; it would have been useless to hold him longer. So much for Iranian justice.

During the night, mechanics removed the seats of our airplane, holding them for another Transocean aircraft due into Tehran the next day with cargo for the Voice of America world-wide broadcasting service. The seats were then reinstalled in the second airplane to accommodate British construction workers who were rotating home to London. The following morning we

*Up again, down again—
on our way to pick up a
load of monkeys at New
Delhi, India, we stopped
briefly to refuel at
Nicosia, Cyprus. Our
airplane?* The Argentine
Queen. *June, 1955.*

ferried the stripped DC-4 to New Delhi in 11 hours and 5 minutes, only to
learn that our monkey flight had been delayed for twenty-four hours. I hired
a taxi and spent the day in the countryside taking pictures.

Record Load

1,350 passengers in a DC-4? Sounds impossible until you realize that I'm
talking about rhesus monkeys. In 1955, Eli-Lilly was involved in the production of the Salk polio vaccine and was using the kidney tissue of these animals
as a culture medium in the manufacture of life-saving polio serum. Exporting
these monkeys from India in large numbers was done so extensively that the
population was threatened, and shipping them out of the country is now
prohibited.

   Among other animals, monkeys are sacred symbols to the Hindus, so
the Indian government expected us to spirit them out of the country secretly,
in the middle of the night. We were scheduled to depart at four in the morning
but a mechanical delay prevented the cages from being loaded until after the
aircraft had been test-flown. By that time there was enough daylight to take
pictures as the little creatures were placed aboard.

Record Stink

Never have I been so close to so many for so long, and even though special venturi tubes had been installed down each side of the cabin for added ventilation, the sickening putrid stench emanating from the cages was overwhelming. Urine and feces collected in trays beneath their cages and there was no way to dispose of it. Accustomed to a hot, humid environment, these small animals were subject to pneumonia when flown to altitudes where temperature and humidity were low, and could die within hours. As many as half a dozen expired during each trip.

(Above) Monkeys are loaded aboard N4726V, the Argentine Queen, *in New Delhi, India, on the morning of June 23, 1955. With no way to circulate the air inside the aircraft while loading, hatches on both sides of the cabin were opened for ventilation. The overwhelming stench from the animal cages was indescribable. (Right) Six very pathetic-looking little creatures per cubicle, (count them), and two cubicles per cage. In spite of the stench we could not help feeling sympathetic. En route from New Delhi, India, to Indianapolis, U.S.A.*

(Left) An attendant was assigned to each monkey flight, whose duty it was to feed and water the animals during the 55 hours it took to fly them from India to the U.S.A. (Below) End of the journey. Two days, eight hours, and fifty-nine minutes after leaving New Delhi, we landed at Indianapolis, Indiana. Immigration officials were flown in from New York's Kennedy International to clear the flight. June 26, 1955.

The chore of feeding and watering the animals en route fell to a monkey handler who also had the unpleasant task of disposing of their carcasses when they died. With the help of some of the crew, the main cabin door could be pried open against the slip stream while in flight, and their bodies shoved out. We laughingly speculated that a future anthropologist might some day startle the world with the announcement that rhesus monkeys had once inhabited Saudi Arabia.

Several of the tiny animals escaped their ultimate fate at Eli-Lilly when ground crews along our route asked for and were given a monkey as a pet. One of the airline's captains took a fancy to the pet idea. Before landing in Indianapolis, he stashed one away in his flight case, but instead of being sent home, his aircraft was diverted to Miami, Florida, for two days. What to do with the monkey? He smuggled the little fellow into his room at the exclusive Fontainebleau Hotel out on Miami's "strip", where he allowed the monkey free run of his room. But when the time came to check out, his entire crew could not catch the little critter. The hotel manager finally had to be notified and the fire department called in. The captain? The police investigated, and a local judge fined him one hundred dollars for littering.

Back home on the hill, my foul-smelling clothing, thoroughly impregnated after three days and nights in monkeyland, was stripped off in the garage, tied securely in a plastic bag and deposited in the garbage can behind the house. Then, heading for the shower, I tried to scrub away the remaining vestiges of that nauseating smell, but it was no use. A faint, but persistent, monkey odor continued to plague me until I finally discovered it was coming from my shoes. They too had to go. I guess you could say that, from then on, I had a nose for monkeys; even my wallet continued to remind me of them for several weeks afterward.

Epitaph to a
Great Airline

I n August 1955, I had borrowed a 90-pound jack-hammer and compressor from Transocean Engineering Company. Chiseling rock day after day with a 90-pound hammer is not for kids, and though I encountered far more rock than I had bargained for, it had to be removed to make way for foundation footings. A couple of hours of continuous jolting and jarring after returning home each evening, left me vibrating the rest of the night; but the job was finally finished.

One Monday morning, after nearly two months of this, the county building inspector was due to arrive. In the bathroom, I was trying to stave off the shakes (a recently acquired complaint, courtesy of the jack-hammer). The telephone rang.

"Can you answer the 'phone, Honey?" I called to Mina.

Proud Parents

Mina picked up the kitchen telephone. Over the noise of the electric razor I caught a few indistinguishable words, then a shout of joy. I knew what the call was about even before she reached me.

Bursting at the seams, she poured out the adoption agency's message in a torrent of words. They had a bright and beautiful two-month-old baby boy waiting for us in Oakland! Delirious with excitement and anticipation, her moment of supreme maternal instinct was finally going to be fulfilled. They had asked her if we could come in to see if he was what we wanted.

"Are those people crazy down there? How could they possibly think we wouldn't want him?" she kept repeating.

The inspection appointment canceled, we shot out of the door before I even had time to put my razor back on the shelf. A thirty-minute ride followed to downtown Oakland with Mina urging me on for fear they might change their minds before we could get there, and decide to give 'our' baby to someone else.

We brought our new son home that day, and within hours from the time the 'phone rang, we found ourselves knee-deep in diapers, bottle sterilizing, and formula preparation. We chose to name him David Earl Lewis ... David, because it was a name well anchored down through the ages, and Earl, after his paternal grandfather. Although he was born on June 23, 1955, we had not been told that he was ours until the middle of August because County policy kept newborn infants under wraps until they were certain there were no physical problems.

The cries of a child in the house now added a new dimension to our lives. We were no longer free to take even short vacation trips. Extended flights brought worries about Mina, who had to be left alone with no one up on our hill with whom she could share this new responsibility. I found myself wishing for Honolulu turnarounds only. As David began to grow, I looked forward to snatching him up in my arms as he ran down the driveway to welcome me home; I don't know which of us missed the other the most.

Publicity and advertising photography, navigation, and new roles as father and house-builder: all these different occupations competed for my time; the days were just not long enough. Increasing demands in photographic assignments eventually reduced my flight schedule to about half normal, allowing even less time to spend at home to be with the family, while work on the new house was restricted to week-ends.

Dirty Politics

For several years in a row, before deregulation, Transocean Air Lines had petitioned the Civil Aeronautics Board for scheduled carrier status, offering to fly passengers, mail, and freight without a subsidy. Yet, in spite of convincing arguments, its applications were as often refused, and the manner in which the precious Certificate of Public Convenience and Necessity was denied was a disgraceful injustice. While flying through Chicago one night, I telephoned my old friend, Paul Harvey, from the airport and asked a favor. Would he do a piece in his column concerning the C.A.B.s repeated denials of Transocean's applications? Some weeks later, Dick Pettit, a company attorney, sent a note to me in the photo lab with a clipping from a local newspaper. Paul had obliged with an excellent article lauding the outstanding performance of supplemental air carriers. "The C.A.B.," he had written, "was pursuing a policy of discrimination."

By 1953, Transocean had pioneered a lucrative new source of revenue. Working through civic groups and chambers of commerce, the company's sales department originated and developed the airline group tour business.

By the time Transocean ceased operations in 1959, its 145 aircraft and some 400 crew members had flown more than 70,000,000 miles. This "flying billboard" lets the whole world know. (Left to right are Radio Operator Joe Conn; Copilot Ed Landwehr; Stewardess unknown; Navigator Wayne Lappi, and Captain Joe Stachon. 1949.)

AEMCO, A Transocean subsidiary, performs on an Air Force C-124 Globemaster maintenance contract at the Oakland Airport. The old control tower, located behind Hangar #5, is seen in the background.

One of the first to sense the potential in this field, and certainly the first in the Pacific, Transocean quickly became successful in promoting and selling tours to Hawaii and to other popular vacation spots; first from California, then from all over the United States.

For the next several years, the company's Pacific operation continued with military contracts to and from Kadena on Okinawa; Tachikawa near Tokyo; and Clark Air Base, north of Manila. Revenue during this period was substantially supplemented by charters and tours originating on both coasts.

Now gradually being retired, the DC-4s were soon to be replaced by more modern equipment that could handle greater passenger loads. In 1958, Transocean acquired three Model 749 and two Model 1049 Lockheed Constellations and, that same year, leased from Boeing Aircraft a fleet of fourteen Boeing B-377 Stratocruisers that had been turned in by B.O.A.C. (British Overseas Airways Corporation), against an order for Boeing 707s. This lease agreement thus established Transocean's place on Boeing's production line for three of the new 707s. Upon receiving this news, Pan American threatened to drop its option orders with Boeing. Consequently, Continental Air Lines wound up with Transocean's three new jets.

This precipitated a multi-million-dollar restraint-of-trade suit in the courts. Lengthy litigation was followed by bitter disappointment when Transocean lost its bid for a favorable settlement in the case.

The Stratocruiser was a pilot's airplane; the flight deck was spacious, and the large wrap-around cockpit windows that extended nearly to the floor provided excellent visibility. A substantial improvement over the DC-4s, the B-377s were radar-equipped, and were pressurized, allowing them to fly much higher and faster. Though fun to fly, this airplane was not a money-maker. Transocean acquired them, hoping to install passenger seats in the lower deck lounge area. The C.A.A. approved the plan and about a dozen seats were installed, but MATS (military air transport), would not approve the additional seating for use on military charters. Only eight of the Boeings were ever placed into Transocean service.

In 1951, Transocean flew several exploratory flights to the Society Islands, using DC-4s, to assess the traffic potential in the area, but soon discontinued them. Then again in 1959, Stratocruisers were used on a second foray into the region to determine if regular air service to Tutuila in the Samoan Islands might be feasible. Double crews were used on these flights. Flown from California cities, fuel stops were made at Honolulu and Canton Island.

Visits to Samoa by the 377s were major events for the islanders, as several hundred residents, many barefooted, brought picnic lunches to the

One DC-4 frames the other in this photo. Note Diamond Head on the Horizon. Honolulu, Hawaii, 1957.

A military charter, bound for Okinawa, boards passengers at gate #6, Honolulu International Airport. 1958.

This B-377 prepares to leave the blocks at Oakland International Airport. 1959.

A tour group rolls up its banner in preparation for departure for Honolulu, while another Transocean DC-4 taxies to the ramp in front of the Oakland International Air Terminal.

Passengers deplane at Honolulu International Airport in 1955, when Transocean was operating two and three round trip common carriage flights daily from the Mainland.

Transocean was a pioneer in economy air travel; no one beat our fares. Vice President of Sales, Bill Leonard, points out a popular vacation destination.

(Above) Captains Joe Stachon and Herb Hudson check out the Royal Hawaiian DC-6B before a flight. This, the only DC-6 Transocean ever operated, was lost in the Pacific approximately 325 miles east of Wake Island early on the morning of July 12, 1953. The cause of the mishap was never determined. Fourteen bodies and all the life rafts were recovered. Captain Bill Word and his entire crew perished, and Captain Hudson, the one on the left in this photo, was one of them. (Below) Transocean Air Lines takes delivery on a Connie L1049G in Los Angeles. Heading for Oakland, it cruises north over the Sierra Madre Mountains. 1958.

*What well-dressed
stewardesses were wearing
in the year 1957. These two
are Pat Lauderback and
Sherry Waterman.*

*Bound for Honolulu
and points east,
passengers board
403Q at Pago Pago,
Samoa. A scheduled
fuel stop at Canton
Island will be made
three hours and thirty
minutes later. Double
crews were used on
these flights. June 24,
1959.*

(Above) Crew members Board a Stratocruiser at Canton Island for the three and a half hour flight to American Samoa. From left are: First Officer Bill Piles; Captain John Russel; Flight Engineer Bert Elliot; and Navigator Don Fraim. (Below) Sitting quietly on the ground, a group of Samoans snacked, read, or just chatted with their neighbors, as they waited at Pago Pago Airport to watch the departure of the Honolulu-bound flight. 1959.

airport to frolic on the grass surrounding the small white terminal building and watch the big airplane land and take off. Along the five- or six-mile ocean drive from the airport to the Pago Pago townsite, groups of Samoan teenagers could often be seen perched in tree branches along the way, playing their ukuleles and singing; a more relaxed atmosphere could not be imagined. Although the trip I made carried capacity loads both ways, these flights, too, were soon abandoned.

All Our Own Work

By David's second birthday, the new house was enclosed. Mina and I made the decision to go back to the adoption agency, this time to apply for a baby girl. Judging from the time involved in clearing the adoption hurdle with David, we knew there would again be many long months of waiting.

Working through the winter, my spare time was spent backpriming cedar siding inside Mr. Forrest's garage, while the wind and rain raged outside. By late spring, our new house was framed and the roof on, and I had managed to enclose the entire structure with 20-pound felt paper, an underlayment for the exterior cedar siding that was to follow. Storms could be especially vicious a thousand feet up on our exposed hill and, in the course of one of them, we experienced a minor setback.

I had barely finished tacking up the felt when unusually heavy rain and gale force winds shredded the paper off the outside walls of the house and scattered it all around the neighborhood. Three days work was lost and it had to be done over. Mina, too, had pitched in, tarring almost the entire foundation by herself. One day, a neighbor, a professional bricklayer who lived on an adjoining hill, made me an offer that I could not refuse: He agreed to put up my fireplace over a week-end if I would keep him supplied with beer as he worked. I was to build the scaffolding and mix the mortar. Well ... He drank his way through two cases of 16-oz. Budweiser in the two days, and when I ran out of large cans, he suggested that small cans would do very well ... if there were enough of them. By the end of the second day, he didn't know a brick from an empty beer can, and only constant vigilance on my part prevented beer cans from showing up as art deco in the fireplace wall.

On a warm spring morning, nearly three years after work on our house had begun, we moved in. What could not be carried by hand across the hundred or so yards that separated the two houses, we loaded into an old Ford pickup truck we had bought to haul supplies. Although inhabitable at this point, the place would need two more years of work to finish it completely.

We decided to move in anyway, hoping to have all three bedrooms in shape by the time the new baby came.

Double Happy Event

One evening after dinner, following a particularly frustrating day, Mina put David to bed and joined me on the divan in the living room. As twilight approached, the two of us relaxed quietly for a while, enjoying the spectacular view through the large glass sliding doors. Like so many luminous tentacles, the distant flicker of lights spread slowly across the length and breadth of the Bay Area below us. Putting an arm around my shoulder, Mina snuggled up close. Neither of us spoke for several minutes; finally, Mina broke the silence.

"Could you have forgotten our twentieth wedding anniversary? It's coming up in less than two weeks, you know." She was looking me straight in the eye. Women have a way of remembering things like that, and I had indeed forgotten. I guess house-building had become a consuming passion to the exclusion of everything else, leading me to the realization that we had not been away together—just the two of us—for a very long time.

My thoughts drifted back to a night some fifteen years before. "Remember Harry Woods's little cottage outside Taos, New Mexico?" I said, recalling a heart warming experience from the past, "Maybe we can find a secluded little cabin like that somewhere in the Santa Cruz mountains. We've been working too hard, Honey. We need a couple of days away, all by ourselves."

"But we can't go away and leave David!"

Mina was suddenly apprehensive, wrinkling her brow at the thought. I shared her concern, of course, and after thinking about it for a moment, I came up with an idea.

"Our company nurse at Transocean, Vi Sharman, may know some one who would consider staying here with him," I said. "We could keep in touch by 'phone while we're away ... I'll drop in at the dispensary first thing tomorrow morning and talk to her."

The sun rose bright and warm on the morning of 17 April 1958, presaging a beautiful day. All the necessary arrangements for a three-day trip to the Monterey Peninsula had been worked out. Vi had helped us find a reliable baby-sitter, the car was packed, and we were all ready to walk out the front door when the telephone rang.

That robotic ringing device, which reposed so innocently on a stand near the kitchen table, had a personality all its own, and at that moment, instinct prompted me to strangle the thing. I was certain that it was about to summon me to the airport, where dispatch would then order me off on another trip to some distant place. Fate has a way of rearranging our lives at the most awkward times. Had we left just a few minutes sooner, we would never have heard the ring. Maybe I should ignore it now and leave anyway, but no ... I could not do that. With considerable misgivings, I picked up the receiver. Then, from the other end of the line, came a cheerful female voice.

"Can you get down here right away? We have a darling little baby girl waiting for you!" It was ... the adoption agency.

The prospect of a three-day vacation in the coastal mountains paled into insignificance in the face of this news. Not even bothering to unpack the car, we dismissed the sitter, grabbed little David, and headed off in an unplanned direction: toward downtown Oakland. The remainder of our twentieth wedding anniversary was spent at home in a repeat scenario, with three of us now, to look after baby sister. Our newest family member was christened Mary Mina Lewis. Mary, because of the permanence of a good Bible name, and Mina, after her new mother and maternal grandmother.

The End of the Line

Transocean Air Lines ceased operations in November 1959, and collapsed into bankruptcy early in 1960. From its first fledgling moments on a dreary morning fourteen years before, until its last wheel skidded to the runway, this company's experience had been my experience; its destiny had been my destiny. It was a very bad day.

Primarily, Transocean's demise resulted from its inability to convince an obdurate Civil Aeronautics Board that it had paid its dues and earned a place in commercial aviation as a scheduled airline; and secondly, from lack of investment capital which, with C.A.B. certification, would have improved the company's credit rating with the banks—a classic case of cause and effect, or, as the saying goes, 'Catch 22.' Transocean Air Lines had served the nation well in every conceivable way, but route certification, though applied for year after year, was never granted. Throughout its entire existence, a full certificate was granted to only one airline, and that one was based in Washington, D.C.

Not in the Inventory

One of the best air carriers the United States ever had, Transocean simply died because, when it needed nourishment during a difficult time, it was allowed to starve. The reasons were complex and political, and I had no part of it. But one small episode in which I was involved epitomized, I think, the sad way in which this great company disintegrated.

When the accounting department issued an inter-office memorandum to all department heads requesting that company-owned equipment be turned in, I reluctantly took my beloved Linhof camera and its three accessory lenses to Senior Vice President Wilson's office. He was sitting at his desk. I watched as he took possession of the camera and placed it in the top drawer of a four-drawer filing cabinet that stood against the wall behind his chair. For the next twenty-five years I felt, somehow, that Sam had taken it home.

Many years later I had occasion to bump into Captain Jess Morrison, who had flown with Transocean almost as long as I had. We were discussing photography when the subject of the Linhof came up. Reminiscing, I remarked to Jess, "I think Sam must have kept it."

A faint sheepish grin crossed his face. "No," he said, "Sam didn't get that camera. I did!"

I was stunned. "But you were a pilot," I reasoned. "You and I weren't close, nor could you have known that that camera meant anything special to anyone."

"No, of course not," he continued, "but let me explain ... some time after the collapse of the company, I got together with a few others to discuss the possibility of putting Transocean Air Lines back in the flying business. The interested parties met at the Oakland Airport, and, of course, the I.R.S. was one of the participants. Their representative that day was a friend of mine ... I won't mention his name."

"After the meeting, my friend asked if I would like to accompany him on an inspection tour of TAL's remaining physical assets which had been impounded in the catwalk area above the Hangar 5 floor. He had a key to the padlock on the access door, which he unlocked, and we went inside. I stood by, watching, as he examined several items in the storage area, and soon he came across this four-drawer filing cabinet. when he opened the top drawer ... there was the camera.

" 'Hey, Jess, come see what I've found!' he said.Lifting the camera out of the cabinet, he examined it briefly, then handed it to me, asking, `Would you have any use for this?' Well ... I hesitated ... but I couldn't say no. My friend knew that I was interested in trying some aerial photography. He didn't wait for me to answer, he simply said, 'Here ... take it. It's yours!' "

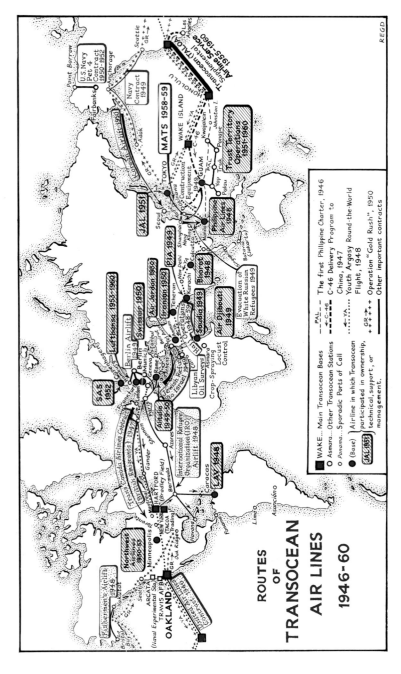

ROUTES
OF
TRANSOCEAN
AIR LINES
1946-60

Tribute to Orvis Nelson

Orvis Marcus Nelson, President and Chief Executive Officer of Transocean Air Lines, was born of Norwegian-American parents at Tamarack, Minnesota, in 1907. He grew up working alongside his father in the timber business. At the age of twenty, he enlisted in the Army Air Corps and, after graduating from Chanute Field, went back to college. Later he returned to the Air Corps, and in 1933, graduated again from training programs at both Kelly and Randolph Fields. Signing on as co-pilot with United Air Lines in 1935, he flew domestic routes until 1943, when United, along with several other American air carriers, contracted to fly military passengers and cargo for the

For thirteen years—1946 to 1959—corporate headquarters of Transocean Air Lines were located in Hangar #5 at Oakland International Airport. The old airport control tower is visible behind the hangar. March 13, 1953.

225

*Transocean Air Lines'
world headquarters in
Hangar #5 at the Oakland
International Airport,
California. President
Orvis Nelson's office was
behind the arched window
above the marquee. Many
an airline subsequently
benefitted from this
Transocean enterprise.
September 10, 1953.*

Air Transport Command. Joining this program, he participated in both the
Alaskan and Pacific Operations. At war's end, in 1945, he left United to form
Transocean Air Lines.

Although I photographed Mr. Nelson dozens of times in the course of
Transocean's fourteen years, we did not enjoy a close personal relationship.
He was the company's Chief Executive Officer, while I hovered at the lower
levels of the company's pecking order. Mina and I, however, did have occasional social contacts with the Nelsons during those years.

Transocean's executive offices at the Oakland Airport were housed on the
second floor of Hangar 5. From that floor, another flight of steps continued
upward to a single alcove-type room which, in whispered parlance, came to be
known as the 'Ivory Tower'. This was President Nelson's office. His chair and
desk faced the center of the room, while at his back was a massive arched
window that overlooked Earhart Drive below. When he was not traveling around
the world making business deals, he managed his empire from this room.

For some reason, Orvis added two letters to my name and invariably
addressed me as Ralphus ... Passing each other in the hallway, his greeting
was usually "How are things goin', Ralphus?"

I remember being called to do some publicity shots in which he was to pose with actors Louis Jourdan and Doris Day between sequences of a movie being shot at Transocean's TALOA Academy ... and my flash bulbs wouldn't flash! After two or three attempts, my subjects' patience was wearing thin, and I was terribly embarrassed. Orvis just seemed amused by the delay and relaxed the charged atmosphere by defending me. "Don't worry about it, Ralphus,", he said with a chuckle, "cameras can be like airplanes; they don't always do what they're supposed to do." I finally took the pictures.

Orvis Nelson was a man whose genius for organization created a new airline almost overnight, with borrowed equipment, even borrowed executives, and precious little money. His dynamic personality and inventive resourcefulness provided the direction that guided and eventually sustained Transocean's entrepreneurial spirit. A man of infinite vision and boundless energy, he inspired confidence and trust in everyone he knew. Add to these attributes an impeccable moral character, and you have Orvis M. Nelson, President of Transocean Air Lines. Though frustrated year after year by the Civil Aeronautics Board's stubborn intransigence, he never gave up hope for Transocean's ultimate triumph as a scheduled air line. But the hope was in vain.

Shown here in the cockpit of the DC-4 simulator at Transocean Air Lines' TALOA School, are from left to right: TAL Vice President Bill Keating; actress Doris Day; and actor Louis Jourdan. In the movie Julie, *the stewardess, played by Miss Day, lands the airplane. The lengthy sequences were filmed in the school's simulator. April, 1956.*

Still in my possession are hundreds of photographs and negatives taken during those years while I was navigating a full schedule and, at the same time, running Transocean's photographic department. Together with Red Emery, Dave Gregory, and several others, I worked with Bert Vanderveen, manager of Transocean's full service print shop, to produce Taloa News.

I do not think anyone could have been more deeply imbued with the spirit of this company than I was. Those of us who flew TAL's routes lived out a real life drama normally found only in story books. The careers of most of our crew members spanned service with many airline companies, but it was Transocean Air Lines, with its glorious spirit of adventure, enterprise, and unpredictability, that captured their hearts and minds.

Transocean's President and Chief Executive Officer,
Orvis Nelson.

The Rest of the Story

During the American occupation of Japan, which began late in 1945, General of the Army, Douglas MacArthur, by this time, supreme commander of the Allied Forces in the Southwest Pacific, had selected the Dai-ichi Building, across the moat from the Japanese Imperial Palace in Tokyo, as his command headquarters. Our Transocean flight crews were billeted at what we knew as the Union Club, also adjacent to the palace grounds, and just up the street a couple of blocks from the Dai-ichi Building.

At exactly 8 a.m. each week-day morning, five-star General MacArthur, in full uniform—including his battered campaign cap and dark glasses—arrived for work in a chauffeured limousine. Alighting from his car, and flanked by a couple of aides, he would sprint from the curb to the building entrance. Military guards on either side of the highly polished double brass doors would snap to attention as the general bounded up half a dozen steps to disappear inside. Rain or shine, a crowd of Japanese citizens was invariably on hand at the marble-fronted building, waiting patiently to bow, in deference to the general, and possibly to catch a glimpse of him as he hurried past. The entire show was over in thirty seconds.

Tokyo Comes Back to Life

During the occupation, American GIs had been unable to read the Tokyo street signs. So with the exception of Ginza Street, all the major downtown thoroughfares were renamed alphabetically: A Ave., B Ave., C Ave., and so on.

Just how a Japanese letter carrier located an addressee in a Tokyo residential neighborhood was difficult to understand. It would seem that if a residence was numbered 24 Siugetsu St., that the house next door would be 26 Siugetsu St., and so on. Therefore, the dwelling directly across the street should be 25 Siugetsu St., right? Wrong! The Japanese, we were told, do not assign house numbers in numerical order; instead, they number structures according to the date they were built. Trying to train a new postman in the Tokyo suburbs must be a tricky exercise.

Judging from the proliferation of face masks as we walked among the hoards of shoppers along the Ginza, it was obvious that half of Tokyo's population was suffering from severe head colds. Seeing so many masked faces on the street was a strange sight, but the Japanese "cover-up" did demonstrate consideration for others.

Every foreigner traveling around the countryside in Japan should know at least a few words of Japanese, and high on that list would surely be the word 'benjo', meaning toilet. While shopping in a large department store on the Ginza during one of my first trips to Tokyo, I sensed the need for one, and was directed to what I thought would be the men's room, but upon entering I soon realized that the 'benjo', at least in this public place, was integrated. I found myself facing the end of a partition which bore symbols directing women to the left and men to the right.

Choosing the proper side, I sailed around the partition ... and came face to face with a young female! I froze, thinking I had mistakenly entered the wrong side, but no ... in front of me was a row of male urinals. The girl, with a towel draped over her arm, stood stiffly at attention beside a small table which held additional towels. Bowing from the waist, she flashed me a warm smile. I returned her look as I nervously sidled up to the urinal nearest the door. Acutely aware now of her presence directly behind me, I stood there for several seconds ... paralyzed. I couldn't; and didn't! This much togetherness takes some kind of getting used to.

The Yamata Line, which circles the city in both directions, together with Tokyo's extensive subway system, provide transportation for the masses. Riders are stacked into cars like upright breadsticks in a drinking glass. Commuting hours on station platforms are so congested that 'pushers' are hired to cram another half dozen commuters aboard before the car's electric doors can snap shut.

When Transocean's brave fight for survival ended in 1960, I walked across the ramp to a neighboring hangar and took a job with Overseas National Airways (O.N.A.), navigating Douglas DC-7s on a one-year military contract involving regular flights to Tokyo. Layovers of two to seven days in this metropolitan city on and off for sixteen years made us quite familiar with it.

During the 1960s, Tokyo was building high rises and we were struck by the incongruity of bamboo scaffolding rising fourteen or fifteen storeys up the outside of modern steel and concrete office buildings (a building technique, incidentally, which is taken to even greater heights in Hong Kong). The old methods had not yet caught up with the new. Then there were the Japanese theater seats ... so narrow that a westerner could barely squeeze himself into one.

I remember too the almost constant stream of small groups of very young school children being shepherded by their teachers through the maze of traffic along the Ginza. Neatly uniformed, the boys, wearing black pants and white shirts, and the girls in black skirts and white blouses, were taken on outings to study Japanese art and culture. Large department stores such as the Takashimaya in Nihonbashi, Mitsukoshi in Ginza, and the Iseton, in suburban Shinjuku, maintained extensive art galleries on their upper floors. Japanese youngsters seemed eager to learn.

Imagine my surprise one day, while passing a primary school in the Tokyo suburbs, to hear a chorus of children's voices singing, 'Way ... down upon the Swa...nee River ... far ... far ... away ...' in English. Then there was the sign on the wall of a public comfort station, which, in large red letters, read 'Charged Toilet'.

In 1963, General Electric was awarded a contract to manage the Pacific Island Missile Base on Kwajalein for the American government. This DC-6 was plushed up for a series of weekly flights by World Airways for G.E. VIPs, who enjoyed superb service prepared by an onboard steward. Originating in Oakland, California, and overnighting in Honolulu, it operated during daylight hours only.

O.N.A. and World Airways

The last employer in my life was World Airways. When the Overseas National contract ran out I switched to World, where my first trip out took me to Africa. A Douglas DC-7, using a double crew, flew a high priority mission from Oakland to Libya, and return. Except for six hours crew rest in Tripoli and gas stops in Charleston, Bermuda, the Azores, and Casablanca, we were back in less than three days, quite a feat for piston-engined aircraft in 1961, as even the jets needed two.

That same year, I navigated a Lockheed Model 1649H Constellation from Tokyo to San Francisco non-stop. We loaded twenty-four tons of fuel into her tanks and, at 19,000 feet, rode the jet stream and 60 knot tailwinds over the entire distance. With a ground speed of 300 nautical mph, we covered the 4,500 nautical miles in fifteen hours. For today's jets, these distances non-stop are commonplace, but at that time, at least for us, it was a record.

Flying to the Far East with World Airways continued in Model 1049 and 1649 Connies, with trips to Tachikawa Air Base near Tokyo and Clark Field, north of Manila. On 22 October 1962, I worked a flight which took a load of rocket launchers into Saigon, Vietnam, and in landing, the captain dragged out a low approach. On the ramp a few minutes later, we learned that our aircraft had taken half a dozen rounds of small arms fire in its underbelly. The Communists off the end of the runway were taking pot shots at us.

Where There's a Will There's a Way

On a leg between Rangoon and Bangkok in a DC-4 one day, a violent explosion in the cargo area shook the entire airplane. A pressure-limiting device on the hydraulic accumulator had failed. The exploding accumulator blew a hole in the side of the airplane big enough for a large man to climb through. Fortunately, no control cables were severed.

On another occasion we had flown a 1649 Connie from Hilo, Hawaii, to Travis Air Base, California, had dropped our passengers, and were headed across the Sacramento delta to the Oakland airport, 30 miles to the southwest. It was 4 a.m.; we were tired and anxious to go home. On the Oakland approach, however, the main gear refused to come down.

After the flight engineer tried unsuccessfully to crank it down by hand, the captain chose a novel approach in solving the problem. Taking the airplane up to a safe altitude, he pulled this seventy-ton, four-engine passenger plane into a convulsive stall and literally shook the landing gear

This picture was taken from a DC-6 General Electric VIP flight as it turned in final approach to Kwajalein Airport in the Marshall Islands. April 23, 1963.

loose. You would never find this remedy listed as an option in any company's operations manual.

My last flight as a crew member was made 10 August 1963, ending a career that spanned 22 years. Included in a total flight time of over 21,000 hours were 700 round trips between the United States mainland and Hawaii alone. The most exciting, yet at the same time, satisfying part of my entire life was ended with the decision to give up commercial flying. Had it been dangerous? Too young to think much about it at the time, I would now have to say yes, I suppose so. Quite a number of my close friends and associates lost their lives during those years.

My Kind of Music

Through the cockpit window of an airplane high above the earth, a lifetime of wonders has unfolded before my eyes. I have thrilled to the everchanging hues and diverse forms of a thousand tranquil sunrises. I have held in awe the towering clouds that refract the sun's crimson rays in a thousand breathtaking sunsets, believing always that each spectacular vista transcended its predecessor. Flying the skies of the world was a sublime, almost religious, experience that earth-bound humans will never know.

I have earned a living as a violinist, radio announcer, broadcast engineer, flight navigator, and photographer, and in the latter years of my working life, as the owner of a retail liquor and grocery business. I seem to have made careers of them all, and each has added its own share of enjoyment that makes the spice of life.

Nearing his eighty-fifth birthday, during a visit with us, my father begged me to play for him once again. "Son," he implored, "I want to hear you play the violin just one more time."

Trying to discourage him, I explained that I had not picked up the instrument in years, but he would not be put off. At least, I decided, I should honor his request. Reluctantly, I brought the violin down from the shelf and ran through a few bars. Dad listened patiently for about ten seconds. Then, abruptly raising his hand, he made the final sad pronouncement on the subject. "Put the violin away, Son!"

Radio operators and navigators alike became extinct when modern technology made them redundant, but during a vital era of air transport development they played their part. Had it not been for the Second World War, I might have pursued a career in music, but airplanes changed all that. Although I never played again, my love of music—and the instrument that expresses it so eloquently—will always be a part of me. Everything I have undertaken in life has been a welcome challenge, and if I could choose to relive it, I would change very little.

To have written many of these stories with any degree of accuracy would have been impossible without my flight logs, eight or ten cancelled passports, and hundreds of photographs and letters. The catalyst for these factual references, of course, has been my memory, and therein lies the likelihood of error. Amid the trivia of unimportant detail, I may occasionally have erred on the side of inaccuracy. Many incidents still burn brightly in my memory, and in this book I have tried, in words and pictures, to recapture the warmth and magic of days past. My music was destined to be played on the octant and the compass; and my conductors were the sun and the stars.

Glossary of Terms

Abaaya–Loosely fitting outer garment worn by women of the Middle East.

ADF–Automatic radio direction finder.

Agal–Double rope cord worn around the crown of the head over a head scarf, by men in the Middle East.

Azimuth–In navigation, the arc of the horizon measured clockwise in degrees from the north point to where a vertical circle through a given heavenly body intersects the horizon.

BOAC (or B.O.A.C.)–British Overseas Airways Corporation.

C.A.A.–Civil Aeronautics Authority.

C.A.B.–Civil Aeronautics Board.

CAVU–Clear and Visibility Unlimited.

C.N.A.C.–China National Aviation Corporation.

CW–Continuous wave (telegraphy). Refers to the transmission of Morse Code (dots and dashes) by breaking the carrier wave of radio signals.

F.C.C.–Federal Communications Commission.

F.I.R.–Flight Information Region.

G.C.A.–Ground Controlled Approach.

Greany Maru–LST landing craft adapted for local use at Wake Island.

Greenwich Mean Time–This is reckoned from the zero meridian at Greenwich in southeast London, England.

Gyro Compass–A compass that uses a motor driven gyroscope, so mounted that its axis of rotation maintains a constant position with reference to true or geographic north—a major component of the automatic pilot.

Gyro Horizon–Artificial horizon—gyro stabilized—which indicates the attitude of the aircraft—a major component of the automatic pilot.

Hack Watch–Slang phrase for a chronometer whose second hand can be set to an exact time.

High Blowers–Air compressors that supply oxygen to aircraft engines while operating in thin air at high altitudes.

ILS–Instrument Landing System.

IRS–Internal Revenue Service.

Jet Stream–Strong, predominantly westerly winds in the upper troposphere.

Kaffiyeh–Head scarf worn by both sexes in the Middle East.

Kapu–Hawaiian word for "Keep Out".

KVM–Call signal of Honolulu CW radio station maintained during WW-II for communication with aircraft en route to Wake Island and/or the west coast of the U.S.

Linear Amplifier–Final stage of frequency amplification in a radio transmitter.

Line Squall–A weather front formed along a more or less straight line that is often associated with moderate to severe turbulence.

LORAN–Acronym for Long Range Navigation.

Mercator Charts–These are used when navigating in mid-latitudes. In such charts all meridians of longitude are parallel. Consequently a straight line will cross them all at the same angle.

Millibar–Unit associated with the measurement of air pressure—a thousandth of a bar.

O.N.A.–Overseas National Airlines.

ONAT–Orvis Nelson Air Transport.

Pasay / Quiapo–Two southern districts in suburban Manila, Philippines.

Phone Patch–A connection between a telephone line and a radio transmitter.

RADAR–Acronym for Radio Detection and Ranging.

Rial–The monetary unit of Iran; a coin.

Rhumb Line–A curve on the surface of a sphere which cuts all meridians at the same compass heading.

SAS (or S.A.S.)–Scandinavian Airlines System.

Seabees–Construction battalions of the U.S. Navy.

St. Elmo's Fire–A luminous electric discharge which occasionally manifests itself as eerie blue fingers of light that radiate from propeller tips and wing surfaces during heavy atmospherics.

Sun Line–A line of position determined by celestial sighting of the sun.

Suwa Maru–Japanese freighter grounded on the beach at Wake Island during WW-II.

Tagalog–National language of the Philippines.

TAL–Transocean Air Lines.

Trim Tabs–Small flaps on trailing edges of aircraft control surfaces used to trim flight attitudes.

VFR–Visual flight rules.

VHF–Very high frequency.

Zebra Time–Greenwich Mean Time as reckoned from the zero meridian at Greenwich, southeast London, England.